CHURCH, STATE
AND SOCIETY

CHURCH, STATE AND SOCIETY

The Attitudes of
JOHN KEBLE,
RICHARD HURRELL FROUDE
AND
JOHN HENRY NEWMAN,
1827–1845

John Henry Lewis Rowlands

CHURCHMAN PUBLISHING
1989

Church, State and Society
by
John Henry Lewis Rowlands
was first published in 1989 by
Churchman Publishing Limited
117 Broomfield Avenue
Worthing, West Sussex BN14 7SF

Publisher: Peter Smith

Copyright © John Henry Lewis Rowlands 1989

Represented in
Dublin; Sydney; Wellington;
Kingston, Ontario and Wilton, Connecticut

Distributed to the book trade by
Bailey Book Distribution Limited
(*a division of the Bailey and Swinfen Holdings Group*)
Warner House, Wear Bay Road
Folkestone, Kent CT19 6PH

All rights reserved

ISBN 1 85093 132 1

Printed in Great Britain by
Bourne Press Limited
Bournemouth

TO MY WIFE, CATRYN,
AND MY CHILDREN,
PARRI, SARA AND ELENA,
WITH LOVE AND GRATITUDE

CONTENTS

Preface ix

Introduction 1

Notes to Introduction 17

1. John Keble: "The True Socialism, the True Liberty, Equality and Fraternity" 27
   1.1 Introduction 27
   1.2 The Christian Year (1827) 29
   1.3 The 1832 Reform Bill 44
   1.4 National Apostasy (1833) 46
   1.5 The Poor Law Amendment Act (1834) 52
   1.6 Primitive Tradition recognised in Holy Scripture 59

   Notes to Chapter 1 66

2. Richard Hurrell Froude: "Let us tell the truth and shame the devil; let us give up a National Church and have a real one" 78
   2.1 Introduction 79
   2.2 "Keble is my fire and I may be his poker" 80
      2.2.1 Froude's Understanding of the Sixteenth Century Settlements 81
      2.2.2 The Constitutional Situation, 1829–1833 83
      2.2.3 The Radical Keble, 1833–1839 85

	2.3	"Let us throw the Z's Overboard"	90
		2.3.1	The Concept of the Church and State advocated by the Friends of the Church	90
		2.3.2	Anathema to Froude	91
		2.3.3	Newman's Position, July 1833	96
		2.3.4	The Night of 13 November, 1833	100
		2.3.5	The Address to the Archbishop (1834)	102
		2.3.6	The Royal Supremacy	104
	2.4	The Political and Social Significance of The Remains	110
		2.4.1	Toryism, Medievalism and Feudalism	113
		2.4.2	The Political and Social Interpretation of The Reformation	116
		2.4.3	The Tory Spirit of The Remains	118
	Notes to Chapter 2	120
3.	John Henry Newman: "To make trial of the age"	134
	3.1	Introduction	134
	3.2	Roman Catholic Emancipation, 1829	136
	3.3	The 1832 Reform Bill	141
	3.4	The History of the Arians (1833)	143
	3.5	Church and Society, 1833–1837	147
		3.5.1	The Church of the Fathers	147
		3.5.2	The episcopal and prophetic Traditions and the individual	150
		3.5.3	The Church's relationship to society	157
		3.5.4	Newman's Social Conscience	159
		3.5.5	The Church of the People	162
	3.6	The Tamworth Reading Room (1841)	166
		3.6.1	Peelite Conservatism	166
		3.6.2	Faith and reason	167
		3.6.3	The man of business and the religious man	168
		3.6.4	The dessication of modern man	170
		3.6.5	One-dimensional man	171
	3.7	Change, development and progress, 1841–1845	173
	3.8	Church, State and society: the imperial image of the Church, 1837–1845	181
	Notes to Chapter 3	197

CONTENTS

4.	Conclusion	214
	4.1.1 John Keble	214
	4.1.2 Hurrell Froude	216
	4.1.3 John Henry Newman	217
4.2	Similarities	220
	4.2.1 Holy Otherworldliness	220
	4.2.2 The Church's mission to society	222
	4.2.3 Rich and poor one in Christ	223
	4.2.4 Detestation of democracy	227
4.3	Differences	229
4.4	The contribution of Keble, Froude and Newman to political and social thought	230
	4.4.1 John Keble	230
	4.4.2 Hurrell Froude	231
	4.4.3 J. H. Newman	231
	Notes to the Conclusion	233
Bibliography		235

PREFACE

This study is a critique of the two popular misconceptions of the Church's relationship to State and society in Tractarian thought. The first sees the leading Tractarians as completely divorced from the realities of their world. In 1834, Thomas Arnold was convinced that the success of the Tractarians would cause the ruin of the Church of England and obstruct the progress of the Church of Christ.[1] F. D. Maurice believed the chief concern of the Tractarians was the setting up of a Church system, "Denisonian Chartism about the rights of the clergy".[2] Similar criticisms can be found in M. B. Reckitt's *From Maurice to Temple*[3] and Valerie Pitt in "The Oxford Movement: a Case of Cultural Distortion?".[4] Dwight Culler wrote of Newman ensconced in his thirty six Volumes of the Fathers, a gift in 1831, for whom the world of cities was little more than a busy and fretful dream.[5]

The second misconception amounts to an apologetic for the political and social beliefs of Keble, Froude and Newman. According to W. G. Peck in *The Social Implications of the Oxford Movement*, the Tractarians, threatened by Liberalism, had no option but to retreat "to the innermost sanctuary of religion as the only safe and sure refuge".[6] R. W. Church, the author of the magisterial history of the Oxford Movement, commented laconically, "Poor Tractarians ... it seems they were expected to exhaust all important subjects in the few years when they were mostly fighting for their lives".[7]

These various scholars show an inadequate grasp of the Tractarian understanding of the Church's relationship to State and society for three reasons. First, it is necessary to emphasise that Keble, Froude and Newman never felt that there was any dichotomy between theology and worship. Recently, Andrew Louth in *The Origins of the Christian Mystical Tradition* and *Discerning the Mystery* has seen this dichotomy as a fairly recent trend in the history of Christian thought. That is why in this study, on the contrary, so much Tractarian social and political thought is found in sermons and meditations. Secondly, Keble, Froude and Newman felt that theology was not a narrow acadamic exercise but was rather concerned about everything which had to do with the glory of God and the destiny of man. That did not only mean reading the more obviously classical works in philosophy, literature and history but also science and political economy. Thirdly, Orthodoxy must always be lived and can never be separated from Orthopraxis. That a thing is true, wrote Newman, is no reason that it should be said but that it should be done, acted upon and made our own inwardly.[8]

For these reasons, this study is primarily theological and considers the political and social thought of Keble, Froude and Newman as an inherent part of their theology, and not as something divorced from it.

During my research and writing I have incurred many debts. I would like to thank the Revd. Professor Stephen Sykes for much encouragement over the years; the Rt. Revd. Dr. J. G. Hughes, Bishop of Kensington and former Warden of Saint Michael's College, Llandaff for his support; the Revd. J. F. H. Henley, former Librarian of Saint Michael's College for much assistance with research into the nineteenth century manuscript and pamphlet collection; the Executive of the Managing Trustees of Saint Michael's College and the Trustees of the Catherine and Lady Grace James Foundation for their assistance and the staff in the Arts and Humanities Library of University College, Cardiff (now the University of Wales College of Cardiff).

My most enduring debt of gratitude must, however, be reserved for Dr. Sheridan Gilley, Senior Lecturer in the Department of Theology in the University of Durham, who suggested this subject, supervised my research and has always been a constant source of help, encouragement and wise counsel. Another enormous debt of gratitude is acknowledged in the dedication to my dear wife, Catryn, and my children, Parri, Sara and Elena.

Saint Michael's College, Llandaff, Cardiff. J. H. L. Rowlands
Michaelmas, 1987.

NOTES

1. A. P. Stanley, *The Life and Correspondence of Thomas Arnold, D. D.*, Vol. II, p. 53.
2. J. F. Maurice, *The Life of F. D. Maurice*, Vol. II, p. 61.
3. M. B. Reckitt, *From Maurice to Temple, A Century of Social Movement in the Church of England*, pp. 52 ff.
4. Valerie Pitt, "The Oxford Movement: A Case of Cultural Distortion?" Kenneth Leech and Rowan Williams, ed., *Essays Catholic and Radical*, pp. 205–224.
5. Dwight Culler, *The Imperial Intellect, A Study in Newman's Educational Method*, pp. 79–83.
6. W. G. Peck, *The Social Implications of the Oxford Movement*, pp. 98 ff.
7. Mary Church, ed., *Life and Letters of Dean Church*, p. 334.
8. *P.P.S.*, Vol. V, pp. 44–45.

INTRODUCTION

Unlike Melchizedek, John Keble, Richard Hurrell Froude and John Henry Newman did have predecessors and progenies. To understand their concepts of the Church in relation to the State and society, it is necessary to outline the exact background against which they were writing. The Enlightenment was a word unknown in the nineteenth century and yet the idea stood for much that many despised.[1] It is not difficult to see why this was so. Most studies of the Enlightenment have portrayed it as a movement which was essentially anti-traditional and anti-Christian. Symptomatic of this approach is Paul Hazard's well-known study, *The European Mind 1680–1715*[2] and Peter Gay's two-volumed work which sees the Enlightenment as "a volatile mixture of classicism, impiety and science"[3] and David Hume as "the complete modern pagan".[4] Bernard Lonergan, the doyen of twentieth century Roman Cathoic theologians, lends his considerable theological weight to this approach to stating that the Enlightenment "replaced the God of the Christians by the God of the *philosophes* and, eventually, the God of the *philosophes* by agnosticism and atheism. It gloried in the achievements of Newton, criticized social structures, promoted political change, and moved towards a materialist, mechanist, determinist interpretation no less of man than of nature".[5] *Christian Theology, An Introduction to Its Traditions and Tasks*, a recent publication which could become a standard text-book in Theological Departments, states that a new understanding of the Church emerged in Enlightenment historiography, which viewed history in pragmatic, functionalist, nonsupernaturalist terms, distinguished between true religion and church doctrine and saw the Church as an association on a similar footing with other human societies such as the state.[6] In 1976, John Redwood published his *Reason, Ridicule and Religion: The Age of Enlightenment 1660–1750*. The seventeenth and eighteenth centuries, he wrote, should be seen as a godless era, socially dissolving, spiritually drifting, morally corrupting, ridiculing everything from God to miracles, to Creation, the origin of Earth, man and society. The deists and theists, instead of providing a more solid framework to the questions of faith, contributed to the spreading of atheism. There is certainly no doubt that the English deists occupied the intellectual stage from 1690 till the middle of the eighteenth century.[7] Charles Blount, Thomas Chubb, Anthony Collins, Conyers Middleton, Matthew Tindal, John Toland, William Wollaston and Thomas Woolston[8] basically asserted the existence of God as a principle and first cause of the Universe, his goodness and benevolence and man's duty to obey him, but they dispensed, hesitatingly, with Revelation and Atonement. Many deists, either under the pressure of their environment or out of conviction, attempted compromises between the God of the Bible and the new God of philosophy. The moral problem exercised the English and Scottish philosophers of the eighteenth century with particular urgency. The British moralists developed either a theory of "moral sense", or attempted to found morality on rational principles, even on the analogy of mathematical truths, or, much more simply, on natural human sympathy, or, finally, on man's desire for the happiness of the greatest numbers.

Yet to see the Enlightenment as a convenient anti-traditional and anti-Christian movement is thoroughly misleading. Indeed, Redwood's work ought to be read with the utmost caution. His main thesis, for instance, that the Enlightenment began the inevitable drift towards secularism and atheism, must be rejected. Whatever the merits of the Deists – it would be churlish to denounce the very serious contribution which they made to the debate about the existence of God – their beliefs, according to orthodox Christian circles, were more than adequately answered by some of the outstanding apologists for Christianity. Bishop Butler's *Analogy of Religion* (1736) was as magisterial a reply to Matthew Tindal's *Christianity as Old as the Creation* (1730) as

Origen Contra Celsum in the third century.[9] Thomas Sherlock's *The Trial of the Witnesses of the Resurrection* (1743) composed an imaginary trial of the witnesses to the Resurrection in answer to the doubts raised by Thomas Woolston.[10] The jury finds for the Apostles who could not have given false evidence. Bishop Richard Watson of Llandaff wrote his *An Apology for Christianity in a Series of Letters Addressed to Edward Gibbon* (1776), attacking Gibbon's account of the rise of Christianity by appealing to the belief in the Resurrection as the central event of human history.[11] Even William Paley, who was to be attacked so vigorously by the Tractarians, outlined in his *Natural Theology* (1802) a world which spoke of supernatural mysteries. His finite and remote God was very much supplemented by the omnipotent God of Revelation.[12]

Hume's anecdote about the lack of atheists in England is justly famous,[13] especially since devotion and sound learning were not confined to holy clerics. Samuel Johnson was the epitome of what a devout Churchman ought to be, praying and fasting regularly, receiving communion with humility, making constant endeavours to be a better servant of Christ.[14] Furthermore, there was no conflict in England between science and religion.[15] Indeed, eighteenth century thinkers continued to profess Christianity within its reasonableness. Enlightenment goals like the progress of society and belief in a benevolent Deity flourished within the realms of piety itself. This was revealed by the good number of clergymen who were members of the Royal Society. From the date of its second Charter on 22 April, 1663, one of the goals of the Royal Society was to illustrate the providential glory of God manifested in the works of His Creation. The new natural philosophy of the Society did not militate against belief in God's acts of miraculous special Providence. If it had, it would have been in direct contravention of the Society's purposes, which were "studia ad rerum naturalium artiumque utilium scientas experimentorum fide alterius promovendas in Dei Creatoris gloriam et generis humani commodum applicanda sunt".[16]

The serenity of England was in marked contrast to the revolutionary atmosphere in France. Anti-clericalism was germane to those lands which were predominantly Roman Catholic. England, on the contrary, actually approved of Voltaire to a large extent. Far from Voltaire hurling the volumes of Newton and Locke into the face of clerical authority, the Church of England approved of Newton and Locke as much as any member of the French Enlightenment. Indeed, Newton became a high point of education at Cambridge while Locke shared the honours with Aristotle and the classics at Oxford.[17]

The eighteenth century Church of England produced no thinker of the stature of Giambattista Vico, the Neapolitan writer who questioned the Enlightenment ideal of progress towards a clear, objective knowledge of the world around us.[18] The reason was that it required no such critic. Science and religion formed such a close alliance of interests that the scientific parson of the English Church symbolised the general sensibility of the age. Furthermore, such a parson knew exactly his role in society. He had plain sense rather than much learning, a sociable temper, was beloved by his parishioners and kept peace in the village. Essentially, he reflected the profound need of most Englishmen for peace after a tumultuous century. A torpid Church and a tepid religion was what a society, preoccupied increasingly with the mysteries of naturalism, demanded and obtained.[19] Little wonder that Christian pastors tended to ignore all but the few essential doctrines of the faith. The maintenance of adaptive fitness was essential for the survival of institutions like the Church of England. What has been termed the treason of the clerks was the sound opinion of many Churchmen that the Church had to move with the times. It preached sound common sense and no more:

> Island of bliss! amid the subject seas,
> That thunder round thy rocky coast, set up,
> At once the wonder, terror, and delight,
> Of distant nations.[20]

Such a view of the eighteenth century, however, would have been anathema to the Tractarians. Indeed, apart from Bishop Butler, the Church of the preceding century was best forgotten, synonymous as it was with materialism, wordliness, simony, pluralism, greed and secularity. Newman, for instance, thought that the parsons portrayed in Jane Austen's novels were vile creatures.[21] Indeed, the majority of Churchmen in the eighteenth century were for the most part neither Apostolic, Evangelical nor Latitudinarian but Conservative, the advocates of the Establishment. The mass of the Church was implicitly Erastian. They did little else but adjust their precepts according to the dictates of each successive challenge. Their after-dinner toast of "The Church and the King", wrote Newman, was their justification for asserting the spiritual over the temporal. Their chief theological dogma was that the Bible contained all necessary truths which each individual could discover for himself. Latitudinarians, Evangelicals, High Churchmen of the Non-Juror variety were all treated with contempt. The Country clergy were respected more for their social position than the influence of their doctrine. In the great towns, orthodoxy amongst the clergy meant a coldness almost devoid of interior life. Their most enthusiastic pursuit was the drinking of port wine to the health of "the Church and King".[22] Such a portrait of the eighteenth century was so popular that it became the standard view amongst the Tractarians. Many historians, however, mistrusted the picture. J. A. Froude, for instance, was always of the opinion that the Tractarians had deliberately exaggerated the evils of the Hanoverian Church. They underestimated the strength, he wrote, which existing institutions and customs possess so long as they are left undisturbed. The majority of eighteenth century Churchmen were quite happy to view religion, taught by the Church of England, as moral obedience to the Will of God. People went to Church on Sundays to learn to be good. But for the Tractarians, scepticism might have continued a harmless speculation of a few philosophers. By exaggerating the importance of the Church – either the Church or nothing – they made many sceptics adopt the latter alternative rather than embrace what they knew to be a lie.[23]

For the Tractarians, the spirit of the Hanoverian Church was symbolised primarily in the life and work of Bishop Hoadly.[24] It is certainly true that the Tractarians were primarily responsible for the bad press which Bishop Hoadly has tended to have. It is frequently the case, however, that it is not the accuracy of the picture of the past which matters primarily in the hearts of men but the supposed image which can be used as a yardstick for reaction and reform. According to the Tractarians, Hoadly was responsible for turning the Church into a mere human invention. Arbitrary rules were invented for the spiritual benefit of the

Church purely by human sagacity. The Church, as a supernatural power, was got rid of by the theology of Hoadly. He had much experience of various episcopacies. In all, he was Father in God successively of the dioceses of Bangor, Hereford, Salisbury and Winchester. During this time, maintained the Tractarians, the Church of England was rendered a shadow, no matter if it was spiritually independent or not. The question was, "Is the Church of England a channel of grace and conservator of doctrine, or not?" In reality, there was no need to worry about the independence of a body which had nothing to effect. Bishop Hoadly thought endowments more important than truth. During his episcopates, the Church had no divine teaching, authority or grace. This was the Hoadleian Free Church. This was Erastianism and Rationalism at its most blatant; both denied the reality of divine rules.

Whether the Church should be a supernatural institution or not was one of the fiercest points of controversy in the Church's relationship to the State and society in the 1820's, 1830's and 1840's.

The period from the French Revolution of 1789 to the eve of the Oxford Movement could be described in terms of alliances. The first of these was between the Church and the government. Many of the clergy, High Church and profoundly Tory in sympathy, were ardent supporters of the government which went to war with revolutionary France.[25] What was more surprising was the attitude of the Evangelicals, who, vehement in their condemnation of Rationalism, prior to 1789 had little time for politics, "which are Satan's most tempting and alluring baits".[26] After 1789 came a dramatic change. Their support of the government and the Constitution was as marked as the Tories. Edmund Burke was the prophet of the age, dubbing the people "the swinish multitude".[27] Loyalist groups like the Association for Preserving Liberty and Property against Republicans and Levellers, the Anti-Jacobin Club and the Crown and Anchor Clubs found the clergy amongst their most vociferous supporters. This close alliance was cemented even further after the War in the Tory government of the day with Church appointments firmly in the hands of many High and Dry Churchmen known as the Hackney Phalanx.[28] From 1817 to 1828 Charles Manners Sutton was Archbishop of Canterbury while his son, also Charles, was Speaker of the House of Commons.[29]

Between 1789 and 1830 there was a more intriguing alliance still. One of the most influential writers of the age was the Reverend T. R. Malthus whose *Essay on Population* appeared in 1798. Defending the "status quo" against the French Revolution's triad of liberty, equality and fraternity, Malthus held that poverty and inequality were inevitable because population unchecked increases at a geometrical rate and subsistence only at an arithmetical rate.[30] Population will always tend to increase to the limit of subsistence, so that no permanent improvement is possible in the lot of the poor. Population growth is checked by necessary misery and probable vice. Such a political economy had to have a theological basis. In the first edition, Malthus attempted this himself, claiming that this situation was providential for the full intellectual and spiritual development of the human race but this section was withdrawn in the later issues.

The field was left open for some of the best known theologians of the age. In his *Natural Theology* of 1802 William Paley argued from Nature that the conditions of life diagnosed by Malthus were necessary to make it a state of discipline and probation. J. B. Sumner, as a good Evangelical, argued more on the basis of Scripture. His two volumes of *A Treatise on the Records of Creation* of 1816 had as its sub-title the "Consistency of the Principle of Population with the Wisdom and the Goodness of the Deity". Edward Copleston in his *A Second Letter to the Rt. Hon. Sir Robert Peel, M.P.* of 1819 and Richard Whately's *Introductory Lectures in Political Economy* of 1831 were as enthusiastic as Malthus on the importance of private property and the appeal to self-interest. Benevolence could not be embodied in law, especially the Poor Laws. The Christian political economists, whose influence upon the Church of England was profound, argued that competition and private property were socially beneficial, poverty and inequality were providentially expedient as a means of bringing out the best in people and true happiness did not depend upon material possessions but moral worth. As the Christian faith is universal, these laws must be applied universally. The developing philosophy of *laissez-faire* received a perfect theological justification.

Alliances led to much social and political cohesion, which did not mean, however, that the Church of England pleased everybody. After 1815, the Church Extension Programme was actively backed by the government. Ultimately, the Church Building Society received support to the extent of £6 million. Many of these Churches, which retain a certain eighteenth century elegance attractive to modern eyes, appalled many serious contemporaries and none more so than A. W. N. Pugin, to whom "they were showy worldly expedients, adapted only for those who live by splendid deception". The mass of paltry Churches, erected under the auspices of the Commissioners, were a disgrace to the age.[31] For Newman, this was the unpoetic Church of England, lacking a divine element, prayers and offices rendered meaningless, the beauty of worship annihilated, an incipient Socinianism everywhere, damp and dust rather than incense, royal arms for the crucifix, boxes of wood for the altar, a frigid, helpless dogmatic for orthodoxy.[32]

The Church of England was attacked from the outside by the Utilitarian, Radical philosophers.[33] In general, many critics were of the opinion that the Anglican clergy possessed much learning and science, sound manners but little theology.[34]

The fact that there were so few, however, who actually thought that the Church of England needed spiritual regeneration is ample testimony to the kind reception of Enlightenment ideas within the Church. In the eighteenth century, apart from Jacobitism, the Good Old Cause, the Hutchinsonians and the Evangelical Revival, the way of the Church of England was benign acceptance of the prevailing political, social and economic philosophies.[35] Those sincerely concerned with true High Church principles were limited to a few pious individuals like William Jones of Nayland and Bishop George Horne of Norwich, both disciples of Hutchinson, William Stevens, Joshua Watson and Thomas Sikes. The most illustrious of all was Dr. Martin Joseph Routh, President of Magdalen College, Oxford, to whom Newman dedicated his *Lectures on the Prophetical Office in the Church* of 1837 and who revived interest in the Fathers of the Church to a forgetful generation.[36] Yet divines like these did not exercise a profound influence upon the Church of England at large. The majority thought of the Church of England as a great national institution, a preserver of peace, good order and culture. The revival of dry bones needed positive visions rather than occasional gleams of light.

By the beginning of the nineteenth century, Church and society had absorbed much of the prevailing atmosphere of the philosophical, literary, social and economic aspects of the Enlightenment. In part, the Romantic Movement was a reaction to much of the spirit of the Enlightenment.[37] To those who were disillusioned with the current order and scheme of things, the Romantic spirit spoke of the rebirth of wonder. It brought inspiration, joy and admiration. This was closely linked to a religious feeling, a sense of immense spiritual power discerned in the mysteries of Nature. The shallow intellectualism and artificial concerns of the eighteenth century were anathema to the Romantic spirit.

Percy Bysshe Shelley, one of the stars of Romanticism,[38] was of the opinion that poets are the unacknowledged legislators of the world, which had far too long been shut up in coffee houses and respectable clubs. Samuel Taylor Coleridge (1772–1834), Robert Southey (1774–1843) and William Wordsworth (1770–1850) came together in what they considered to be a hard and shallow age. In contrast to Locke, Coleridge thought that poetry could transform the world.[39] Through the imagination, a transcendental order could be found which explained the world of appearances and accounted for the effect visible events have upon people. Coleridge, who, according to de Quincey, was "the greatest and most spacious, the subtlest and most comprehensive, that has yet existed among men",[40] became the fiercest critic of the Rationalists and Utilitarians, for whom people and truth were always in opposition. An enlightened people will always be philosophical, only half civilised people are poetical.[41]

The regeneration of the world was Coleridge's vision. The poet and the philosopher dealt with the same subject-matter, the great problems of the world and of human life. As poet, mystic, philosopher and theologian, he challenged the prevailing intellectual, social and political climate with the depth of knowledge and breadth of application which only the polymath can muster. The Scriptures were hailed as the living educts of the imagination and contrasted with political economy as the products of an "unenlivened generalised understanding". The false dichotomy between subject and object, self and the world, the conscious and the unconscious, was overcome. As an acute critic of society, Coleridge realised that if poetry without the mystic or spiritual element meant Darwin's *Botanic Gardens*, so too in theology this meant Paley's *Evidences* and in morals Benthamite Utilitarianism. Since the world was composed exclusively of either Platonists or Aristotelians, with reason and imagination of great importance for the former and only understanding, signifying prudence in morality, external evidence in theology and pure expediency in politics for the latter, it was perfectly clear that the Aristotelians had come to dominate the world since the beginning of the eighteenth century. Society was consequently seen very much according to the principles of *laissez-faire*, a mere mechanism for distributing certain attributes of happiness. In contrast, Coleridge visualised society as an organism which had grown and developed over the centuries, to be studied as a whole in its vital principles.

Robert Southey was no less dedicated to the regeneration of the world than Coleridge.[42] In him there was that deep combination of passion, romance and righteousness which made such an impression upon the Tractarians.[43] His *Book of the Church* of 1824[44] illustrated his supreme faith in the Church of England, idealised in a romantic, nationalist, Tory sense as a bulwark of defence against heathenism, papal idolatry, superstition and triumphant secularism. His ideal reformer was the average Church of England clergyman who performed his duties with immense pastoral care and was rewarded by the devotion of his parishioners.[45]

The art of poetry had sunk to an unprecedented nadir, claimed the Romantics, during the latter half of the eighteenth century. Pope was rebuked for turning poetry into "a mere mechanic art".[46] Those who thought of poetry as an idle pleasure were castigated by William Wordsworth.[47] The dissociation of sensibility and the dessication of art had reached its apotheosis by the 1790's. The way was led by the most eminent moral theologian of the age, William Paley, whose trilogy of books, *The Principles of Moral and Political Philosophy* of 1785, *View of the Evidences of Christianity* of 1794 and *Natural Theology* of 1802 were widely read as standard text-books. For the Romantics, however, this was a mechanical view of Nature and an ignoble view of mankind. Here no mystery, beauty or divinity could be discovered. No attempt was made to lift the veil. Religious poetry was considered a strange concept, since poetry could not deal with God. Indeed, religion had little to do with liturgy or the aesthetic sense of beauty but only with proving God's existence and an appropriately suitable moral code. The Romantics seriously believed that Paley had reduced Nature to an inventory.[48] Encountering a culture which visualised poetry as belonging to an uncivilised age, religion increasingly adopting the theories of the evidence school of Religion and Nature conceived as a backcloth against which God's existence could be proved, Wordsworth wrote of the poet's role in prophetic, mystical terms. Instead of merely addressing the bourgeoisie, Wordsworth spoke to the whole nation.[49]

In contrast to the prevailing culture which did not wish to see any connection between religion and poetry, Wordsworth affirmed the essential complementarity of both disciplines with total dedication.[50] In the *Essay* of 1815, Wordsworth wrote, "The concerns of religion refer to indefinite objects and are too weighty for the mind to support them without relieving itself by resting a great part of the burthen upon words and symbols. The commerce between man and his Maker cannot be carried on but by a process where much is represented in little, and the Infinite Being accommodates himself to a finite capacity. In all this may be perceived the affinity between religion and poetry".[51]

Whereas Johnson had considered the language of rustics barbarous,[52] Wordsworth was at pains to illustrate their particular spiritual significance. In *The Preface to the Lyrical Ballads* both Coleridge and Wordsworth spoke of their intent to use the language of men in low and rustic life because they "hourly communicate with the best objects from which the best part of the language is derived".[53] While Paley, representing symbolically the prevailing trends of his age, severed the connection between Nature, Religion and Poetry, seeing the poor as objects for possible fodder material for the bourgeoisie, Wordsworth revolutionised the world-view in favour of making poetry not only the best medium for religious truth but also of portraying the poet as the harbinger of prophecy and vision. The poor were raised from their status as pitiable objects of pity to that of emblems of true humanity.

The concepts of Nature, Religion and Poetry were brought into the safe haven of holy Church in Wordsworth's *Ecclesiastical Sketches* of 1822.[54] Their theme was similar to Southey's *Book of the Church* of 1824. Both authors saw the Church as a divine institution, not the human product of the Reformation, a national English affair which had existed since early times, the perfect moulder of the English character and alongside the hearth and the Throne, the most naturally blessed of English establishments.[55]

It was Newman's opinion that John Keble made the Church of England poetical.[56] Keble introduced into the Church a note which had not been heard for many years, the music of a new school.[57] *The Christian Year*, written as a work of religious devotion rather than as an act of literary self-sufficiency, was not divorced from the tumult of the bustling, active world but addressed to real people with real needs.[58] By understanding the universe in a sacramental, mythological way, Keble was possibly the greatest Wordsworthian of them all.[59] Keble's poetry was aimed at directing the minds of its hearers away from the materialism of this world to the realities of the eternal world, not by ignoring the banalities of this world but by transcending them.

Nature, Religion and Poetry reflected a synthesis which was essentially Wordsworthian. In his *Lectures on Poetry* of 1844,[60] Keble stressed that the function of poetry was moral and religious, "to lift to a higher plane all the emotions of our minds, and to make them take their part in a diviner philosophy".[61] Religion and poetry are alike in their powers of healing. Truth is difficult for both and will yield only to devotion. Poetry and Religion are equally subject to "the vision of something more beautiful, greater and more lovable, than all that the mortal eye can see". They make common use of the external world. Poetry leads men "to the secret sources of Nature" for images and symbols which it lends to religion, which in turn clothes them with its splendour and returns them to poetry as sacraments.[62] Poetry has preceded all the great religious revivals of mankind, Plato and Virgil in antiquity, Spenser and Shakespeare in the Renaissance. This was Keble's poetic vision of the regenerate society, with the Church's ministerial Ordinances and Sacraments restored to her rightful position at the centre of society. The poor were no longer seen as objects of derision but as signs of God's presence. Poverty was no longer an inevitable, sinful calamity but a source of rich blessings. Keble's poetry became the vehicle of all that he held dear, the doctrines of Reserve and Tradition and the mystical interpretation of Scripture, all of which he had learned from the Fathers. As poetry had become the vehicle of social criticism for Coleridge, Southey and Wordsworth, Chapter 1 deals with the inherent political and social appraisal which Keble made of his society in *The Christian Year* with references to his Sermons, Tracts, Treatises and letters.

If the aim of *The Christian Year* was to make the spirit of the Prayer Book a living reality and to bring the feelings and thoughts of the men of his age into harmony with such a spirit, the result could only reflect the general feeling which Keble had for the society in which he lived. His poem "King Charles the Martyr" was a vivid illustration of the way the Caroline heritage and the tradition of the Non-Jurors was still alive. Already in 1827 Keble was aware of how the poetic Church was being stifled by the increasingly encroaching policies of the State. The sermon "National Apostasy" is discussed in Chapter 1 as an example of what Keble felt to be the supreme sacrilege, the meddling of politicians with God's Church.

Richard Hurrell Froude's political and social thought was formed very much during the revolutionary years of 1828–1833 when it seemed that two hundred years of history were being condensed into five. Since 1789 two alliances, that between the clergy of most religious outlooks and the government and that between the political economists and some leading Churchmen, seemed to augur well for the Church's material and spiritual fortunes. By the 1820's, however, another alliance, less well defined in composition but unreservedly clear about its aims, threatened the exalted position of the Church of England. Radicals, Roman Catholics, Utilitarian philosophers and anti-clerical Whigs acted as if they were possessed by one supreme mission in life, to break utterly the Church's monopoly of national and local government, to abolish rates or tithes, and to abrogate the laws and customs by which for centuries the whole population in England had been baptised, married and buried.[63] In such an atmosphere, Froude showed himself to be a true child of the Romantic spirit.[64] Unlike the Whigs, who loathed the Middle Ages, Froude's Romantic spirit embraced all things medieval with unbounded enthusiasm.[65] Even his illness reflected a Romantic trend. Both Coleridge and Froude were called the Hamlet of their times.[66]

In 1828 the Test and Corporation Acts were repealed, thus

destroying at a stroke the traditional view that Parliament was the Lay Synod of the Church of England. The Roman Catholic Emancipation Act of 1829 seemed to threaten the whole delicate balance of the Elizabethan Settlement. The Church of England's central role as the Church of the English nation appeared to look absurd as persons, whose main role in life was to subvert the Church, were given political power in the State.[67] In 1829 Froude was deeply impressed by Robert Southey's *Colloquies on the Progress and Prospects of Society* with its portrayal of the advantages of feudal times, its rational defence of the Established Church with the Constitution as the greatest bulwark of defence against an unstable world, its inculcation of spiritual rather than material values and the revival of monasteries and sisterhoods. Equally impressive in its defence of the Old Order was Coleridge's *On the Constitution of Church and State* of 1830 which idealised the dialectical unity between Church and State.[68] For the Tractarians the 1832 Reform Bill was the final blow, as ecclesiastical reform seemed inevitable. The Whigs' Temporalities Bill of 1833 proposed to abolish ten bishoprics in Ireland and redistribute their income to support the poorer clergy and maintain Church fabric.

In these radical months, Froude set the scene for the counter-revolution. With the skill, if occasionally intemperate, of the canon lawyer, Froude wrote articles for *The British Magazine* on "State Interference in Matters Spiritual". In 1832 Froude went with his father and Newman on their Mediterranean tour and became unconsciously the main connection between the Oxford Movement and similar events in France. Chapter 2 discusses the political significance of Froude's articles and their effect upon Keble and Newman. The significance of the posthumously published *Remains* is discussed in the final part of the Chapter.

In 1829 Newman published his "Poetry, with Reference to Aristotle's Poetics" in the newly founded *London Review*. Religion is essentially poetical, since it is a duty for Christians to colour all things with hues of faith, to see a divine meaning in every event. Poetry is a most sanitary medicine in a period of crisis in values.[69] Realising the need for a reaction from what was considered to be the dry and superficial character of eighteenth century religious teaching, Newman praised Scott, Coleridge, Wordsworth and Southey for penetrating below the surface of things and drawing men from the material to the invisible world.⁷⁰ When Newman read Coleridge for the first time in 1835, he was surprised to find so much of what he thought to be his own there.⁷¹ By 1835 Newman had been reading the Fathers for many years. The Romantic spirit did much to arouse Newman. Coleridge confirmed much of what he had read about the Church of Alexandria. In many respects, there were many similarities between the Alexandrian school of thought and the Romantics.⁷²

In Chapter 3 Newman is considered first and foremost as the theologian of the Church. Only then can his concepts of the Church's relation to State and society be assessed. Newman's reading of Romantic literature confirmed his greatest passion, the Church of the Fathers.⁷³ "How are we to prevent the Church from being liberalised?" was Newman's question in 1833.⁷⁴ The Church of Alexandria provided the answer.⁷⁵ Having read the Fathers for the first time at the age of fifteen in Joseph Milner's *Church History*,⁷⁶ it was in 1829 that Newman set about to read them chronologically, beginning with St Ignatius and St Justin. His love of the Alexandrian tradition was amply illustrated in his first great work, *The Arians of the Fourth Century* of 1833.

When Newman considered the Church in her relationship with the State and society, he had three prevalent norms in mind, the Bible, the Fathers and the Anglican Divines of the seventeenth century. The emphasis was on the Fathers as they were the authoritative interpreters of the Bible and the basic source of the Anglican Divines in their attempt to shape Anglicanism. This belief was reflected in Newman's most powerful work on the nature of the Church of England, his *Lectures on the Prophetical Office of the Church* of 1837. After 1837 Newman became persuaded that there could be no rashness in giving to the world in fullest measure the teaching of the Fathers, as the Church of England was very largely founded upon them.⁷⁷ From 1840 to 1845 Newman's complete interest in the Fathers was illustrated in *The Church of the Fathers* of 1840, itself a seris of articles which had appeared in *The British Magazine*; his critical review of Milman's *History of Christianity* of 1841;⁷⁸ his fascination with the theology of Saint Athanasius, especially the famous treatises, *Orationes contra Arianos*, appearing as *Select Treatises of Saint Athanasius* of 1842; his *Tracts: Theological and Ecclesiastical* (two Volumes), being essentially patristic and his translation of the

French Fleury's *Church History* of 1842 to 1844, convincing him of the primary significance of the fourth century Fathers. Till the end of his Anglican career, Newman was reading voraciously Justin Martyr, Athanasius, Tertullian, Ambrose, Lactantius and Cyril.[79] It is only through the eyes of the patristic scholar that Newman's understanding of the Church through the ages and her present position in regard to State and society can be understood.

To understand Newman's social and political thought in its fulness during his Anglican period, it is also necessary to consider his constant emphasis upon the salvation of the individual soul.[80] Reacting to the prevalent culture which he saw as seeing man purely in terms of mechanical thought and analysis,[81] Newman was at pains to show that it is not man's reason which thinks but his whole being. When a person thinks, he uses all his cognitive powers in a whole system of interconnected activities. Nowhere is this more obvious than in the inner life of conscience when, to all intents and purposes, a man stands on his own but in reality face to face with two luminously evident beings, his true self and the living God. Newman's opposition to Sir Robert Peel over Catholic Emancipation in 1829 was a matter of conscience. The more a man obeyed his conscience, the more he felt alarmed at himself for obeying it so imperfectly. He realised his need for clearer guidance and more strength. Our conscience is a personal guide but, since men do not live alone, external assistance may be necessary to help it into action. In an age when so many books were being published to prove what men ought to believe and why, the best argument, even for those who cannot read, for proving the existence of God is "that which arises out of a careful attention to the teachings of the heart, and a comparison between the claims of conscience and the announcements of the gospel".[82]

Newman considered that he was living at the end of the age of evidences, "when love was cold", when the invincible character of the Argument from Design was still being accepted by the devout. Newman was fiercely opposed to the evidential school of theologians like Paley. Southey commented, "in came calculation and out went feeling".[83] Newman wrote of the usurpation of reason.[84] In Chapter 3 "The Tamworth Reading Room" of 1841 is considered as a piece of social criticism of the age. In his reaction to what many considered the Enlightenment emphasis upon separating the intellect from feeling, causing that dissociation of sensibility,[85] Newman has been compared with Pascal, Schleiermacher and Kierkegaard.[86] A comparison with Wordsworth would be more immediately relevant. In his *Preface to the Lyrical Ballads*, Wordsworth made a strong claim for the holiness of the heart's affections and preferred instinct to formal learning. Far more powerful than reason are the faculties of perception which transcend rational analysis; that love, that holy passion and sense of excitement which lead to the apprehension of a divine unity at the heart of Creation.[87] Newman lived in the Oriel Common Room which stank of logic; poetry, eloquence and devotion were chiefly intended to feed syllogisms.[88] In contrast, Newman preferred to speak about instinct, feeling, truth and genius. This emphasis upon feeling differentiated Newman from the Evangelicals, who, for all their attachment to the religion of the heart, devalued the importance of the sacraments by their excessive emphasis upon the Atonement. This was an inadequate response to Rationalism. "Right feeling" also meant listening to the promptings of the Church. Yet feelings on their own do not lead to the salvation of souls. Feelings must lead to actions, for which man is born. The Enlightenment had said, according to Newman, Dare to Know. Newman was at one with the Romantics who declared, Dare to feel. He went one crucial step further, however, than the Romantics. It is inadequate to say, Dare to feel without also adding, Dare to act.

The General Conclusion assesses the importance of the attitudes of Keble, Froude and Newman to the Church in her relationship with the State and society.

NOTES

1. See O. Chadwick, *The Secularisation of the European Mind in the Nineteenth Century*, pp. 143 ff. On the general history of Enlightenment scholarship, see M. S. Anderson, *Historians and Eighteenth Century Europe 1715–1789*. A useful discussion of the bibliography of eighteenth century church history is found in J. Danielou, A. H. Couratin and John Kent, *Historical Theology: The Pelican Guide to Modern Theology, Vol. 2*, pp. 292–306. The best known studies on the European Enlightenment are, L. G. Crocker, ed., *The Age of Enlightenment*; Peter Gay, *The Enlightenment, An*

Interpretation. *Vol. 1, The Rise of Modern Paganism. vol. 2, The Science of Freedom*; Peter Hazard, *The European Mind 1680–1715*, Eng. trans. J. L. May; J. G. Hibben, *The Philosophy of the Enlightenment*. On the Enlightenment in England, see G. R. Cragg, *Reason and Authority in the Eighteenth Century*; E. Halevy, *The Growth of Philosophic Radicalism*; J. H. Plumb, *The Commercialisation of Leisure in Eighteenth Century England*; J. Redwood, *Reason, Ridicule and Religion: The Age of Enlightenment in England 1660–1750*; A. Richardson, *History Sacred and Profane*; L. Stephen, *History of English Thought in the Eighteenth Century*, 2 Vols; B. Willey, *The Eighteenth Century Background*.

For a recent reassessment of the Enlightenment, see especially S. W. Gilley, "Christianity and Enlightenment, An Historical Survey", *History of European Ideas*, Vol. 1, pp. 103–121; Jack Lively, "The Europe of the Enlightenment", *History of European Ideas*, vol. 1, pp. 91–102; Roy Porter, "The Enlightenment in England" in R. Porter and M. Teich, *The Enlightenment in National Context*.

On the attitudes of the Tractarians to Church and society, see Ruth Kenyon, "The Social Aspects of the Catholic Revival" in N. P. Williams and C. Harris, ed., *Norhtern Catholicism, Centenary Studies in the Oxford and Parallel Movements*, pp. 367–400; W. G. Peck, *The Social Implications of the Oxford Movement*. On Tractarian attitudes to Church and State, see J. R. Griffin, *Tractarian Politics* (unpublished PhD thesis, Trinity College, Dublin); H. Laski, *Studies in the Problem of Sovereignty*. On Church, State and society, see C. K. Gloyn, *The Church in the Social Order, A Study of Anglican Social Theory from Coleridge to Maurice*, pp. 47 ff.
2. Paul Hazard, *The European Mind*, op. cit.
3. Peter Gay, *The Enlightenment*, Vol. 1, p. 8.
4. Gay, ibid. pp. 401–19.
5. Bernard Lonergan, S. J., *A Second Collection*, p. 57.
6. Peter Hodgson and Robert King, ed., *Christian Theology, An Introduction to Its Traditions and Tasks*, p. 232.
7. J. Redwood, *Reason, Ridicule and Religion: The Age of Enlightenment in England 1660–1750*, pp. 150–220.
8. Charles Blount, *Miscellaneous Works*. In this edition, Blount (1654–93) attacked miracles and the belief in immortality. Thomas Chubb (1679–1746), *The Comparative Excellence and Obligation of Moral and Positive Duties* (1730) taught that Reason was a sufficient guide to God's favour. Anthony Collins (1676–1729), *A Discourse on Free-thinking Occasion'd by the Rise and Growth of a Sect Call'd Free-Thinkers* (1713) was a friend of John Locke and was the most prominent spokesman for complete tolerance. Conyers Middleton

(1683–1750), *A Free Inquiry into the Miraculous Powers, which are Supposed to have subsisted in the Christian Church* (1749). His assault on miracles was incomparably the most effective of the whole deist controversy. Matthew Tindal (1657?–1733), *Christianity as Old as Creation or the Gospel, A Republication of the Religion of Nature* (1730) was called "the deists' Bible". John Toland (1670–1722), *Christianity Not Mysterious* (1696) was one of the most influential deist writers. William Woolaston (1660–1724), *The Religion of Nature Delineated* (1722) was a rationalist deist, for whom the God of Nature was also the God of reason and justice. Thomas Woolston (1670–1731), *Discourses on the Miracles of Our Saviour* (1727–30) was the most outspoken deist, questioning the New Testament miracles.

9. On Bishop Butler's refutation of deism, see David Brown, *The Divine Trinity*, pp. 3–51. Similarly, George Berkeley wrote his *Principles of Human Knowledge* (1710) in explicit opposition to "scepticism, atheism and religion" which he saw as the ultimate consequence of the Lockean philosophy and the scientific approach which it formulated and rejected. See Edward A. Sillem, *George Berkeley and the Proofs for the Existence of God*.
10. Thomas Sherlock (1678–1761), Bishop of London (1748–61) wrote his *Trial of the Witnesses of the Resurrection of Jesus* (1729) which was a highly apologetic writing, characteristic of the age.
11. Richard Watson (1773–1816), Bishop of Llandaff (1782–1816), was considered one of the outstanding apologists for Christianity.
12. On William Paley (1743–1805), see M. L. Clarke, *Paley, Evidences for the Man*; Tess Cosslett, ed., *Science and Religion in the Nineteenth Century*, pp. 25–45.
13. See E. C. Mossner, *The Life of David Hume*, p. 483.
14. See W. T. Cairns, *The Religion of Dr Johnson and Other Essays*, pp. 1–23.
15. Stephen Prickett, *Romanticism and Religion, The Tradition of Coleridge and Wordsworth in the Victorian Church*, pp. 76 ff. Roy Porter, "The Enlightenment in England", op. cit. makes much of this important point, pp. 15 ff.
16. Thomas Birch, *The History of the Royal Society* (4 Vols.) (London, 1756), Vol. I, pp. 222–30, quoted by J. E. Force, "Hume and the Relation of Science to Religion among Certain Members of the Royal Society", *Jl of the History of Ideas*, Vol. XLV, No. 4, pp. 517–36. See also Force, "Secularisation, The Language of God and the Royal Society at the Turn of the Seventeenth Century", *History of European Ideas*, Vol. 2, No. 3, pp. 221–35.
17. Gay, Vol. 1, op. cit. pp. 266 ff. For a discussion of this development, see Mark Pattison, "Tendencies of Religious

Thought in England 1688–1750" in *Essays and Reviews*, pp. 254–329.
18. For a brief discussion, see Andrew Louth's assessment of Vico, *Discerning the Mystery, An Essay on the Nature of Theology*, pp. 18 ff. A recent study of Vico is G. Tagliacozzo, *Vico And Contemporary Thought*.
19. Gay, I, op. cit. pp. 345 ff.
20. See A. Plummer, *The Church of England in the Eighteenth Century*, p. 239. Some older studies still retain their value: C. J. Abbey and J. H. Overton, *The English Church in the Eighteenth Century*, (2 Vols.); J. H. Overton and F. Relton, *The English Church from The Accession of George I to the end of the Eighteenth Century (1714–1800)*. The magisterial treatment of the Church in the eighteenth century is Norman Sykes, *Church and State in England in the Eighteenth Century, From Sheldon to Secker, Aspects of English Church History 1660–1768*. A more recent survey is James L. Clifford, ed., *Man Versus Society in Eighteenth Century Britain: six points of view*. In this collection of essays, it is maintained that while involvement in the world often led the Hanoverian Church to forfeit its prophetic role, it also often led to a heightened social and moral concern for that world.

For two recent surveys of the Church in the eighteenth century, see Richard Sharp, "New Perspectives on the High Church Tradition: historical background 1730–1780" and Peter Nockles, "The Oxford Movement: Historical background 1780–1833" in Geoffrey Rowell, ed., *Tradition Renewed, The Oxford Movement Conference Papers*, pp. 4–50.
21. *L. & C.* II, p. 200.
22. W. Ward (intro.), *Newman's Apologia Pro Vita Sua, the two Versions of 1864 and 1865 preceded by Newman's and Kingsley's Pamphlets*, pp. xxiii–xxvii.
23. For these views, see J. A. Froude, "The Oxford Counter-Reformation" in *Short Studies on Great Subjects* (4 Vols.), Vol. IV, pp. 231–252.
24. For the Tractarian view which follows, see R. I. Wilberforce, *A Sketch of the History of Erastianism together with two Sermons on the Reality of the Church's Ordinances, and on the Principle of Church Authority*, pp. 65–86. For a detailed treatment of Bishop Hoadly which sees him as representing a certain trend in the eighteenth century, see N. Sykes, "Benjamin Hoadly, Bishop of Bangor" in F. J. C. Hearnshaw, ed., *The Social and Political Ideals of some English Thinkers of the Augustan Age*, pp. 112–157; *Church and State in the Eighteenth Century*, pp. 332–362; Norman Ravitch, *Sword and Mitre. Government and Episcopate in France and*

England in the Age of Aristocracy; H. D. Rock, "Christ's Kingdom Not of this World, Benjamin Hoadly Versus William Law" in Derek Baker, ed., *Studies in Church History,* Vol. 12, *Church, Society and Politics.*
25. On the Evangelicals, see F. K. Brown, *Fathers of the Victorians,* which is highly critical of William Wilberforce's generation; Michael Hennell, *Sons of the Prophets, Evangelical Leaders of the Victorian Church* which is a very uncritical history of the lives of Fowell Buxton, Edward Bickersteth, Lord Shaftesbury, Alexander Haldane, Henry Venn, James Stephen and Francis Close.
26. James of Creaton, quoted by G. V. Bennett and J. D. Walsh, *Essays in English Church History,* p. 351.
27. For Burke's contribution, see E. R. Norman, *Church and Society in England, 1770–1970,* pp. 21 ff.
28. There is no proper history of the Phalanx. The best back-ground material is found in A. Webster, *Joshua Watson, The Story of a Layman* and Francis Warre Cornish, *The English Church in the Nineteenth Century* (2 parts), Vol. I, pp. 62–76. From a Church patronage viewpoint, the Church by 1827 was certainly flourishing, Keble, writing *The Christian Year*, published "in a time of peace and plenty for his Church, when Lord Liverpool's government was in power, when Church patronage was dispensed more respectably perhaps than it had ever been, and when Church Reform had not showed itself on paper". Yet even though these were the palmy days of the Establishment, Keble discerned that neither in doctrine nor in ethical standard was it even as much as it might have been according to its own principles. See J. H. Newman, *Ess.* II, p. 428.
29. A. D. Gilbert, *Religion and Society in Industrial England,* p. 57.
30. For the nature of this alliance, see A. M. C. Waterman, "The Ideological Alliance of Political Economy and Christian Theology, 1798–1833", *The Jl of Ecclesiastical History,* Vol. 34, No. 2, April 1983. William Paley (1743–1805) wrote *The Principles of Moral and Political Philosophy*, which became a standard text-book for Cambridge Undergraduates. J. B. Sumner (1780–1862) became Archbishop of Canterbury in 1848. Edward Copleston (1787–1863) was Provost of Oriel, 1814–1827 and Bishop of Llandaff (1827–1849). Richard Whately (1787–1863) was Fellow of Oriel in 1811, Drummond Professor of Political Economy at Oxford in 1829, Archbishop of Dublin in 1831. His *Letters on the Church by an Episcopalian* of 1826 did influence Newman though later he became an opponent of the Oxford Movement.
31. A. W. N. Pugin, *The True Principles of Pointed or Christian Architecture,* pp. 45 ff.
32. J. H. Newman, *Ess.* II, pp. 443–4.

33. For the attacks of Jeremy Bentham and James Mill in *The Westminster Review* of 1824, see E. L. Halevy, *The Liberal Awakening, A History of the English People in the Nineteenth Century*, Vol. II, pp. 30 ff; Leslie Stephen, *The English Utilitarians* (3 Vols.), Vol. 1 is a good introduction to the thought of the Utilitarians generally.
34. See J. H. Overton, *The English Church in the Nineteenth Century 1800–1833*, pp. 217 ff.
35. For Jacobitism generally, see I. Kenwick, *Bolingbroke and his Circle, the Politics of Nostalgia in the Age of Walpole*. On John Hutchinson, see Leslie Stephen, *History of English Thought in the Eighteenth Century* (2 Vols.), Vol. 1, pp. 389–91.

    On Evangelicalism, see F. K. Brown op. cit. and M. Hennell, op. cit. See also E. Jay, *The Evangelical and Oxford Movements*.
36. On the Orthodox party, see L. E. Elliott-Binns, *Religion in the Victorian Era*, pp. 46 ff; F. Warre, *The English Church in the Nineteenth Century*, (2 Vols.), Vol. 1, pp. 62–76; on Routh, see J. W. Burgon, *The Lives of Twelve Good Men*, pp. 1–115.
37. Some of the main studies of Romanticism are J. B. Halsted, ed., *Romanticism: Definition, Explanation and Evaluation*; Hugh Honour, *Romanticism*. For much of the political background, see M. Bowra, *The Romantic Imagination*; Crane Brinton, *The Political Ideas of the English Romanticists*; M. Butler, *Romantics, Rebels and Reactionaries, English Literature and its Background, 1760–1830*; A. Cobban, *Edmund Burke and the Revolt against the Eighteenth Century, A Study of the Political and Social Thinking of Burke, Wordsworth, Coleridge and Southey*; S. Prickett, *Romanticism and Religion*, op. cit.; M. B. Reckitt, *From Maurice to Temple, A Century of the Social Movement in the Church of England*, pp. 37–74; Carl Woodring, *Politics in English Romantic Poetry*.
38. Bowra, op. cit., pp. 117–121.
39. ibid., p. 3. In the *Apo.*, pp. 93 ff., Newman praised Scott, Coleridge Southey and Wordsworth as the advocates of a deeper philosophy in reaction to the dry and superficial character of the religious teaching and literature of the last generation.
40. Cited by Leslie Stephen, *Hours in a Library* (3 Vols.), Vol. III, p. 319. A recent study of Coleridge is David Jasper, *Coleridge as Poet and Religious Thinker, Inspiration and Revelation*. Good studies of Coleridge as a political and social thinker are David P. Calleo, *Coleridge and the Idea of the Modern State*; John Colmer, *Coleridge, Critic of Society*; John Coulson, *Newman and the Common Tradition, A Study in the Language of Church and Society*, pp. 1–51; W. F. Kennedy, "Humanist Versus Economist. The Economic Thought of Samuel Taylor Coleridge", *Univ. of*

INTRODUCTION 23

California Publications in Economics (Vol. XVII); R. J. White, *The Political Thought of Samuel Taylor Coleridge*.
41. See Carl Dawson, *Victorian Noon, English Literature in 1850*, pp. 222 ff.
42. See G. Carnall, *Robert Southey in his Age, The Development of a Conservative Mind*.
43. Cf. *Apo.*, pp. 93 ff. Newman referred to Southey's "Thalaba"for which he had much affection. See W. Ward, *Life of John Henry Cardinal Newman* (2 Vols.), Vol. II, p. 315. "Thalaba" is found in Robert Southey, *The Poetical Works*, Vol. IV. For contemporary criticism of "Thalaba", see L. Madden, ed., *Robert Southey, The Critical Heritage*, pp. 63–95; K. Curry, *Southey*, pp. 159–160. For Southey's influence upon Newman, see T. Vargish, *Newman: The Contemplation of Mind*, pp. 99–100.
44. For a full discussion, see Sheridan Gilley, "Nationality and Liberty, Protestant and Catholic; Robert Southey's Book of the Church" in S. Mews, ed., *Studies in Church History*, Vol. 18, *Religion and National Identity*, pp. 409 ff.
45. See Carnall, op. cit., p. 191 for John Keble's letter to Southey on the spiritual strength of the Church in 1833.
46. See M. Bright, "English Literary Romanticism and the Oxford Movement" in *The Jl of the History of Ideas*, Vol. XL, pp. 389 ff. This was Cowper's verdict upon Pope's poetry.
47. "Those who talk of Poetry as a matter of amusement and idle pleasure; who will converse with us gravely about a taste for poetry, as they express it, as if it were a thing as indifferent as taste for rope-dancing, or Frontiniac or Sherry". See R. L. Brett and A. R. Jones, ed., "Preface", *Lyrical Ballads*, p. 257.
48. See Prickett, op. cit., p. 84 for Wordsworth's reaction to Paley who saw Nature purely as a mechanism and not as involvement.
49. See M. Butler, op. cit., p. 66 on Wordsworth's adaptation of Milton's heroic style.
50. A very important contemporary theme. See David Jasper, ed., *Images of Belief in Literature*.
51. W. J. B. Owen and J. W. Smyser, *William Wordsworth, The Prose Works*, Vol. III, p. 65.
52. This was a common enough eighteenth century insight. Joseph Priestley thought "vulgar words and phrases unsuitable for a gentleman". In *The Plan of a Dictionary of the English Language*, Samuel Johnson wished to include "words and phrases used in the general intercourse of life, or found in the works of those we commonly style polite writers". There could be no slang in the English language, that is, a corrupt dialect used by beggars and vagabonds, or particular forms of speaking used by certain classes of

men, and barbarous jargon. See Mona Wilson, ed., *The Plan of a Dictionary of the English Language in Samuel Johnson; Prose and Poetry*, p. 23.
53. R. L. Brett and A. R. Jones, ed., *Wordsworth and Coleridge; Lyrical Ballads*, p. 239. For the general significance attributed by Coleridge and Wordsworth to rustic language, see M. Stonyk, *Nineteenth Century English Literature*, pp. 5 ff.
54. See G. B. Tennyson, *Victorian Devotional Poetry, The Tractarian Mode*, pp. 224–225.
55. For Wordsworth's adherence to Anglicanism, see Gilley, op. cit., pp. 416–418. Fuller references to Wordsworth's influences upon Keble are found in chapter 1, "The Christian Year".
56. J. H. Newman, *Ess.*, II, p. 442. For the connection between the Oxford Movement and Romanticism, see M. Bright, op. cit., pp. 385–404; C. F. Harrold, "The Oxford Movement, A Reconsideration" in J. E. Baker, ed., *The Reinterpretation of Victorian Literature*, pp. 39 ff.; S. Prickett, op. cit.; G. B. Tennyson, op. cit.; A. H. Warren, *English Poetic Theory, 1825–1865*. For Keble's connection with the Romantic Movement, see Sheridan Gilley, "John Keble and the Victorian Churching of Romanticism" in J. R. Watson, ed., *An Infinite Complexity, Essays in Romanticism*, pp. 226–239.
57. *Apo.*, op. cit., p. 26.
58. Tennyson, op. cit., p. 74. For the influence of *The Christian Year*, ibid., pp. 226–232.
59. Prickett, op. cit., pp. 68, 71.
60. John Keble, *Praelectiones Academicae, De Poeticae Vi Medica*, transl. into English by E. K. Francis (2 Vols.), *Lectures on Poetry, 1832–1841*.
61. *Lectures on Poetry*, II, p. 157.
62. ibid., II, p. 481.
63. Owen Chadwick, *The Victorian Church* (2 Parts), Part 1, pp. 7–166; W. I. Mathieson, *English Church Reform 1815–1840*.
For the view that a whole social, political and religious order was destroyed by the events of 1828–32, see J. C. D. Clark, *English Society, 1688–1832, Ideology, Social Structure and Political Practice During the Ancien Regime*. The Hanoverian Constitution in Church and State was formidably well entrenched and strongly supported. The Revolution Settlement and the social structure were upheld by a religious, even more than a secular ideology. The Hanoverian polity was an "ancien régime", similar to Bourbon France. England was a "confesional state" with a "one-class society" throughout the years. Eighteenth century religious belief was crucial. Clergy played a significant role in the debates on the usefulness of religion in society

from skirmishes with the Deists to the defence of the Test Acts against the Dissenters. The Tractarians, amongst many others, did not retreat from "the spirit of the age" as much as read in the events of 1828–32 the most dramatic and profound changes ever affected in English society since the Reformation without recourse to widespread armed conflict.
64. Piers Brendon, *Hurrell Froude and the Oxford Movement*, pp. 26–40.
65. Brendon, ibid. For the Middle Ages as an ideal age of the Faith for many in the nineteenth century, see Owen Chadwick, *The Secularisation of the European Mind*, pp. 3 ff; for the view of the Whigs on the same period, ibid., pp. 210 ff.
66. For the illnesses from which Romantic poets seemed to suffer, thus symbolising much of the pathos of their writings, see M. Butler op. cit., pp. 76, 93. For the comparison of Froude with Hamlet, see Brendon op. cit., pp. 107–108, 166–167, 176–177.
67. See E. R. Norman, *Anti-Catholicism in Victorian England*. More detailed references are found in Chapter 3, "Newman and Roman Catholic Emancipation".
68. For an assessment, see Raymond Williams, *Culture and Society, 1780–1950*, pp. 21 ff; Curry, op. cit., pp. 82–88; Madden, op. cit., pp. 334–389; Prickett, op. cit., p. 255.
69. On Newman's relationship to the Romantic Movement, see Vargish, op. cit., pp. 98–108; H. L. Weatherby, *Cardinal Newman in his Age, His Place in English Theology and Literature*, pp. 97–134. For a discussion of "Poetry, with references to Aristotle's Poetics", found in *Ess.*, I, pp. 1–26, see Weatherby, op. cit., pp. 264 ff.; Tennyson, op. cit., pp. 37 ff; Warren, op. cit., pp. 35 ff.
70. *Apo.*, p. 94.
71. *L. & C., II,* p. 35. See also Coulson, op. cit., pp. 254–256 on "How much of Coleridge had Newman read?"
72. Weatherby, op. cit., pp. 98 ff. C. F. Harrold argued to the contrary, stating that the Fathers saved Newman from a vague Nature mysticism. See his "Newman and the Alexandrian Platonists" in *Modern Philology*, Vol. XXXVII (1939–1940), pp. 279–291. Such a view, however, seriously underrates the Platonic and mystical content of the Romantics.
73. T. M. Parker, "The Rediscovery of the Fathers in the Seventeenth Century Anglican Tradition" in John Coulson and A. M. Allchin, ed., *The Rediscovery of Newman*, pp. 31–49.
74. *Apo.* p. 39.
75. ibid. p. 36.
76. ibid. p. 22.
77. ibid. pp. 60 ff.

78. Published in *Ess.*, II, pp. 186 ff.
79. Owen Chadwick, *From Bossuet to Newman, The Idea of Doctrinal Development*, p. 119.
80. *U.S.*, Sermon V, pp. 75 ff.
81. For Newman's reaction to the Enlightenment, see Louth, op. cit., pp. 136 ff.
82. *O.S.*, p. 74. The main studies of the conscience in Newman are found in Chapter 3, "Newman and Roman Catholic Emancipaton".
83. Robert Southey, *Colloquies on the Progress and Prospects of Society*, p. 79.
84. *U.S.*, Sermon IV, pp. 54 ff.
85. Louth, op. cit., pp. 1–66.
86. For the comparison with Pascal, see J. M. Cameron, "Newman and the Empiricist Tradition" in John Coulson and A. M. Allchin, op. cit., pp. 76 ff; with Schleiermacher, see Stephen Sykes, *The Identity of Christianity, Theologians and the Essence of Christianity from Schleiermacher to Barth*, pp. 122 ff; with Kierkegaard, see John Macquarrie, "The Theological Implications of the Oxford Movement" in J. R. Wright, *Lift High the Cross*, pp. 15 ff.
87. Vargish, op. cit., pp. 100 ff.
88. *Apo.*, p. 156.

1

JOHN KEBLE
"The True Socialism, the True Liberty, Equality and Fraternity"

1.1 INTRODUCTION

These sentiments, expressed by Keble in one of his most memorable sermons, point to one of his favourite themes, that "in the Holy Catholic Church, the rich and the poor are indeed met together in the Name of the Lord, Whom they know to be not only the Maker but also the Redeemer and Regenerator of them all".[1] That this is a profound conviction is proved by the frequency of his references to it, around which, like rising and falling stars, everything else revolves.[2]

For Newman, Keble was never a man of indeterminate shades and shadows. Authority was everything, conscience, the Bible, the Church and Antiquity. What Keble hated most was "heresy, insubordination, resistance to things established, claims of independence, disloyalty, innovation, a critical censorious spirit".[3] Keble did once describe Jesus as "a poor Carpenter, obeying orders, working for his bread".[4] Obedience is essentially being "subject to law, and the rules of society".[5] Such an attitude, however, should not disguise the fact that there was also a note of subversion in much that Keble wrote. He was a sentimental Jacobite and, although appearing to accept the Establishment, in fact never missed a chance to cause mischievous trouble, as long as he was not involved personally.[6]

For Keble, England was similar to Nineveh in its national inclinations[7] for

> Wild thoughts within, bad men without,
> All evils spirits round about,
> Are banded in unblest device,
> To spoil Love's earthly Paradise.[8]

Keble liked to speak of "that sin of our age and nation which is even now written with a pen of iron and the point of a diamond in the records of eternity".[9] Indeed, England was very similar to Israel in the times of Solomon, for "high civilisation, so far as it goes, what is it but that very condition, which proved so fatal to this great king?", a condition which is nothing less than that which enables "each person to take to himself more and more of the very best in the several departments of life which come within the range of each respectively".[10]

Yet Keble never turned his back on such a state of affairs. Although he disliked unnecessary change,

> Since all that is not Heaven's must fade,
> Light be the hand of Ruin laid
> Upon the home I love:
> With lulling spells left soft Decay
> Steal on, and spare the giant sway,
> The crash of tower and grove,[11]

yet his main protest was not so much against change as such but against all that is base. It was one of the great merits of Coplestone's *Praelectiones Academicae* that it was "full of honest and holy indignation against all that is debasing, immoral or irreligious".[12] Although Keble disliked politics, thinking it only secondary in comparison with eternal realities,

> Some of us think much of politics,
> And of the great doings of this world;
> But what of them all in that Day?,[13]

yet his main aim in life was to strengthen what had decayed. "Our fears, our jealousies, our prayers, our efforts", he wrote, "should be mainly, not to say exclusively, directed to the preservation and well-being of the Catholic Church among us, as such; that we may restore what is gone to decay and strengthen the things which remain and are ready to die; lest our work be found at last wilfully imperfect before our God".[14] Keble was in no doubt as to the Church's role in this situation. If "universal consent among Christians is moral demonstration", then there must be a visible Church, full of sacramental grace and governed by succession from the Apostles. All of which means, according to Keble, "Ask for the Church of England, and we know which way people will point".[15]

1.2. The Christian Year (1827)

In his *Romanticism and Religion*, Stephen Prickett writes that, compared with Maurice and Ludlow, Keble merely evaded the issue of poverty, since to speak of "honourable poverty" is plain hypocrisy on the lips of a priest of the wealthy Established Church.[16] Many of Keble's expressions concerning the poor were, in fact, little more than echoes of the insights of Bishop Wilson of Sodor and Man, whose works Keble later edited. The poor ought to bless their state, since, compared with the rich, they have very few temptations, having no reckonings to make when they are dead. The poor are able to put their trust in God rather than in riches.[17]

Keble reiterated the same kind of counsel to the poor, who make up the masses of mankind. That is why they above all must have the Gospel preached to them.[18] There is a great advantage in being poor, for "they are comparatively free from several ensnaring temptations to which the rich are exposed.[19] Keble was convinced that there is much to be said for any poor cottage, since it is there that "very scanty wages will go towards providing the real comforts of life".[20] In the seventy four years of his life, from 1792 to 1866, Keble spent no fewer than forty three of them in rural parishes, first, as his father's Curate from 1823 to 1836 and, secondly, as parish priest of Hursley from 1836 to 1866. He saw how the exercise of prudence, courage and patience could make much of little. Who would not prefer to be like John the Baptist in the wilderness, eating his meat locusts and wild honey than be a wealthy King like Herod, "making a feast to his lords, high captains, and chief estates of Galilee?".[21]

In *The Christian Year*, Keble felt that the poor ought not to be too concerned about their daily sustenance, since daily bread could only mean the bread from heaven:

> Or rather help us, Lord, to choose the good,
> to pray for nought, to seek to none, but Thee,
> Nor by "our daily bread" mean common food,
> Nor say, "From this world's evil set us free;"
> Teach us to love, with Christ, our sole true bliss,
> Else, though in Christ's own words, we surely pray amiss.[22]

In any case, poverty is spiritually uplifting, for it is nothing else than a kind of fasting. If a poor man had been well taught how precisely to fast, if he were used to present his hunger and thirst as a kind of sacrifice to Christ, then he need not steal or cheat to live, since God would keep him alive, by any means that He may judge best. Keble never told his father's parishioners nor his own at Hursley how God would actually do this, but it would all be done in His own time, not man's.

Far from evading the issue of poverty, as Prickett has claimed, Keble wrote more about the issue of poverty than many theologians. Keble was always enthusiastic about the ability of the poor to understand, reason and appreciate so much in this mortal, sinful, fallen world. In his sermon, "Implicit Faith recognised by Reason", Keble quoted the story of an old peasant woman who silenced her Arian critic by merely reciting the Apostles' Creed, reflecting not bigotry or prejudice but true practical wisdom.[24] This reflects one of Keble's profound convictions, that the age thirsts so much after knowledge that there is no corresponding growth in holiness. This is to gain knowledge for its own sake. Yet there is much to be learned from those who do not profess to be well educated, especially since the simple and unlearned are able to reason and even follow intricate arguments.[25]

Keble did not see the toil of the poor man as an utilitarian exercise in merely tilling the land and gaining his daily livelihood. Keble asked his parishioners, "He that is poorest and lives hardest among you, has he not many spare hours in every week, which he is too apt to fill up with idleness or mischief? Has he not, even when he is doing his work, leisure to think on what he has read and heard of the promises and threatenings of God, of the state and hopes of man, of the forgiveness of sins, of death, judgement, heaven and hell?".[26] Indeed, the poor man is conscious of the diseases and cravings of the soul as well as the body. The rustic believer has much in common with the enlightened sceptic, as both have many problems to be solved. They are both engaged in the intellectual struggle, looking, as they are, for medicines and cures.[27]

The poor have another vital quality, since "particular usages or expressions of uneducated men are said to have more or less of 'unconscious poetry' in them".[28] It was Keble's conviction not only that the poor man could reason about his faith but also that he had the gift of poetry in his veins. In his review of Monro's *Parochial Work* Keble delighted to quote from the latter's insistence that "there are few people amongst whom the subject-matter of deep poetry resides more than among the English poor".[29] On the most dramatic occasions in this life, bodily pain, the death of a dear friend, intense hope, fear or disappointment, exile, the poor have the ability to express themselves in deeply poetic ways. Thus, they are able to arise above the turmoils, disappointments and weaknesses of this mortal life and "contrive imaginary escapes and little images of the repose" for which they long.[30]

What was the source of Keble's enlightened view of the reasoning and poetic powers of the poor man? Prickett has called Keble "the greatest Wordsworthian of them all".[31] This is the only way to understand not only Keble's dedication of his *Lectures on Poetry* to Wordsworth but also his praises of the Poet Laureate when the latter was awarded an honorary doctorate at Oxford. Wordsworth was unique in Keble's eyes as the perfect exponent of the manners, pursuits and traditional feelings of the poor. Indeed, all must read Wordsworth's poetry who wish "to feel that secret and harmonious intimacy which exists between honourable Poverty and the severer Muses, sublime Philosophy, yea, even our most holy Religion".[32] Excessive familiarity with this supreme tribute, however, has hidden the real significance of its inner meaning. Compare, for instance, Faber's dedication of his *Sights and Thoughts in Foreign Churches and among Foreign Peoples* to the same Wordsworth: " . . . in affectionate remembrance of much personal kindness, and many thoughtful considerations on the rites, prerogatives, and doctrines of the Holy

Church".[33] The contrast between the two tributes could not be more marked. Faber's is purely religious, a direct appeal in one kind only. Keble's combines what for him were three vital ingredients of his trinity of concepts, Nature, poverty and poetry.

Keble's tribute to Wordsworth reveals that he had learned from his inspired poetry the abiding truth, that this is a harsh world, yet the poet is able to transcend it and find solace in the perfect, unchanging world of Nature. M. H. Friedman makes this point when he refers to Wordsworth as one who "creates a fictive world in which men can find objects and circumstances that correspond with the dignity and intensity of human desires". What is more, Wordsworth's desire to take "subjects ... chosen from ordinary life" and apply to them "the power of giving the interest of novelty by the modifying colours of imagination" becomes more understandable.[34]

No person is better able to enter this sacred, mysterious and poetic world than the poor man. This is Wordsworth's constant theme, acknowledged by Keble. Wordsworth had no illusions about those who kept on insisting that the enjoyment of poetry was the preserve of the learned, who were unable to admit

> How little those formalities, to which
> With overweening trust alone we give
> The name of Education, have to do
> With real feelings and just sense.[35]

"Real feelings and just sense" is a good summary of the attitudes of the unlearned members of society. It was this precious insight which provoked so much admiration from Keble. Poetry has nothing at all to do with man's social state as such. It is available to all, especially the poor, as a source of new life. Here is the ever constant springing-well, the very stuff of which dreams and visions are made. The later Wordsworth had no concept of actually reforming the poor out of their social conditions. The station in which they found themselves in society was no dark hole from which they must dig themselves out at the earliest opportunity. Rather, Wordsworth's aim was to evoke sympathetic understanding of the suffering of the poor, among whom were heard truths

Replete with honour; sounds in unison
With loftiest promises of good and fair.[36]

All this was familiar to Keble. His *Lectures on Poetry* reflect on almost every page the same blessed trinity of Nature, poverty and poetry. Indeed, the poor prefer starvation to leaving their familiar fields and landmarks.[37] Keble, like Wordsworth, felt that poetry makes a man dignified. It makes him less materialistic and more spiritual. As the poor man has so little, he is particularly well placed to enjoy the spiritual maturity which is poetry's greatest pleasure, as it "disencumbers him of earthly affections, and lifts him nearer where he once was, and what he may be again".[38]

Lifting people out of their position, not in any social sense but purely in terms spiritual, poetic and religious, this is the aim of the poetic impulse. It is what Wordsworth had mainly in mind in his poem "The Excursion" with which Keble was familiar. Mary Moorman has paid this poem the ultimate tribute, as it is nothing less than "the poetic charter of the poor, the ignorant and the underprivileged in a way that no English poem has been before or since".[39] This is a realistic assessment, for the Wanderer is the voice of traditional Pastoral wisdom, who "could afford to suffer/ with those whom he saw suffer".[40] Wordsworth described a poor household as

A virtuous household, though exceeding poor!
Pure lives were they all, austere and gran,
And fearing God;[41]

The Wanderer trusts Nature. Above all, he gains through her renovative powers Resurrection and becomes

A Being made/of many beings.[42]

He remains untouched by the "disesteem of life". After every difficulty, he is able to recuperate in Nature's loving arms, as Nature breathes

immortality, revolving life/And greatness still revolving; infinite.[43]

Rather than lying down to be overtaken by the difficulties which life brings, the message of "The Excursion" is that the poor of the earth should transcend their environment, not politically or socially but poetically and spiritually. Then hope cannot decay, love cannot end, fulfilment cannot cease as

> The food of hope
> Is mediated action; robbed of this
> Her sole support, she languishes and dies.
> We perish also; we see by the glad light
> And breathe the sweet air of futurity;
> And so we live, or else we have no life.[44]

According to Hough in *The Romantic Poets*, "one must read 'The Excursion' to understand the nineteenth century".[45] This is Wordsworth's philosophy concerning the poor, that they are privileged to be nothing less than the repositories of undisturbed, undeflected, poor humanity. For this he gained the immortal affection and respect of Keble.

Wordsworth belonged to a tradition which lay great store by the lower subordinate orders forming the substantial ethos of a society, since "the subordinate orders tamed and made familiar aspects of the human character that would otherwise be terrifying to view".[46] This is the supreme privilege of the poor, that through the sacred medium of poetry they are able to enter the mystical world of Nature and thus transcend the miseries, travails and despondencies of ordinary life. That is the message of the later Wordsworth. There is no advocacy of reforming the poor out of their condition but rather constant praise of their honourable, privileged and unassailable position in contemporary society. This is no mere literary exercise. For Wordsworth there is no divorce between literature and politics. Romanticism is a political, religious and philosophical phenomenon by its very nature.[47] The aim of the Romantic poet is to influence society not by changing but by soothing it.[48]

Such is the essential background to Keble's high praise of Wordsworth's sympathy with the poor. The sacred trinity of Nature, poverty and poetry is as real for Keble as it was for Wordsworth. This is not to claim, however, any kind of political or social status for *The Christian Year*.[49] This is no manifesto for the socially underprivileged, even though its popular appeal was immense, cutting across all differences of Churchmanship.[50] *The Christian Year* was, however, a work of devotional poetry from which the poor were able to draw much sustenance. Echoing Wordsworth, Keble knew the secret of the hermits who

> talk with God in shadowy glades,
> Free from rude cares and mirth;
> To whom some viewless teacher brings
> The secret lore of rural things,
> The moral of each fleeting cloud and gale,
> The whispers from above, that haunt the twilight vale:[51]

Keble drew upon the rich resource centre of Nature, where there is no corruption. Nature is herself irreformable as there dwell in her the secrets of the divine Being. The hermit is particularly well placed by his station in life to penetrate the inner veil of Nature, where even the clouds and gales have moral lessons to impart.

Keble's poem for "The Fifteenth Sunday after Trinity" on the lilies of the field has much to teach the poor of the earth. It does not matter what stresses there are in life since the poor, like the lilies, have their hearts warmed by Christ's blessing. The poor partake of Nature's most abiding symbol, calm loveliness. As the lilies close at night, their future is assured as they feel their Maker's smile. So, too, the poor are protected from

> Reasons's world what storms are rife,
> What passions range and glare.[52]

The lilies survive all winter's storms for they are especially close to the caring Providence of God. The poor, untroubled by vexing moods, have their compensations as they penetrate the inner recesses of life's meaning and discover therin all the bounteous gifts which Nature can offer in her unbounded generosity.

There is no need for the poor "to crave the worldling's wreath", neither need they shun their daily tasks and hide themselves, for the herbs grow at hand and the common air is balm. More significantly still,

> The prayers of hungry souls and poor,
> Like armed Angels at the door,
> Our unseen foes appal.[53]

For Keble, the compensations of Nature are immense. The beauties that surround common humanity like the herbs, bright flowers and hearths, reach their climax in the particular efficacy of the prayers of the poor and hungry. Here is the fragrance of daily offering, since the poor and hungry are not like leaves which wither away but rather resemble violets, wafted high in death, as soon as their task is done.

Like Wordsworth, Keble held a high view of poverty and lowliness;

> And thou, too curious ear, that fain,
> Wouldst thread the maze of Harmony,
> Content thee with one simple strain,
> The lowlier, sure, the worthier thee.[54]

True, the world is waxing old but the poor are able to see that their Lord is there, even in the midst of storms and tempests. In many of his sermons, Keble was critical of those who were only able to read the signs of the weather without seeing any further.[55] Who are the best suited to read the weather? Not the wealthy in their stately homes, not the town dweller who has no time to look heavenward; only the poor man who tills the fields of God's land is as wise as the leaves of spring or

> birds that cower with folded wing.[56]

However, there are occasions when Nature, which mirrors God's characteristics, veils her round,

> Not to be traced by sight or sound,
> Nor soil'd by ruder breath?[57]

Nature is sometimes too mystical even for the poor to understand. Yet Nature is not always so reserved in her dealings with mortal man, especially as the poor are more than royal heirs,

> Framed by Heaven's peculiar grace,
> God's own work to do on earth,
> (If the Word be not too bold),
> Giving virtue a new birth,
> And a life that ne'er grows old.[58]

The poor are not only in an honourable position in society but they are also enriched with many blessings, a subject which formed a vital part of Keble's evening intercessions.[59] Keble was in no doubt where Christ could be found,

> In quiet ever, and in shade,
> Shepherd and sage may find;
> They, who have bow'd untaught to Nature's sway,
> And they, who follow Truth along her star-paved way.[60]

Keble was keen to point out that on Christmas Day it is those who "in lowly thoughts are nursed" who come first to approach the Babe divine. The poor, the unlearned, the hermits, the shepherds and peasants must be the pattern for the rest of mankind. They reflect that calm tranquillity, that godliness of life, that perfect resignation to God's providential care. Through the sacred medium of poetry Keble showed that with their poetic impulses, nearness to the eternal truths which Nature has to offer, the lessons learned daily by the hour, the poor, like the lilies of the field, are constantly renewing the face of the earth.

Keble was no mere idle versifier, imagining the poor attending poetry reading sessions and receiving much assurance about their spiritual destiny. There was never any doubt in Keble's mind about the harshness of the daily round. It is not

> upon a tranquil lake
> Our pleasant task we ply,
> Where all along our glistening wake
> The softest moonbeams lie

but rather

> Full many a dreary anxious hour
> We watch our nets alone

> In drenching spray, and driving shower
> And hear the night-bird's moan.[61]

But Keble's insight was that work is not merely a laborious exercise. It is not just "a way of procuring employment, of spending time, getting bread or maintaining the state of the world".[62] Whatever happens to us is not a meaningless event but rather "one token more of God's aweful and gracious Presence".[63] Always

> Meek souls there are, who little dream
> Their daily strife an Angel's theme,
> Or that the rod they take so calm
> Shall prove in Heaven a martyr's palm.[64]

All the daily trials and tribulations of the lives of the labouring poor are imbued already with the signs of eternity. Keble's prospective was not temporal, seeing everything in a prosaic way. He believed that the trials of life were very wholesome for the souls of individual believers, even in their abject poverty, even

> If niggard Earth her treasures hide,
> To all but labouring hands denied,
> Lavish of thorns and worthless weeds alone,
> The doom is half in mercy given
> To train us in our way to Heaven,
> And show our lagging souls how glory must be won.[65]

All poverty, all suffering, all deprivations, all "bitter thoughts of low-born care begun" are purified as Christians "learn their lessons at the Throne of Love".[66] God will provide for the needs of the poor in His own time,

> From darkness, here, and dreariness
> We ask not full repose,
> Only be Thou at hand to bless
> Our trial hour of woes.
> Is not the pilgrim's toil o'erpaid
> By the clear rill and palmy shade?
> And see we not, up Earth's dark glade,
> The gate of Heaven unclose?[67]

Keble persevered with his central theme of spiritual compensations for the poor till the end. Despite the drawbacks, the misfortunes of inclement weather and harsh housing conditions, the lessons of Nature are always there for the poor not only to behold and understand but also to grasp and make their own. Of course, God's anger rolls through His darkly round, yet His

> sunshine smiles beneath the gloom,
> for God's purpose is to warn, not confound, as His showers pierce the harden'd ground,
> And win it to give out its brightness and perfume.[68]

Keble faced the problem of the suffering poor not only with sympathy but also with theological feeling. Thus

> every where we find our suffering God,
> And where He trod
> May set our steps: the Cross on Calvary
> Uplifted high
> Beams on the martyr host, a beacon light
> In open fight.[69]

There is no suffering which has not already been encountered upon the Cross, no path trod, no cup of bitterness drunk, which has not already been dignified by the Sacrifice of the Son of Man. The suffering Christian is able to look back and smile

> On thoughts that bitterest seem'd erstwhile,
> And bless the pangs that made thee see
> This was no world of rest for thee![70]

Keble was familiar with Wordsworth's Cumberland beggar who did perform a moral function in society. Simple social action is no answer to the sufferings of Michael or the leechgatherer. Rather, they are symbols of all that is frail, vulnerable and mortal in this life. They are imbued with a sense of infinitude, an almighty power, for they alone have the ability

> To look with feelings of fraternal love
> Upon the unassuming things, that hold
> A silent station in this beauteous world.[71]

This is no strange world but, rather, the animals, plants and hermits are spokesmen for mankind's fate and glory. And at the heart of it all, wrote Keble, there is a God whose love "is a restless ever-active principle",[72] which is not sentimental but a profound trust always in God's Providence.[73]

This is a great mystery, to expect not only bounteous blessings but also calamitous disasters, since "if we have no persecution, no tribulation to endure; if we are such that the world cannot hate us; not some reason to fear that we are not such as He would approve? The Cross is distinctly declared to be Christ's mark. If we have it not clearly upon us, we have the more reason to stand on our guard and tremble, lest after all we should prove not to have been His true soldiers and servants".[74] Keble was no fatalist. Rather, he faced the whole problem of suffering theologically. It is the theology of the suffering God whose marks are to be seen everywhere in His universe. In one of his meditations for Holy Week, Keble wrote,

> How much better to go on mourning,
> And even sinking to the end,
> Than to fall asleep in false comfort,
> And to wake, and find it a dream.
> God preserve us from all that![75]

Keble's theology was founded very firmly on the pattern of the Cross and the Christ who "condescended to be in agony, or strife of spirit".[76]

The Cross is not on the periphery of the world. Indeed, God's work is still not finished, despite the fact that the sufferings, the victory over the Devil, all that has been accomplished. Yet it remains that all this actually has to be applied to the fallen world, "in respect of grace and cleansing; in respect of active righteousness, growing communion with Him, knowledge of God and ourselves and Heavenly joy".[77] Keble's God was no tyrannical monster, whose work was done, whose hands were washed daily in absent benevolence. This is the suffering God, the God of poverty and despair. As he looked at the suffering poor, Keble wrote,

Almighty God needs these distressed brethren.[78]

This may sound contradictory, that God actually needs anything, let alone the suffering of the innocent poor. Keble acknowledged this fact; "How can the great God of Heaven and earth, the Creator of those innumerable worlds which we see in the vast Heaven on a starry night and of infinitely more which we do not see or guess at, He Whom all the angels worship, the Almighty, the Eternal, the All-Sufficient?"[79] How can God need anything? Yet, answered Keble, although by His divine nature God is obviously not in need of anything, even so His love "causes Him to have, as it were, need of us".[80]

The crucial question of theodicy, however, is still unanswered. Why does God act as if He were powerless? When He dwelt among men, wrote Keble, He felt for the multitudes in their hunger.[81] Keble could not have ascribed any apathy to God, only a true compassion for the suffering of humanity. God needs these distressed bretheren to acquire a moral balance in the world. As the suffering of Christ is pleaded daily by earthly priests before the Throne of love, so too the glorified Christ offers His wounds and scars to his Heavenly Father. As true priest, God and man, the suffering of God and man meet in Christ.

Amidst the suffering of the world's poor, the presence of the compassionate God is especially real. It is not merely a poor father or mother, a sea captain, leader of a caravan, the army commander, the governor of a besieged city, Hagar in the wilderness, Jacob in Canaan, Moses before the advent of the manna, the woman of Sarepta, King Joram in Samaria, the Jewish mothers when Jerusalem was besieged, it is none of those who asks the eternally relevant question of starving humanity, "Whence shall we buy bread that these may eat?" but

> the Great God, Who here asks it,
> The Creator and Owner of all things,
> He Who "daily openeth His hand,
> And filleth all things living with plenteousness".[82]

For Keble, the Cross of Christ stood at the centre of the suffering world:

> Lovest thou praise? the Cross is shame:
> Or ease? the Cross is bitter grief:

> More pangs than tongue or heart can frame
> Were suffer'd there without relief.[83]

Suffering brings its own form of glory. The Christian's prayer is

> to have it united to the Sufferings of Christ.
> See how this frame of mind will last you through life;
> How it will support you in the hour of death;
> Who knows how it may be in the Day of Judgement!
> And so, at last, the Mystery may be realised,
> The Mystery of sinful souls entering into union with God,
> And, in Him, becoming pure in Eternity.[84]

All suffering, all poverty is pleaded in the spirit of Calvary on a daily basis before the Throne of Heaven, as "Christ presents to the Father the Body and Blood, which He, this day, took up with Him to Heaven, for a constant memorial of that sacrifice; and thus, although His bloody Atoning Sacrifice is completed, never to be renewed, yet is He for ever offering for us in Heaven: He hath an unchangeable Priesthood: He is our High Priest for ever, after the order of Melchizedek".[85]

Of all places, Christ is to be found most amongst the poor. Christ is not reserved purely for holy places and Holy Communion, since "you know that He is to be found in His poor"[86] who, as Saints of the Most High, will reign for ever. Unlike the wise politicians, valiant warriors, knowing counsellors and powerful speakers, all of whom are held in such high esteem and honour, it is not so with the poor and despised of the earth who take the Kingdom and reign for ever.[87]

The suffering of the poor, however, did not only have a Godward but also a manward dimension. Keble wrote that

> The Almighty God made us without ourselves,
> he does not save us without ourselves.
> So He condescended here to call in His creatures' aid;
> He made us as though He had need.[88]

What a terrible shame, wrote Keble, if people, having the opportunity to be charitable, "lose the comfort of having shared in a good work, itself a bond among classes". God needs the help of men, otherwise He would not put the poor masses within their reach.[89]

Keble, influenced so much by Bishop Butler,[90] was familiar with that Bishop's counsel, that "He who has distributed men into these different ranks, and at the same time united them into one society, in such sort as men are united, has by the constitution of things, formally put the poor under the super-intendency and patronage of the rich. The rich, then, are charged, by natural providence, as much as by revealed appointment with the care of the poor".[91] Keble preached as many sermons on charity as he did on poverty. The times were urgent as even the wealthy were forgetting their primal duties, decreed by Nature and Providence alike. The power of the Cross is nothing less than to fill men's hearts with holy charity. Keble was explicit in his reasoning as he told his parishioners, "God has raised up men and women, who, for mere love of Him, have left their comforts and enjoyments, to which they had been used all their lives, in order to wait on those who were struck down by it".[92] The end of soft-handed charity, "tempering her gifts, that seem so free/By time and place" is that "not a woe the bleak world see,/But finds her grace".[93] Caring for poor is nothing less than a sign of having been with Jesus.[94]

The ideal was the local community, having its own laws of social hierarchy. The longing for community is one of the most important themes of the Romantic Revival. Of course, the poet must occasionally retreat into the desert places but he prophesies for his people publicly.[95] Grasmere and Hursley featured largely on any map of Romantic places, as there was in both places so much emphasis on the local hierarchy, domesticity, the hearth. Keble and his lay patron, Heathcote, worked hand in hand, caring for this one's lease, that one's debts.[96] All of which was perfectly consitent with Keble's emphasis on the Prayer Book and a clergyman in every parish. All efforts must be made to preserve the parochial system.[97] The presence of a priest in every parish was a sure sign that God would be there and that the inhabitants of the parish would have a strict account to give.[98] Ideally, charity ought to be administered on a local basis and people consoled "in a thousand little ways and great".[99]

1.3. The 1832 Reform Bill

Georgina Battiscombe wrote that Keble was opposed to the spirit of the Reform Bill because it would not give purity of election, the balance or equilibrium between the landed and commercial classes would be destroyed, the understanding between the Monarch and the Commons would be undermined, leading to hostility between Lords and Commons.[100] But behind all these worldly reasons there was the theological presupposition that the whole spirit of the Reform Bill smacked unmistakably of irreverence which was at the root of every doctrinal disease. As in the theological sphere, wrote Keble, "We are handling the Words of the Most High as the materials of a system which we are to plan out for ourselves, instead of marking them with a silent reverence, as the foundations of a vast Temple, the outline whereof, as far as we can trace it, has been previously delivered into our hands by an unerring Architect",[101] so too in the political sphere men were devising their own systems of government instead of accepting what had been handed down to them by a caring and providential God.[102]

What Keble detested most was exhibitionist behaviour, from theologians, poets or politicians. It offended his whole understanding of the doctrine of reserve.[103] In Volume I of his *Lectures on Poetry* Keble complained about one of the age's besetting sins as "no room for what is dignified, simple and genuine; there is a want of repose, of clearness; only that which is startling, not to say monstrous and uncouth, makes a noise and is talked about".[104] If theologians indulged themselves in exhibitionist behaviour, promoting their own man-made doctrines at the expense of those of the Church, they would repeat the mischievous nonsense of Paul of Samosota, who "in his preaching, constantly aimed at making a show of ingenuity, and producing a splendid effect for the time". This resulted in rude exhibitionism in Church, expressions of applause, shaking of handkerchiefs, just like the theatre. Indeed, this Bishop of Antioch was more like one telling fortunes for hire than a genuine Christian theologian. Little wonder that such a charlatan preached that Christ was from beneath, not from above, merely a human prophet and not the Son of God descended from heaven.[105] Paul of Samosota was the forerunner of all who have ignored the doctrine of Reserve in communicating Religious Knowledge.[106]

Keble's mind was of the saints and sinners variety. Without exception, he asked, "had not the saints, the holy men in society always been reserved and reverent as regards holy things, bearing themselves religiously in religious worship, and only in the narrow circle of intimate friends ever spoken of God's forgiveness or their hopes of heaven?"[107] Keble feared that people would be taught the greater truths of Christianity at random. Ignorance is no security against sin since "so near akin is the piety of the ignorant to the purity of the child; the first involuntary whisper of an evil thought is enough to taint its virgin glories for ever. There is need of some higher principle, some goodness more than merely negative, to keep the heart 'among the faithless, faithful', blameless and unspotted in an adulterous and sinful generation".[108] Keble had found this principle in his reading of the Fathers. He has been aptly compared to Clement of Alexandria.[109] Each person must receive only what he is able to bear. There is no purpose in deliberately trying to confuse the ignorant with the controversies of the day. Keble was convinced that infidels were busy colonizing the parishes of England with their latest devices, promoting infidelity and licentiousness. The lesson was obvious. Great care must be taken among religious teachers in "rightly apportioning, timing and selecting the truths to be communicated".[110]

Keble always had his theology of the few, disliking the excessive show of large churches and their huge congregations.[111] That the few would remain as an island of refuge, a remnant of the true Church of England was an exciting possibility for Keble, especially if Protestantism and Roman Catholicism swept over the land.[112] This did not mean, however, that the laity should never be consulted. No one less eminent than St Cyprian "regarded the laity as so deserving of confidence that (the Fathers) never did anything without consultation with them". Yet this consultation never extended as far as the guardianship of the truth,[113] which remains the domain of the Apostles' successors.[114] That is why Keble was opposed to the laity receiving any votes in ecclesiastical government. "We do not find in Antiquity", he wrote, "that (the laity) ever had power, either in a body as represented by their chief governor, directly to reverse what the clergy, after due deliberation, had freely decreed".[115]

A hierarchical ecclesiastical government must correspond to an equally similar state in the political realm. As the laity had no spiritual rights as such, apart from asking doctrinal cases to be reheard, thus signifying their disapproval, so too they had no political rights apart from having their interests represented in the High Court of Parliament by those whom God had chosen to stand in their stead. Keble's reasoning was founded upon the theological principle that God has His own channels of pouring out His grace upon His people. If the laity were actually allowed to make Christian doctrines as well, the result would be a chaotic interference with the divine machinery of handing down the sacred deposit of religious truth. So, too, in the political sphere reverence for the established order would be replaced by that most symptomatic sign of the times, irreverence, a particularly marked penchant of those who substituted man made creations for the divine order of things.[116]

In a brilliant passage of his *Lectures on Poetry*, Keble encapsulated his whole understanding of the doctrine of reserve with its inherent opposition to the spirit of democracy. Keble was writing about the nature of poetry in a democratic state: "Once the revolutionary and mercenary passion prevails, whether it be with individuals or communities, forthwith a certain unreasoning contempt for poetry possesses them ... poetry will be unappreciated under a democracy; unquestionably we must allow that one most essential feature of all poetry is a due reserve which always shrinks from pouring forth everything, worthy or unworthy, without selection or modesty. A certain reverence must be observed; as with sacred things, so here everything must be touched upon with due reserve; nor could it be otherwise, for he who sings because he must and is no mere versifier, well knows that he is betraying the secrets of his heart and the innermost aspirations of his soul".[117] No profounder indictment of the spirit of democracy can be found in Keble's writings.

1.4. "National Apostasy" (1833)

The most famous sermon which Keble ever preached on 14 July, 1833 was a direct response to what he considered to be an immediate emergency. The repeal of the Test and Corporation Acts against Protestant Dissenters in 1828, Catholic Emancipation in 1829 and the 1832 Reform Act had effectively opened up a hitherto exclusively Anglican Parliament to the Church's enemies.[118] Above all, the measure that prompted Keble's sermon, the spoliation of the Irish Church by the parliamentary suppression of ten bishoprics and two archbishoprics, seemed to Keble nothing less than a nakedly utilitarian approach to the Church's welfare by the government of the day.[119] It was the principle which motivated the Irish Temporalities Bill[120] which met with Keble's stern disapproval.

Keble was well aware that the spirit which had prompted the Irish Temporalities Bill was in itself a reflection of the Whig Latitudinarian attitude to Church and State relationships which had been so prominent in the eighteenth century. According to William Warburton and William Paley, the Church had no inherent spiritual rights or independence apart from the civil power.[121] A totally different attitude, however, was expressed by those who continued to practise genuine High Church views. The Establishment was not merely an utilitarian matter but, far more profoundly, embodied an *iure divino* ideal of a divinely ordained inseparable union of the two mutually interrelated powers of Church and State. After the French Revolution, this attitude was firmly expressed in the political writings of Edmund Burke.[122]

Throughout his life, Keble firmly upheld the *iure divino* ideal which had been so prominent in the works of the Caroline divines, the Nonjurors and the Hutchinsonians.[123] Above all, however, the ideal played such an important part in Keble's life because it had been expressed with such unsurpassed brilliance and lucidity in the works of Richard Hooker. Although Keble's edition of *The Works of the Learned and Judicious Divine, Mr. Richard Hooker* was not published till 1836, yet even in 1833 he was more thoroughly acquainted with the works of that writer than any other English Churchman.[124] Keble's maxim that politics could not be divorced from morality[125] was a reflection of his profound conviction that the spiritual interests of the Church could not be separated from principles which governed her legislative welfare.[126] Similarly, Hooker had written that "a true understanding of politics puts religion as its chief concern, and of religion, Christianity as the true religion. A Christian polity is then a Church".[127] This Church was meant to comprise the whole body of believers who were at once members of politic society and believers in Christ. Church and Commonwealth could thus be together one society. Some members might be appointed to one office according to the form of secular law and regiment, and some to another after "the spiritual law of Jesus Christ", yet without making "two several impaled societies".[128]

It was the abandonment of principle which Keble abhorred in the Irish Temporalities Bill. A nation had decided through its Parliament to do well enough without God and His Church. A Christian nation was always constitutionally bound in all its legislative policies by the fundamental rules of Christ's Church. As the Jews had clamoured for an earthly King, an act of gross apostasy, so too the English nation was about to disavow the basic principle of its existence, its obligation to care for Christ's Church. All that matters is motive and purpose. Christians were responsible for the temper in which they dealt with God's Holy Church, established among them for the salvation of souls. The temper of a nation which had deliberately abandoned its sacred trust could only be described as APOSTASY. Profane conduct was always synonymous with ill-religion. Once religious resignation was separated altogether from men's notions of civil duty, the result was always profanation of sacred rights and duties.[129] The Apostolic Church, forsaken, degraded, despoiled by the State and people of England, must still not cease from intercession, public and private, for the English nation.[130]

Keble's argument in "National Apostasy" was morally inspired. Men had dared to put asunder what God had solemnly joined together. The wholeness of Church and State had been shattered by the whims and devices of statesmen and politicians, turning the Church of England into "a mere Parliamentarian Church".[131] Yet the calculations of human expediency could not interfere with the divine authority of the Church, let alone untie the oaths and obligations by which Christians were bound to her. What Hooker had deemed essential, the indissolubility of Church and State, could not be eradicated by the legislative measures passed by mere Parliamentarians. Keble's position, like Hooker's, was essentially idealistic. The past could not be undone. The *vinculum* of Church and State was an unalterable reality in English religious, political and social life.

On 31 December, 1833, the Bishop of Leighlin and Ferns wrote a letter to *The British Magazine* concerning the spiritual rights of the Church after the passing of the Irish Temporalities Act.[132] Keble's reply to this letter, unpublished at the time, in January 1834 contains some of his finest sentiments about the spiritual prerogatives of the Church of God.[133] Although Keble maintained the high moral tone of "National Apostasy" in this letter, his main concern was to show the inadequacy of the Irish Bishop's reaction to the Irish Church Temporalities Act, a view which seemed to sacrifice all points of episcopal jurisdiction which this or any future Parliament might claim.[134] Not only does the power of Order reside in Bishops, wrote Keble, but also Bishops must have a share in Ecclesiastical Legislation. The Thirty-fourth Article states clearly, "Every particular or national Church hath power to ordain, change, or abolish ceremonies or rites of the Church". Keble pointed out that the statutes of the Realm acknowledged the first four general Councils as a main foundation of English ecclesiastical law. The second canon of the Council of Constantinople "commits the ecclesiastical legislation of each province to the Bishops of that province, excluding foreign Bishops, and much more aliens and laymen".[135]

Echoing the sentiments expressed in "National Apostasy", Keble asked the crucial question whether, in fact, Parliament had any right to legislate for the Church. The changes were so vital as to amount to a virtual breach of the terms of union between Church and State. Consequently the governors of the Church are now at Liberty, provided that their consciences will allow it, to decline submitting themselves to the ecclesiastical laws of the Parliament. The rationale behind Keble's claim was the two societies, according to Hooker's theory and the practice of the days of Queen Elizabeth, were no longer identical. Every Christian, wrote Keble, must "obey the customs of the Realm" but whether the law of God actually permitted the continued acquiescence "of those entrusted with the Church in a system which permits aliens and heretics to bear the chief sway in legislating for her",[136] that was precisely the point at issue. Of course, concluded Keble, it may be possible that on the grounds of "conciliation" or economy the Hierarchy might be reduced to one single Bishop. That could be a confirmation of assenting to "the customs of the Realm". Far more probable, however, is to understand fully the commission of our Lord to His Apostles and their successors, which means that, were such events to take place, it would be the sacred duty of all to exert themselves "for the breaking of such an unhallowed bond".[137]

In 1833 and 1834 Keble was at pains to reveal the Erastian nature of Parliament. In his advocacy of the Royal Supremacy, Keble wished to expound his basic belief in the godly prince, an idea which expressed exactly the ideal of the Christian ruler found in Hooker.[138] Article Thirty-seven states, "We give not to our Princes the ministering either of God's Word, or of the sacraments". Hooker was perfectly clear as to what the Royal Supremacy involved: "We must note that their power is termed supremacy as being the highest, not simply without exception or anything. For what man is so brain sick as not to except in such speeches God Himself, the King of all dominion? Who doubteth but that the King who received it, must hold of it and under the law according to the old axiom, 'The King assigns to the law that power which the law has assigned to him'. And again, 'The King ought not to be under man but under God and the Law'".[139] Keble, like Hooker, was adamant, that this ideal was simply not Erastian. The spiritual independence of the Church was not sacrificed but rather upheld.

In his sermon "Church and State", preached before the University of Oxford on 26 June, 1835, the anniversary of William IV's Accession, Keble took as his text Isaiah xlix.23., "And kings shall be thy nursing fathers, and their queens thy nursing mothers".[140] This did not mean that the Church as an infant was lodged in the arms of the civil power but that, as a mother, she lodged her children in its arms. The monarchs and princesses of this world were as foster fathers and foster mothers in the family of Our Lord Jesus Christ, and of His Spouse, the Holy Church Universal. The King, holding a sacred office, was not simply stationed over his people by God's providence, without any special commission for the Church's welfare but, rather, was ordained in a certain sense to perform duties in the Church of God.[141]

On the King's Accession in 1836, Keble preached his sermon, "Kings to be honoured for their Office sake".[142] Although Keble considered political discussions akin to profaneness, yet as true Churchmen and as loyal subjects to the King, Christians were bound to be aware of their real condition, which was that the successors of the Apostles, the heads and ordainers of all the clergy of God, were nominated and appointed by those who had neither part nor lot in the faith of the Apostles.[143] Keble's counsel was that Christians must continue to pray for their King, not merely as one in high authority who keeps good order but as the anointed of the Lord, a living type of the supreme dominion of Jesus Christ, made by God an image of His Majesty.[144] Keble's sermon, "On the Death of a King", preached 9 July, 1837, emphasised once again that as Moses, taking God's message, was said himself to be a god to Pharaoh, so kings were called gods, as being in Christ's place on earth. That is why sovereigns have always been anointed with holy oil, crowns placed on their heads not by great noblemen but by a Bishop of the Church of God and the oath taken on the Bible to those duties especially in which he most nearly represents Jesus Christ glorified, the protection of the Church and the administration of judgement with mercy.[145] Keble always had historical precedents in mind for attributing such an exalted status to the King's person. But the emphasis was always that of Hooker's, that the King does indeed rule, he calls ecclesiastical convocations, makes ecclesiastical laws, judges ecclesiastical disputes and appoints bishops but he is not a shaping stamp; the king's is a stamp of approval, not a mold.[146]

This was precisely the vital insight which Keble wished to affirm when he reviewed Gladstone's *The State in its Relations with the Church* for the *British Critic* in October, 1839.[147] In spiritual matters kings were meant to execute the laws of Christ's Church, not impose laws upon her. This is precisely why Constantine refused to take his seat at the Council of Nicaea until he was requested by the Bishops to do so. St Ambrose resisted Valentinian and excommunicated Theodosius while St Basil refused to change the Church formularies, though it might have brought Valens into Church communion. The happy emperors were those who made their power a handmaid to the majesty of God.[148]

Keble maintained that Hooker's insights were still valid. An indissoluble unity, reflected in the anointed, sacred person of the Monarch, the nursing Father to his children, the Church of God, was an ideal which looked increasingly irrelevant in a world of

Erastian Parliaments and Ecclesiastical Commissions. Such a charge would not have worried Keble excessively. His interest was not in devising temporary, expedient schemes for Church reform, the preoccupation of politicians and statesmen, but in interpreting what he considered to be God's eternal will for His holy Church and His equally sacred state.

1.5. The Poor Law Amendment Act (1834)

In 1834 the Poor Law Amendment Act was passed which was very much the creation of the Reverend T. R. Malthus, one of the outstanding political economists of the age.[149] Although Keble had been taught by his greatest teacher, his own father, that Malthus was "hard and vulgar", yet he thought that Malthus had "hit the right nail on the head" with his exhortation to abolish the Poor Laws.[150] Why did Keble change his mind so dramatically? Why did he think initially that 1834 was a sound piece of legislation? There is much in Malthus's writings which gives the impression that he was not only concerned about the welfare of the poor but also about local, private and voluntary charity. Bonar, for instance, commented in 1885 that Malthus was the father not only of the 1834 Act but also of the latter-day societies for the organisation of charity.[151]

Malthus appeared to be exhorting the poor masses to be more responsible for themselves: "when the poor were once taught, by the abolition of the Poor Laws, and a proper knowledge of their real situation, to depend upon themselves, we might rest secure that they would be faithful enough in resources, and that the evils which were absolutely irremediable, they would bear with the fortitude of them and the resignation of Christians".[152] All this appeared to be most expedient. Politicians were impressed, like William Pitt, the Prime Minister, Copleston, the Provost of Oriel, Hallam the historian, James Mill, senior and Ricardo the economists. Far from wishing to abolish charity, either of the public or private kind, Malthus merely wished to guide it in the right direction. So many large charities were as ridiculously wayward as the Poor Laws themselves. There was no discrimination, direction or sense of utility.[153] Malthus wished voluntary charity to raise its head above the debris and vestiges of the old Poor Law and once again reassure the genuinely poor that they need never starve. Only indolence, imprudence and sloth would be reprehensible. All this seemed to be sound common sense. However, after the passing of the 1834 Act, Keble soon realised that his original impressions about Malthus, that he was hard and vulgar, were sound. Battiscombe gives vivid details of Keble's reactions to the harshness of the workhouse conditions. In reality, the 1834 Act, inspired by Malthus and his disciples, viewed poverty in terms which completely contradicted those of Keble. In 1816 James Graham had attacked the political economists for treating the poor "according to the consumer demand that regulates the production of spirits and saucepans, chairs and tables, and all the other commodities of life".[154]

The 1834 Act regarded poverty, not as honourable, let alone sacred, but as a fundamental crime. Behind the 1834 programme lay the profound conviction that poverty stemmed from a lack of moral fibre, thriftlessness, imprudence, immorality or drunkenness.[155] The poor are not only lazy but also have no right to subsistence. In fact, they have no right to anything for "to sanction by law a right which in the nature of things cannot be adequately justified, may terminate in disappointment, irritation, or aggravated poverty".[156] Despite Malthus's appeals for local charity, the impression, though never explicit, was firmly ingrained upon the human mind that it only ought to be on a temporary lease as well.

Keble's mind had always been firmly set against the notorious Speenhamland system which, established in 1795, had been born as the result of a decision by the magistrates not to try to adjust local wages to rising costs but to supplement agricultural wages with Poor Law allowances, related to the price of bread and the size of the labourer's family. This was far too facile a solution to a complicated social problem. The labourer became too dependent on the local parish, making him a slave in all but name. Abuse of the system had been accompanied by bad harvests and the strains and excesses of war. The amateurishness of the Justices of the Peace had exacerbated an already muddled and confused administration. The result was chaos. Keble offered an alternative in 1831 in an unpublished pamphlet, *A Plan for the*

Gradual Amendment of Parochial Relief in the Southern Counties of England.[157]

This pamphlet was a mature, constructive and rational plan, a kind of Via Media between the 1817 Act, in which he had expressed so much interest[158] and the 1834 Act, which had gone too far. The abolitionists were a powerful school of thought and Keble was momentarily attracted to them. Yet he did feel intuitively that the Poor Laws, far from being abolished, ought to be drastically and substantially overhauled. This is why he was interested in the 1817 Select Committee which led to the Regulation of Parish Vestries Act of 1818 and an Act to Amend the Laws for the Relief of the Poor of 1819. Basically, these Acts attempted to make local administration more effective by restoring daily business to the ideally more capable hands of the landowners and wealthier farmers, the parish élites.[159] Unfortunately, both Acts were of limited effectiveness.[160] In another sphere, however, the Acts promoted an activity in which Keble showed much interest. Enclosures and large-scale farming at the end of the eighteenth century had led inevitably to the loss of lands which would normaly have been available for smal cottageowners. As a result, the cottage allotment, formerly a source of income for rural families, was becoming more important as an alternative livelihood for the poor masses. The 1819 Act had encouraged parishes to let small portions of land to any poor and industrious inhabitant of the parish. But the 1834 Act set its face firmly against such dangerous innovations, for to encourage the poor to live off their own vegetable gardens alone would surely make them vulnerable to real famine in poor seasons. Keble himself was not so pessimistic, seeing allotments as, at worst, a peasant subsistence economy and, at best, a sound local arrangement, encouraged gently by official government policies.[161]

As far as the problem of mass poverty was a constant perplexity, challenge and threat, Keble realised that local, private charity on its own was simply inadequate. A reliance solely on voluntary activity for economic aid represented in the 1830's and 1840's a reversal of sound social responsibility. Removal of all government aid spelt chaos and catastrophe for all local administrators and the rich and poor in society. Keble's ideal was always private charity, healthily, steadily and progressively supported by public charity in the form of humane legislation.

Little distinction would be made between magistrates, overseers, landlords and philanthropists, all working for the greater good of the poor masses. Charity, local and private, far from being a footnote or appendix, as the Malthusians would have it, ought to be the main heading on every page. But the book itself must be public charity in the form of the more efficient Poor Laws. 1834 struck at the power of the landed gentry, substituting the cynicism of the wealthy mill-owner for the charity of the landlord. Keble's ideals were those "of the pre-industrial culture in which the political structure is dominated by upper-class leadership and in which social tensions are resolved by upper-class paternalism".[162] In such a climate, the needs of the individual pauper were meticulously cared for[163] and the result was suitably efficacious.[164]

Keble's protest against the spirit of the age, however, went deeper than constantly referring to "wicked, worldly-minded Christians".[165] Spending his time in all kinds of research from Homer and Virgil to Irenaeus, Burke and Malthus, his knowledge of current affairs was not limited. Furthermore, he saw for himself what unromantic, dull and wicked men could achieve in society. Wordsworth, too, was in accord with Parson Lot's denunciation of those who "arrogantly talk of Political Economy as a science, so completely perfected, so universal and all-important, that common humanity and morality, reason and religion, must be pooh-poohed down, if they seem to interfere with its infallible conclusions".[166] For the convenience of the theory of the economists, the suffering, poor individual, though eternally hopeful, was replaced by the political, sincere, economic man of mind and body, who is both soulless and heartless.[167]

What was at stake was the preservation of a kind of society which Keble felt was a reflection of eternal values. Diametrically opposed to this local, hierarchical and patriarchal society was the view of Malthus, the forerunner of the consumer society and the advocates of the wealth of nations, who are for ever looking at the balance-sheet of exports and imports and judge from that the prosperity of a country. The followers of Malthus examine the quantity of goods produced without bestowing a thought upon the producer. A calculation of the expenses of the Poor Laws leads to the dreadful conclusion that Nature's table is full, and that, in consequence, the new-born child of a pauper should be starved.[168] Malthus was the chief apostle of *laissez-faire* as he saw labour, its use and need, purely in utilitarian terms, without any consideration of motives. The emphasis was on greed and expolitation of classes. Writing of labour employment, Malthus wrote of the poor that they should work "in roads and public works" accompanied by "a tendency among landlords and persons of property to build, to improve and beautify their grounds, and to employ workmen and menial servants". These, wrote Malthus, "are the means most within our power and most directly calculated to remedy the evils arising from that disturbance in the balance of produce and consumption, which has been occasioned by the sudden conversion of soldiers, sailors, and various other classes which the War employed, into productive labourers".[169] Malthus, seeing the masses of mankind as unproductive consumers, felt that they must be employed to relieve the post-war situation, always liable to erupt, by a public works programme which would increase effective demand. The dynamic influnce, Malthus's chief concern, would be to produce money for the economy. This was the essence of Malthus's vision, the complete eradication of poverty, the annihilation of any sense of dependence between the classes, the exhortation to each individual to be utterly responsible for his own destiny. This would have created the comfortable society, full of good, decent, responsible citizens.

Keble had different ideas, however, about the kind of society which ought to exist. Keble admitted that it was difficult to give up so many temptations in this life, "a little more money, a little more worldly credit, a little more amusement and pleasure; while thrones are being got ready for us in the royal palace of heaven".[170] Keble exhorted his parishioners to shun "that which is unreal, a mere show, which will presently come to an end ... nothing here can be truly called our own; it is only lent for a short time: just to see how we will employ it".[171] For Keble the world was not a place to be exploited unscrupulously, selfishly and meaninglessly but a garden to be taken on trust, a place where there is nourishment, trials and happiness.

The common view was of "the village sinking into poverty and crime and shame that are the shadow of its power and pride"[172] while Sir Edwin Chadwick, an eminent reformer, was of the opinion that "an increase of wages to any considerable extent would be equivalent to a proportionate increase in drink".[173] Poverty, crime and drunkenness, this was no holy trinity but what was to economists and reformers a realistic assessment of the contemporary situation. This is why Malthus was so adamant that the poor had no right to rely with confidence on the aid of the wealthy, since "those given relief would be grateful and those refused could not complain of injustice" as "every man has the right to do what he will with his own".[174] Malthus was as concerned about personal morality as Keble. True moral restraint is the antidote to poverty. "Wider practice of moral restraint", wrote Malthus, "would raise wages and remove all squalid poverty from society, except, of course, that arising from an inevitable misfortune. It would also purify society since the passion of love, no longer satiated by early sensuality, would burn with a brighter, purer and steadier flame ... the lower classes would not only be more comfortable, but would be freed from irrational discontents against forms of governmental or social inequality".[175]

This was the happy society, full of love, moral restraint and reasonableness. It would lead to contentment of spirit, wealth and prudence. Malthus allied Anglicanism with two irresistible phenomena, the middle classes and Evangelical uprightness. Malthus's hope was that the lower classes, rude, vulgar and dirty though they were, might still progress through the ranks of society and become middle class. All this was manna from heaven for the growing number of Evangelicals in middle class society. Here were the paragons of sobriety, honesty and thrift. Indeed, such was Malthus's optimism that he even felt the lower classes, rising above their crime, drunkenness and vulgarity, might become capable of romantic love, the sole prerogative, as he conceived it, of the middle classes.[176] This new recipe for the happy, enlightened and meaningful society was most palatable to John Bird Sumner, Bishop of Chester and later Archbishop of Canterbury. On reading Malthus, he became convinced that he was the apostle for the times. He made Malthus obligatory reading for his clergy. At no other time in Victorian England was there to be such perfect harmony between Malthusian principles and "the wisdom and godess of the Deity".[177] This meant that charity ought to be curtailed, thus discouraging the poor from thinking that this was a kind of birthright. It was far better to change the conditions of the poor. Dirty, vulgar and loathsome, they might become clean, respectable and civilized members of the middle classes.

Keble never sat on any Poor Law Commissions. He never commended the general economic theories of the day to his hearers. He never encouraged the poor to abandon their station in life and become respectable like the middle classes. Rather, he had a view of society which was based on the mutuality of need. Malthus, on the contrary, was typical of that utilitarian or rationalistic error, essentially "cold and unpoetical".[178] Keble's vision of society was essentially poetical. It was based on al those insights which he had gained by reading the Greek and Roman poets, confirmed by the poetry of Wordsworth, that there is a way of managing the affairs of men that has to do with motives, the value of one's preordained station in life and mutuality of need. There was a place in Keble's ideal society for rich and poor, since it could not do without their separate existences, for each was vital to the other. Hence, there was no individualism, only collectivity; no independence, only interdependence. If we were making a world for ourselves, then we would be like the political economists, giving everybody a comfortable existence. But "mark what we should have lost by doing so. We should have had no room left for the exercise of charity in giving alms to our neighbour ... we see what good uses God intended us to make of the difference which He has established, between rich and poor, in the world wherein we live ... the rich man wants the poor man's labour, and the poor man wants the rich man's meat, and both want the love and prayers of each other".[179] What Keble considered to be the society ordained by God purposefully with "all differences of rank, fortune, age, relation, and the like being carefully taken into account"[180] was being undermined by the protagonists of a society where there was little room for poverty and less for heavenly charity. Keble was well aware of these views. "Even now", he warned his parishioners, "in public affairs, and in high places, the old foundations seem to be greatly shaken, not in this land only, but throughout the Christian world". In 1840 it was crucial that the people of Hursley remembered that "in our stations, both rich and poor ... we have great need to learn holy calmness".[181]

In what was Keble's finest vision, he gave the perfect precept of the society which he thought his parishioners ought to imitate, founded primarily on those three pillars of Anglicanism, Revelation, Nature and experience. Keble was in no doubt that the society which occupied so much of his prayers and thoughts was ordained by God's gracious Providence. It was a natural society, composed of different component parts, each vital to the other. Above all, he knew that it worked. As priest, poet and academic, he experienced the wonder of that mutuality of need, without which the Christian society could not exist. "Do not trust in your own riches", he warned his parishioners, "beware of thinking that you can do without the poor, that you need them not. You cannot do without them; you have the greatest need of them; you need their prayers and blessings in return for your alms, to guard you daily against the deadly snare of setting your heart upon this world, or anything in it". To the poor, he had equally apposite counsel, for they must beware of envying the rich, as God saw fit "to make this difference between my brother and myself".[182]

Keble's Anglicanism in its social manifestations accorded well with the poetic, pre-industrial, anti-commercialist spirit about which he wrote, spoke, preached and prayed with such intensity, vehemence and commitment. Within its confines, the rich and poor had their appointed destinies and destinations.

1.6. "Primitive Tradition Recognized in Holy Scripture" (1836)

Keble preached this sermon on 27 September, 1836 at the Cathedral Church of Winchester.[183] According to B. W. Martin, Tradition was vital for an understanding of Keble's poetic genius.[184] One of Keble's daily concerns was that Tradition was being replaced by Utilitarianism. Orthodoxy was under attack. Christianity had been upheld for centuries against unbelief by the doctrine of Analogy. Judaism and Christianity stood in the same tradition as childhood to youth training and manhood. As Butler and Pascal were able to defend the Faith against unbelief, these same principles should be applied in the present crisis of faith, for Orthodoxy must be maintained against heresy.[185] For Keble one could either be a Christian or an infidel, a conformist or an infidel.[186] The fashion in Keble's day was to abide in the religious condition in which one found oneself. What, then, asked Keble, became of "Magna est veritas, et praevalebit? Are we not sacrificing truth to peace, divine doctrines to hereditary yearnings and impressions?"[187] The challenge of the Rationalists was not so much that they had their own private theories and interpretations but had no idea of the classical Church Formularies. Give these up, wrote Keble, and whole races and nations were disturbed. The elements of change were in abundance, leading not to stability but to "the risk of perplexing the simple, encouraging the presumptuous, and promoting a general scepticism".[188]

What the Church consequently encountered was a sad sight as orthodox teachers were falling off from the very truths which they had previously defended. New modes of evidence were devised and men were "disposed to be restless and unsatisfied with the old".[189] Men were simply not leaving God's dispensations alone. Instead of belonging to a Church which referred to Scripture as "the standard and treasure of all necessary doctrine" and expounded that same Scripture "according to the consent of the ancient Fathers", the enemies of Tradition were partaking of a poisonous medicine, "that idle and not very innocent employment of forming imaginary models of a world, and schemes of governing it".[190] The results were inevitable. Once traditional theology was abandoned, all sacred doctrines went the way of all flesh. The deposit of faith was in the hands of aliens. Those who denied sacramental grace, the Incarnation and the Trinity were in the ascendant. Those who scorned the Creeds, the Sacred Ministry and the sacraments seemed to be in charge of doctrinal decisions.[191]

For Keble, Renn Dickson Hampden[192] represented all his worst fears. Indeed, Hampden was little better than Marcion or Simon Magus, let alone Arius or the writers of the Puritan letter in Hooker's time. Hampden was in no doubt about the orthodoxy of his own position. Appealing to the Thirty-Nine Articles of Religion, he declared boldly in the Divinity School at Oxford that the Articles nowhere referred to the authority of Tradition or of the Church in controversies of faith. The Bible and the three Creeds were sufficient as standards of doctrine.[193] It was Hampden's Bampton Lectures on *The Scholastic Philosophy considered in its Relation to Christian Theology*, delivered in

1832, ten years before those on the Thirty-Nine Articles, which caused the greatest stir. Hampden wrote of the Trinity, that "the truth itself of the Trinitarian doctrine emerges from these mists of human speculation, like the bold naked land on which an atmosphere of fog has for a while rested and then dispersed".[194] In fact, Hampden was standing Orthodoxy, as Keble understood it, on its own head, for the fog was the "theoretic air", the "atmosphere of repulsion" in which divine mysteries had been invested by nothing more than ecclesiastical definitions and distinctions from heresy. All this was a true stumbling-block, as the wisdom of God was received as the foolishness of man. "The pretended exactness of thought on which our technical language is based", which was Hampden's reference to the Athanasian symbol, must be discarded. Hampden thought it much better to admit that when the inspired Legislator declared, "Hear, O Israel, the Lord Thy God is one God", he was only opposing the polytheism of existing Heathenism. Hampden was actually claiming that the objectivity of exact definitions of the Trinity, as understood by Athanasius and the Greek Fathers of the fourth century, must be discarded in favour of a loosely defined Trinity of Names. Hampden was a thoroughgoing Rationalist. For him the doctrine of the Trinity as understood in the Catholic Tradition was the fabrication of human minds. The Scriptures merely referred to the three Names of the Divine Being.

Keble was convinced that the Church of England was breaking with Tradition. If Keble belonged to a school, then this was it.[195] Keble was of the opinion that Hampden, aided and abetted by his future episcopal colleagues, was substituting man-made theories for the Tradition of the one, holy, Catholic and Apostolic Church. In 1836, when he preached his sermon on Tradition,[196] his fellow Tractarians were most impressed. On reading the text of the sermon sent to him beforehand, Newman commented, "What a magnificent sermon Keble's is! I think it is the boldest and most powerful composition we have yet put out".[197] Tradition was the life-blood of Keble's theology. Speaking of "the good thing" committed by the Holy Ghost, Keble identified it with the whole doctrine of Jesus Christ, committed by St Paul to Timothy, a doctrine of which only some aspects have been written down in the epistles. As it is summed up in the Apostles' Creed, Keble drew the conclusion that in consequence "the unwritten Word of God", if it could anyhow be authenticated, must necessarily demand the same reverence from us as the written Word.[198] Answering the question as to how much traditional doctrine could be ascertained in practice for the life of the Church today, Keble said: "We answer by application of the well-known rule, 'Quod semper, quod ubique, quod ab omnibus'".[199]

Both Hampden and Arius suffered from the same disease. One kind of profaneness drew on another, leading to a disdain of apostolic privileges and unscrupulous use of civil power.[200] Hampden's challenge was hardly new. Anglican divines in the past had to face such impertinences. In Hooker's day there were forms of apostasy and deadly heresy amongst those who disparaged primitive episcopacy, all of which smacked of arrogant innovations.[201]

It is dangerous to trust in human theories when God has spoken, this was one of Keble's, echoing Hooker, theological "raison d' êtres". Theology is about God, speaking to man, who listens and obeys. Tradition is there to be navigated thoroughly if theology is to remain God's voice for modern man, for, like Scripture, "it is a stream flowing down from the mountain of God, but their waters presently become blended".[202] "Blending" was an important word in Keble's theological vocabulary. "The English Church", he wrote, "does not so violently sever the different parts of the constitution of the Kingdom of Heaven, but acknowledging Scripture as her written charter, and Tradition as the common law, whereby both the validity and practical meaning of that charter is ascertained, venerates both as inseparable members of one great providential system".[203] In such a way, the English Church system was able to preserve the essentials of the faith, the canon of Scripture, the full doctrines of the Trinity and the Incarnation, the oblation and consecration of the Eucharist, the Apostolical Succession, to which, for good measure, should also be added baptismal regeneration.[204]

Keble was constantly aware of the dangers of novelty. In contemporary theology truths were becoming a matter for selection and rejection.[205] This was not the way to study theology. "We ought with all diligence to love what belongs to the Church, and to lay hold of the Tradition of the truth. For why? though the dispute were but of some ordinary question, would it not be meet to recur to the most ancient churches, where the Apostles went in and out, and from them to receive, on any present question, that which is certain and clear indeed?".[206]

To receive advice on any present question, this was Irenaeus but Keble's translation was not merely an academic exercise. It was a profound conviction, shared over the centuries. The emphasis was constantly the same, beating the drum not of "mere private opinion but rather the constant tradition of the Church Universal".[207] Keble rarely relaxed when he wrote about Tradition. The prose, like the theology, is tense, robust and powerful: "We are to look before all things to the integrity of the good deposit, the orthodox faith, the creed of the Apostolical Church, and by consent of pure antiquity. Present opportunities of doing good; external quietness, peace, and order; a good understanding with the temporal and civil power; the love and co-operation of those committed to our charge; – these, and all other pastoral consolations, must be given up, though it be with a heavy heart, rather than we should yield one jot or tittle of the faith once delivered to the Saints".[208]

Keble asked the question, how were the poor to know what is heresy? The plain sense of the Prayer Book was a powerful medicine but how would the poor and simple know if heresy were taught in some sermon or tract by this or that Church leader?[209] Keble's advice to the poor was direct: "Many false prophets are abroad, saying this or that against it: let us at once refuse to listen to them: let us put their books in the fire".[210] This battle against the spirit of the times was a total affair, embracing body, mind and spirit.

The order and decency which Keble thought were reflected in the Tradition of eighteen hundred years could not be confined to the Church alone. Having the deepest suspicion of "a bare word from man", Keble's abiding panacea was to assure his hearers of "the unfolding of God's Word by His own undoubted warrant and authority".[211] The ordering of the Church's ordinances, instruction in God's Word, no person allowed to preach without Christ's warrant, holy lessons selected and read in an orderly way, the holy sacraments correctly administered, these were the maxims for society in its political, social and commercial relationships. The vision which Keble had of the ideal society was hierarchical, authoritatively structured and scrupulously ordered along traditional lines.[212]

If the ordered society were to come into being, certain conditions had to be met. Men had to be content with their position in society. The main reason why Keble advocated this particular social outlook is summarised by Crane Brinton; "If men accept subordination in society, it must be, because they are themselves dignified by the achievements of that society, and because they can throw over the limitations of their lot the veil of a mystic attachment to something greater than themselves, yet of which they are an integral part".[213] Keble preached that Christ was content with his station in life, who formed "the vital link in the chain of God's mysterious mercy"[214] precisely because he enabled sinful, lost, wicked man to have communion with God through his own incarnation, "the foundation laid from the beginning, besides which no man can lay any other".[215] Keble was certain that each station in life was there by nothing less than divine appointment.

The idea that all things come from God was explicit in Keble's finest sermon on this theme, "Resignation the School of Piety", preached in 1843:[216] "For they see plainly, that as the weather and the seasons are of God's own sending, so is the Master whom we serve, so are the companions who work with us, so are all the circumstances, little and great, of our station; even that which is most amiss in them, that which is really perverse and sinful, He allows for wise and good purposes: and to rebel against it, or to complain of it in a bitter, discontented way, is the same kind of impiety, though it may not startle us so much, as rebelling against God, or complaining of the weather". Keble always had in mind the safest way to form the moral community which had as its basis the operation of the moral sense in each of its members: "I am where God has seen fit to place me; surely this one consideration entitles me to throw the burden of proof entirely on those who call me to alter my profession".[217]

Keble's daily intercessions were: "Deliver us, O Lord, from discontented spirits, heresy and schism, strife and debate, a scornful temper and reliance on our own understanding, whatever might disturb the Church".[218] For Keble, rebellion was nothing short of blasphemy. The sins of sensuality and rebellion were rife in the 1830's. There was much love of excitement with no room for pure and quiet satisfactions. The world was full of wanton pleasures.[219]

The inter-relation of the sins of rebellion, sedition and strife in Church and society was assessed by Keble in one of his sermons on "The Litany": "In the state we pray to be delivered from sedition, privy conspiracy and rebellion; in the Church from false doctrine, heresy and schism. Three bad things in the state, and three bad things in the Church, in either case going from bad to worse. In the state sedition, privy conspiracy and rebellion: sedition, that is, when people allow themselves to dishonour and disobey the King, and those in authority under him; privy conspiracy, when they band themselves secretly together, to do something against the law by fraud or by force; rebellion, when they actually lift up their hands against the Lord's anointed, the appointed Governor of the land. And nearly as these sins are in the State, so are false doctrine, heresy, and schism, in the Church".[220]

In Keble's Christian society, there was no room for insubordination, let alone rebellion. Keble's protest was based on the fundamental principle of Tradition, which nowhere allows deviations in doctrine. All things are ordained by God. Rebellion was not merely against the King and society. It was also an open assault upon the domain of God, since "Christians, when anything troubles them in the Holy Commandments of their God, should use themselves steadily to consider, that, nevertheless, they are God's; and that to shrink from them, as too strict, is direct rebellion; the grossest affront to Him, who made us what we are, and loves too well to bid us do anything, but what is really good and necessary for us".[221]

Keble expressed the perfect antidote to all rebellious thoughts: "Be watchful, and strengthen the things which remain, and are ready to die".[222] This was one of Keble's favourite sentiments when blessings were forfeited, privileges wasted, irreverence, self-will, unbelief and sensuality were indulged to such an uncanny degree.[223] There was only one perfect way to strengthen the foundations of the tottering society. The Prayer Book was always the Church's manifesto for such a sad state of affairs. There the hierarchical, sacramental and supernatural way of doing things, practised in the prayers and ordinances, had to be reflected in contemporary society, since that was the only perfect way to perfect peace and joy.[224] Disturbers of the peace, in doctrine or in social life, were anathematised by Keble for they had no fixed law of social life.[225] In Keble's society the corporateness, homogeneity and totality of things took precedence over all that was individualistic, personal and subjective. Personal assurances alone were insufficient for they led to much disquiet, condemning and unsettling others in their wake.[226] A far sounder way was to imitate the members of Keble's congregation, more than half of them women and children, "getting their bread and doing their part in the quiet offices of ordinary life".[227] This was the Christian society, nurtured by Tradition, which encouraged that perfect resignation, that humility of character which was conducive to sanctification.[228]

NOTES

1. "Rich and Poor One in Christ", A Sermon preached at St Peter's Church, Sudbury, 1858.
2. *The Christian Year*, p. 242.
3. J. H. Newman, *Apo.*, p. 257.
4. John Keble, *Outlines of Instructions and Meditations for the Church's Seasons*, p. 53.
5. ibid., p. 51.
6. See H. C. G. Matthew, "Edward Bouverie Pusey, From Scholar to Tractarian" in *The Jl. of Theological Studies*, Vol. XXXII, Part 1, p. 105.
7. *Sermons for the Christian Year, From Lent to Passiontide*, p. 285.
8. *The Christian Year*, p. 153.
9. *Sermons Occasional and Parochial*, p. 112.
10. *Occasional Papers and Reviews*, p. 433.
11. *The Christian Year*, p. 138.
12. *Occasional Papers and Reviews*, p. 162.
13. *Outlines of Instructions*, p. 2. Keble had the Day of the Lord's coming in mind.
14. *Occasional Papers*, p. 434.
15. *Sermons Academical and Occasional*, p. lix, lx.
16. Stephen Prickett, *Romanticism and Religion, The Tradition of Coleridge and Wordsworth in the Victorian Church*, p. 98.
17. John Keble, ed., *The Life of the Right Reverend Father in God,*

Thomas Wilson, DD, Lord Bishop of Sodor and Man, (7 Vols.), vol. VII, pp. 38–40.
18. *Sermons Academical*, pp. 18–19.
19. *Sermons Occasional*, p. 143.
20. *Sermons by Contributors to the Tracts for the Times*, Vol. VI, p. 161.
21. ibid., p. 122.
22. *The Christian Year*, p. 195.
23. *Sermons for the Christian Year, From Lent to Passiontide*, p. 49.
24. *Sermons Academical*, p. 35.
25. ibid., p. 55.
26. *Sermons Occasional*, p. 45.
27. *Occasional Papers*, p. 176.
28. ibid., p. 6.
29. ibid., p. 348.
30. ibid., pp. 10–11.
31. S. Prickett, op. cit., p. 71. For an assessment of Wordsworth's influence upon Keble, see also B. W. Martin, *John Keble, Priest, Professor and Poet*, pp. 73–89; Georgina Battiscombe, *John Keble, A Study In Limitations*, pp. 36 ff.
32. J. T. Coleridge, *A Memoir of the Rev. John Keble, MA, Vicar of Hursley*, p. 259.
33. See B. W. Martin, "Wordsworth, Faber and Keble, A Commentary on a Triangular Relationship", *Review of English Studies*, Vol. XXVI.
34. The best study of Wordsworth's political and social thought is M. H. Friedman, *The Making of a Tory Humanist*. Other studies are: E. C. Batho, *The Later Wordsworth*, pp. 190 ff.; Crane Brinton, *The Political Ideas of the English Romanticists*, pp. 38 ff.; Marilyn Butler, *Romantics, Rebels and Reactionaries, English Literature and its Background, 1760–1830*, pp. 58 ff.; P. Hamill, "Other People's Faces; The English Romantics and the Paradox of Fraternity", *Studies in Romanticism*, Vol. 17; C. F. Harrold, "The Oxford Movement; A Reinterpretation" in J. E. Baker, ed., *The Reinterpretation of Victorian Literature*; G. H. Hartman, *Wordsworth's Poetry*; P. J. Manning, "Wordsworth, Margaret and the Pedlar", *Studies in Romanticism*, Vol. 15; F. M. Todd, *Politics and the Poet*; Carl Woodring, *Wordsworth*; *Politics in English Romantic Poetry*. The most comprehensive selection of Wordsworth's poetry is Ernest de Selincourt and Helen Darbishire, Ed., *The Poetical Works of William Wordsworth*, (5 Vols.); Ernest de Selincourt, ed., *The Prelude*; W. J. B. Owen and J. W. Smyser, ed., *The Prose Works*, (3 Vols.). A recent study of Wordsworth is J. R. Watson, *Wordsworth's Vital Soul*.

35. Wordsworth, *The Prelude*, Book XIII, 169.
36. ibid., 183.
37. John Keble, *Lectures on Poetry*, transl. by E. K. Francis, (2 Vols.), Vol. I, p. 30.
38. *Occasional Papers*, p. 158.
39. See B. W. Martin, *John Keble*, op. cit., p. 84. For the tribute to "The Excursion", see Mary Moorman, *William Wordsworth, A Biography, The Later Years, 1803–1850*, p. 182.
40. Wordsworth, "The Excursion", I, pp. 386–7.
41. ibid., pp. 108–10.
42. ibid., pp. 430–1.
43. ibid., pp. 228–9.
44. ibid., IX, pp. 20–6.
45. G. Hough, *The Romantic Poets*, p. 90.
46. See Paul Hamill, op. cit.
47. Stephen Prickett, op. cit., pp. 5–11.
48. ibid., p. 197.
49. On *The Christian Year*, see M. H. Abrams, *The Mirror and the Lamp*, pp. 138–47, which is still the most comprehensive study; B. W. Martin, *John Keble*, op. cit., pp. 108–68; C. J. Stranks, *Anglican Devotion, Studies in the Spiritual Life of the Church of England Between the Reformation and the Oxford Movement*, pp. 236–66; G. B. Tennyson, *Victorian Devotional Poetry, The Tractarian Mode*, pp. 72–113; S. Prickett, op. cit., pp. 91–119.
50. See Tennyson, op. cit., pp. 226–8 for the popularity of *The Christian Year* and the kind of readership involved.
51. *The Christian Year*, p. 260.
52. ibid., p. 188.
53. ibid., pp. 116–7.
54. ibid., p. 17.
55. Such sentiments abound in *The Sermons for The Christian Year*, Vols. I–III.
56. *The Christian Year*, p. 10.
57. ibid., p. 79.
58. ibid., p. 85.
59. ibid., p. 6.
60. ibid., p. 20.
61. ibid., pp. 160–1.
62. *Sermons for the Christian Year, From Ascension Day to Trinity Sunday*, p. 226.
63. ibid., p. 226.
64. *The Christian Year*, p. 95.
65. ibid., p. 63.
66. ibid., p. 155.

67. ibid., p. 37.
68. ibid., p. 30.
69. *The Christian Year*, p. 95.
70. ibid., p. 178.
71. Wordsworth, *The Prelude*, XII, 50–2.
72. *Sermons, From Ascension Day*, p. 71.
73. *Sermons, Sundays After Trinity, I–XII*, p. 244.
74. *Sermons by Contributors to the Tracts for The Times*, Vol. VI, p. 60.
75. *Outlines of Instructions*, op. cit., 119.
76. ibid., p. 119.
77. ibid., p. 136.
78. *Outlines of Instructions*, p. 251. For a very different attitude to the sufferings of the poor, see Jennifer Hart, "Sir Charles Trevelyan at the Treasury", *English Historical Review*, Vol. LXXV, p. 99. Trevelyan thought that the 1846 Irish famine was God's punishment on an indolent people. It had been sent by God to teach the Irish a lesson. The famine need not be mitigated excessively.
79. *Sermons, From Advent to Christman Eve*, p. 6.
80. ibid., p. 7.
81. *Outlines of Instructions*, op. cit., p. 251.
82. ibid., p. 249.
83. *The Christian Year*, p. 191.
84. *Outlines of Instructions*, p. 230.
85. *Sermons, From Ascension Day to Trinity Sunday*, pp. 46 ff.
86. *Sermons, From Advent to Christmas Eve*, p. 45.
87. ibid., p. 283.
88. *Outlines of Instructions*, p. 249.
89. ibid., p. 249.
90. B. W. Martin, op. cit., pp. 119–25.
91. W. E. Gladstone, ed., *The Works of Joseph Butler* (2 Vols), Vol. II, pp. 65 ff.
92. *Sermons Occasional*, p. 522.
93. *The Christian Year*, p. 134.
94. *Outlines of Instructions*, p. 211.
95. See Friedman, op. cit. for Wordsworth's craving for the re-creation of local communities. Chapter IV.
96. F. Awdry, *A Country Gentleman in the Nineteenth Century*, pp. 75 ff.
97. *Occasional Essays*, p. 249.
98. *Sermons, From Advent to Christmas Eve*, p. 207.
99. *Sermons, From Lent to Passiontide*, pp. 163–4.
100. Battiscombe, op. cit., p. 136.
101. *Sermons Academical and Occasional*, p. 381.

102. In his preface to the works of Hooker, Keble half rebuked the learned divine that government should have the consent of the governed. See Editor's Preface, pp. lxxviii, lxxix.
103. See B. W. Martin, op. cit., pp. 135–154.
104. *Lectures on Poetry*, I. p. 17.
105. *Tract No. 54, Tracts for The Times*, Vol. II, p. 54.
106. See Isaac Williams, Tract No. 87, "On Reserve in Communicating Religious Knowledge" in Elizabeth Jay, ed., *The Evangelical and Oxford Movements*, pp. 106–30.
107. *Lectures on Poetry*, I. p. 75. See also G. B. Tennyson, op. cit. pp. 45–7 for a discussion of the doctrine of Reserve. Keble's *locus classicus* for this doctrine is Tract No. 89, "On the Mysticism attributed to the Early Fathers of the Church" in Jay, op. cit., pp. 131–147.
108. *Occ. Papers and Reviews*, p. 167.
109. See R. C. Selby, *The Principle of Reserve in the Writings of John Henry Cardinal Newman*, p. 11.
110. *Occ. Papers and Reviews*, p. 165.
111. ibid., p. xxii (footnote).
112. ibid., p. 306.
113. ibid., p. 281.
114. ibid., p. 282.
115. ibid., p. 281.
116. For the general reaction of the Church of England to the spirit of the Reform Bill, see E. R. Norman, *Church and Society in England, 1770–1970, A Historical Study*, pp. 84 ff.
117. *Lectures on Poetry*, I. p. 257.
118. For the constitutional background, see O. Chadwick, *The Victorian Church*, Part 1, Chap. 1; O. Brose, *Church and Parliament: the Reshaping of the Church of England*; E. R. Norman, *Church and Society in England, 1770–1970, A Historical Study*.
119. For a study of the significance of "National Apostasy", see J. R. Griffin, *Tractarian Politics*, pp. 21 ff. For many of Keble's more Radical utterances between February and July, 1833, see the section in Chapter 2, "Froude and Keble"; J. R. Griffin, "John Keble, Radical", *Anglican Theological Review*, Vol. LIX; "The Radical Phase of the Oxford Movement", *The Jl. of Ecclesiastical History*, Vol. XXVII. For very different views, see E. L. Woodward, *The Age of Reform, 1815–1870*, p. 493: "The whole protest had about it something feverish, a touch of absurdity"; C. Egner, *Apologia Pro Charles Kingsley*, p. 81: "It would indeed be hard to imagine a more disreputable cause for which to enlist the help of the Scriptures" than that "Parliament, against the suffrage

of the Established English and Irish Bishops, was decreeing the suppression and uniting of certain Irish sees".

120. See Chadwick, I, op. cit., pp. 56 ff.
121. William Warburton (1698–1779) was the author of *The Alliance between Church and State* in which he argued that while the Church, by accepting the protection of the State, must abandon its own independence, the toleration of those who differ from it in doctrine and worship should be allowed. Warburton never enjoyed a good press amongst the Tractarians. See William Palmer, *A Treatise on the Church of Christ: Designed Chiefly for the Use of Students in Theology*, (2 Vols.), II. p. 313; John Keble, "Unpublished Papers of Bishop Warburton", *The British Critic*, Vol. XXIX, pp. 427 ff.

William Paley (1743–1805) maintained in his *Principles of Moral and Political Philosophy*, II., p. 325, that "there is nothing in the nature of religion as such which exempts it from the authority of the legislator when the safety or welfare of the community requires his interposition". For a Tractarian critique of Paley, see Palmer, op. cit., p. 313.

For views which see Warburton and Paley merely echoing the sentiments of their age, see Norman Sykes, *Church and State in England in the Eighteenth Century*, pp. 326 ff; on Warburton especially, see J. N. Figgis, "William Warburton" in W. E. Collins, ed., *Typical English Churchmen from Parker to Maurice*, pp. 215–253; R. W. Greaves, "The Working of the Alliance: a comment on Warburton" in G. V. Bennett and J. D. Walsh, edd., *Essays in Modern English Church History in Memory of Norman Sykes*, pp. 163–180.

122. Burke's High Church Anglicanism was very different from the Tory Utilitarian kind. There is no doubt that Keble shared a unity of vision with Burke about Church and State relationships and with his general political views. Keble referred to Burke in his *Lectures on Poetry*, I., p. 50. A good introduction to Burke is Conor Cruise O'Brien, ed., *Burke's Reflections on the Revolution in France*. Other studies of Burke's political views are M. Freeman, *Edmund Burke and the Critique of Political Radicalism*; D. D. Murphy, *Modern Social and Political Philosophies, Burkean Conservatism and Classical Liberalism*; F. O'Gorman, *Edmund Burke, His Political Philosophy*; for Burke's religious views and his ideas on Church and State, see C. Parkin, *The Moral Basis of Burke's Political Thought*, pp. 131–138; P. J. Stanlis, *Edmund Burke and the Natural Law*, pp. 195–230. Burke's views were utterly different from many contemporary Tories. He had a mystical understanding of the Church's relationship to the State. The fixed estate of the

Church must never be converted into a pension or depend on the Treasury.
123. For these schools of thought, see R. D. Townsend, "The Caroline Divines" in Gordon Wakefield, ed., *A Dictionary of Christian Spirituality*, pp. 73–5. The two most comprehensive studies are P. E. More and F. L. Cross, *Anglicanism. The Thought and Practice of the Church of England, illustrated from the Religious Literature of the Seventeenth Century* and H. R. MacAdoo, *The Spirit of Anglicanism, A Survey of Anglican Theological Method in the Seventeenth Century*. See also H. R. Bloxap, *The Later Non-Jurors*. For John Hutchinson (1674–1737), see Leslie Stephen, *The History of English Thought in the Eighteenth Century*, Vol. 1, pp. 389–91.
124. Older but still valuable studies of Richard Hooker are P. Munz, *The Place of Hooker in the history of Thought* (London 1952); F. J. Shirley, *Richard Hooker and Contemporary Political Ideas* (London 1949). For modern assessments, see R. Eccleshall, *Order and Reason in Politics, Theories of Absolute and Limited Monarchy in Early Modern England*; R. K. Faulkner, *Richard Hooker and the Politics of a Christian England*; W. Speed Hill, ed., *Studies in Richard Hooker*. For a general survey of Church and State relationships in the period, see Paul D. L. Avis, *The Church in the Theology of the Reformers*, pp. 63–68, 85–93, 116–130.
125. *Sermons Acad. and Occ.*, p. 113.
126. "National Apostasy" is in *Sermons Acad. and Occ.*, pp. 127–148.
127. John Keble, ed., *The Works of the Learned and Judicious Divine, Mr. Richard Hooker: With an account of his Life and Death by Isaac Walton* (3 Vols.). Book VIII of *The Laws of Ecclesiastical Polity* is in Vol. III, pp. 326–455. See especially Chapter 1, 2, 3, 4 and Chapter VI, 13, pp. 329–334, 413–414.
128. ibid.
129. *Sermons Acad. and Occ.*, pp. 136–9.
130. ibid., p. 145.
131. "Advertisement to the first edition of the sermon on 'National Apostasy'", ibid., p. 128.
132. Letter of the Bishop of Leighlin and Ferns to the Editor of *The British Magazine*, Vol. IV, 31 December, 1833, pp. 742–6.
133. Keble's letter is found in H. P. Liddon, (preface), John Keble, "The State in is relations with the Church", *a Paper re-printed from the British Critic, October 1839 and including an Appendix, a Letter to the Editor of the British Magazine, January 1834*.
134. ibid., p. 59.
135. ibid., p. 60.
136. ibid., pp. 61–2.
137. ibid., p. 63.

138. On the idea of the godly prince in Hooker, see Avis, op. cit., pp. 131–166; Eccleshall, 126–149; Faulkner, op. cit., pp. 161–165. J. N. Figgis, *The Divine Right of Kings*, p. 199, wrote that "Elizabeth I, like Henry VIII may appear harsh and be regarded as depriving the Church of its due rights. Yet no less could have been claimed by any self-respecting monarch". E. T. Davies, *Episcopacy and the Royal Supremacy in the Church of England in the Sixteenth Century*, p. 125, claimed "in all that she did, Elizabeth acted according to the precepts of the Christian emperors like Theodosius". For views, however, which maintain that Elizabeth superseded her authority over Parliament and the Church, thus illustrating a vast discrepancy between Hooker's ideals regarding the Royal Supremacy and the way the Queen actually did act, see Claire Cross, *The Royal Supremacy in the Elizabethan Church*, pp. 35–6; Faulkner op. cit., pp. 177–8: "Some commentators suppose that she shaped the Church out of policy, while others suppose her motive was religious conviction. No one denies that she shaped the Church".
139. Keble, ed., *The Works of the Learned and Judicious Divine*, III., p. 342.
140. *Sermons Acad. and Occ.*, p. 149.
141. ibid., pp. 152–159.
142. *Plain Sermons*, by Contributors to the *Tracts for the Times*, Vol. 1, pp. 241 ff.
143. ibid., p. 241.
144. ibid., pp. 243–4.
145. *Plain Sermons* by Contributors to the *Tracts for the Times*, Vol. IV, pp. 76 ff.
146. Faulkner, op. cit., p. 165.
147. For Gladstone's views, see Perry Butler, *Gladstone, Church, State and Tractarianism, A Study of his Religious Ideas and Attitudes, 1809–1859*, pp. 77–99 and Keble's review, pp. 85–89.
148. Liddon, op. cit., pp. 27–8.
149. On Malthus's ideas on political economy and towards poverty, see T. R. Malthus, *An Essay on the Principle of Population: or, a View of its Past and Present Effects on Human Happiness; with an Enquiry into our Prospects respecting the Future Removal or Mitigation of the Evil which it occasions* (with an introduction by T. H. Hollingworth); *A Letter to Samuel Whitbread, Esq., MP on His Proposed Bill for the Amendment of the Poor Laws*; *The Principles of Political Economy with a View to their Practical Application*. The main studies of Malthus are M. Blaug, "The Myth of the Old Poor Law and the Making of the New", *The Jl. of Economic History*, Vol. XXIII, No. 2; J. Bonar, *Malthus and his Work*; A. Brundage,

The making of the New Poor Law; S. G. and E. O. A. Checkland, *The Poor Law Report of 1834*; A. W. Coots, ed., *Poverty in the Victorian Age* (4 Vols.); F. M. Eden, *The State of the Poor* (ed. by A. L. Rogers); J. P. Huzel, "Malthus, the Poor Law and Population in Early Nineteenth Century England", *Economic History Review*, Vol. XXII; "The Demographic Impact of the Old Poor Law: more Reflections on Malthus", *Economic History Review*, Vol. XXXIII; B. Inglis, *Poverty and the Industrial Revolution*; D. V. Glass, ed., *Introduction to Malthus*; J. M. Keynes, *Essays in Biography*, pp. 95–150; E. W. Martin, *From Parish to Union: Poor Law Administration, 1601–1865*; Samuel Mencher, *Poor Law to Poverty Programme*; J. C. O'Leary, "Malthus's General Theory of Employment and the Post-Napolenoic Depression", *Economic History Review*, Vol. III; G. W. Oxley, *Poor Relief in England and Wales*; J. R. Poynter, *Society and Pauperism: English Ideas on Poor Relief, 1795–1834*; M. E. Rose, *The English Poor Law, 1780–1930*; Sidney and Beatrice Webb, ed., *The Break-up of the Poor Law: Being Part 1 of the Minority Report of the Poor Law Commission*.

150. J. T. Coleridge, op. cit., p. 191.
151. Bonar, op. cit., p. 305.
152. Malthus, *Essay*, op. cit., p. 539.
153. See Poynter, op. cit., p. 157.
154. On this point, see Battiscombe, op. cit., pp. 162–3. See also James Graham, *Inquiry into the Principles of Population: including a Defence of the Poor Law*, p. 18.
155. See Sidney and Beatrice Webb, *English Poor Law History, Part II, The Last Hundred Years*, pp. 16 ff.
156. Malthus, *Letter to Samuel Whitbread*, op. cit., p. 190.
157. Battiscome, op. cit., p. 163.
158. B. W. Martin, *John Keble*, op. cit., p. 177.
159. See Brundage, op. cit., pp. 10 ff. for details.
160. ibid., pp. 182 ff.
161. Battiscombe, op. cit., p. 162.
162. W. C. Lubenow, *The Politics of Government Growth*, p. 52.
163. F. Awdry, op. cit., p. 134.
164. See, for instance, J. T. Coleridge, op. cit., pp. 576 ff. See also A. B. Donaldson, *Five Great Oxford Leaders*, p. 39.
165. J. T. Coleridge, op. cit., p. 89.
166. E. C. Batho, op. cit., p. 229.
167. On this point, see W. F. Kennedy's study of Samuel Taylor Coleridge's protest against the political economists in his "Humanist v's. Economist. The Economic Thought of Samuel Taylor Coleridge", *Univ. of California Publications in Economics, Vol. XVII.*

168. D. V. Glass, op. cit., pp. 10–11.
169. Malthus, *Principles*, op. cit., pp. 511–512.
170. *Sermons, From Ascension Day to Trinity Sunday*, p. 390.
171. *Sermons after Trinity, I–XII*, p. 290.
172. J. L. and B. Hammond, *The Village Labourer, 1760–1832, A Study in the Government of England before the Reform Bill*, p. 137.
173. Sir Edwin Chadwick, *An Article on the Principles and Progress of the Poor Law Amendment Act*, pp. 14–15.
174. Malthus, *Essay*, p. 565.
175. ibid.
176. ibid., p. 254.
177. For a good account of Malthus's influnce over Sumner, see R. A. Soloway, *Prelates and People: Ecclesiastical Social Thought in England, 1783–1852*, pp. 95 ff.
178. *Occ. Papers and Reviews*, p. 8.
179. *Sermons Acad. and Occ.*, p. 173.
180. ibid., p. 270.
181. ibid., pp. 418–419.
182. *Sermons, From Ascension Day to Trinity Sunday*, pp. 289–290.
183. *Sermons Acad. and Occ.*, pp. 173–231.
184. B. W. Martin, *John Keble*, pp. 23 ff.
185. *Sermons Acad. and Occ.*, p. vii.
186. ibid., p. 4.
187. ibid., p. lv.
188. ibid., pp. lviii, lix.
189. ibid., p. 39.
190. ibid., p. 414. Keble was quoting from Jeremy Taylor, *Works*, Vol. X, p. 322 and Bishop Butler, Preface to *Anal. sub fine*.
191. *Occ. Papers and Reviews*, pp. 213, 214, 231, 243.
192. Renn Dickson Hampden (1793–1868), Fellow of Oriel, he became Principal of St Mary's Hall, Oxford in 1833. In 1836 the Tractarians unsuccessfully attempted to prevent his becoming Regius Professor of Divinity. In 1847 he was offered the see of Hereford by Lord John Russell.
193. R. D. Hampden, *The Thirty Nine Articles of Religion*. The Eleventh of the Public Courses of Lectures in the Trinity Term, read before the University in the Divinity School, Oxford, 1 June, 1842, pp. 14, 22, 42.
194. R. D. Hampden, *The Scholastic Philosophy considered in its Relation to Christian Theology*. For a reaction from the Tractarian side, see W. H. Mill, *A Letter to a Clergyman in London on the Theological Character of Dr. Hampden's Bampton Lectures and the Extent and Value of Subsequent Qualifications of Their Meaning*. Mill (1792–1853) was made Regius Professor of

Hebrew at Cambridge in 1848 and his support of the Cambridge Camden Society did much to further the Tractarian cause at that University.
195. Contrast with Hampden: "I have stood alone, except so far as my teaching might associate me with other members of our common faith and common church", *The Thirty Nine Articles of Religion*, p. 44. Hampden was not exaggerating. He was consistently patronised by Lord John Russell. See A. R. Ashwell, *The Life of Samuel Wilberforce*, I. p. 441; O. Chadwick, op. cit., pp. 232, 296 ff.
196. "Primitive Tradition Recognised in Holy Scripture": a sermon preached in the Cathedral Church of Winchester, at the Visitation of the Worshipful and Reverend William Dealtry, DD, Chancellor of the Diocese, 27 September, 1836. See *Sermons Acad. and Occ.*, pp. 173–231.
197. Anne Mozley, ed., *L.&.C.*, II. p. 192.
198. *Sermons Acad. and Occ.*, p. 198.
199. ibid., p. 199.
200. *Tract No. 57* of *Tracts for the Times*, Vol. II, pt. I.
201. *The Works of the Learned Divine, Mr. Richard Hooker*, op. cit., Editor's Preface, pp. liii, lx, lxiii.
202. Hooker's theological motif was, "Trust in God rather than in man". See Editor's Preface, p. lxxix.
203. ibid., p. 348.
204. ibid., p. 349.
205. ibid., p. 212.
206. J. Keble (transl.), *The Five Books of S. Irenaeus, Bishop of Lyons against Heresies*, p. 209.
207. *Tract No. 52* of *Tracts for the Times*, Vol. II, pt. I, p. 6.
208. *Sermons Acad. and Occ.*, pp. 210–211.
209. *Occ. Papers and Reviews*, p. 329.
210. *Sermons, From Ascension Day to Trinity Sunday*, p. 401.
211. *Sermons, From Trinity XIII to the End*, p. 391.
212. For the idea of the organic society, see Prickett, op. cit., p. 103.
213. Crane Brinton, op. cit., p. 46.
214. *Tract No. 54* of *Tracts for the Times*, Vol. II, pt. I, p. 1.
215. ibid.
216. Sermon CXCII in *Plain Sermons* by Contributors to the *Tracts for the Times*, Vol. VI, p. 213.
217. *Sermons Acad. and Occ.*, p. xviii.
218. ibid., p. lxiii.
219. ibid., pp. 107–8.
220. *Sermons, From Septuagesima to Ash Wednesday*, p. 388.
221. *Plain Sermons* by Contributors to the *Tracts for the Times*, Vol. II, p. 299.

JOHN KEBLE

Little wonder that Keble had been so opposed, for instance, to the riots in the winter of discontent in 1830, when there had been much tumult in many agricultural districts, occasioned by the use of threshing machines. Keble had asked, "Was there anything like the Christian temper to be seen in that shameful tumult? Was there any sudden wrong done, any provocation which might seem to excuse the disorder? Was any quiet method of redress resorted to? Can any man shew the slightest authority from God or the King to use violence on such an occasion?" See *Sermons Occ. and Parochial*, p. 278. For Keble's similar reaction to the 1831 Bristol rioters, see W. Lock, *John Keble*, p. 27.

222. *Sermons Occ. and Parochial*, p. 368.
223. *Sermons Acad. and Occ.*, p. 329.
224. ibid., p. 330.
225. See *The Works of the Learned and Judicious Divine*, I. p. 285; Keble would certainly have agreed with Hooker's counsel; "The seat of the Law is the bosom of God, her voice the harmony of the world: all things in heaven and earth do her homage, the very least as feeling her care, and the greatest as not exempted from her power: both Angels and men and creatures of what condition soever, though each in different sort and manner, yet all with uniform consent, admiring her as the mother of their peace and joy". *The Laws of Ecclesiastical Polity*, Book I, xvi, 8. See also *Lectures on Poetry*, II, where Keble praised Homer and the major poets for their constancy.
226. *Sermons Acad. and Occ.*, p. lxvii.
227. *Sermons after Trinity I–XII*, p. 34.
228. *Sermons Acad. and Occ.*, p. lxviii.

2

RICHARD HURRELL FROUDE
"Let us Tell the Truth and Shame the Devil; Let us give up a National Church, and have a real one"[1]

2.1 INTRODUCTION

This sentiment encapsulates Hurrell Foude's profound contribution to the Tractarian Movement. His was politically and socially the most advanced, sophisticated and penetrating of the triumvirate under review.[2] G. F. A. Best has written of the originality of Froude's *Tract No. 59*,[3] the only Tract with an overtly political theme while Piers Brendon, whose *Hurrell Froude and the Oxford Movement*[4] is an excellent study of his achievement, mentions his partisan zeal as one of his chief gifts to Tractarianism.

W. G. Roe has devoted much time and space to the reception of Lamennais's ideas by the Oxford Movement.[5] He has written of the similarities between Froude and Lamennais – in England and France the Church was under the thumb of a civil authority, now largely infidel. Froude was nothing less, wrote Roe, than the first attested point of contact between Lamennais and the Oxford Movement.[6] It is curious, however, that Roe is of the opinion that because Froude, unlike Lamennais, was a conservative, he consequently had little or no concept of the social implications of his teaching. His main concern was with preserving the purity of the Church of England.[7] It is certainly true that Froude, along with Keble, Newman and Pusey thought that ecclesiastical purity was essential. This does not, however, preclude an acute consciousness, for instance, of the Church's mission to society. Froude, like Pusey, was very aware of the need to Christianise the large industrial towns.[8] Roe also believes that of all the

Tractarians only Froude and Newman had that breadth of vision which enabled them to embrace the ideas not only of antiquity but also of their own day.[9] This overrates the breadth of Newman's mind. He could only have been truly happy during his Anglican days at Oxford. His was the quintessentially English mind. He could not bear to see the Tricolour flying on a French vessel at Algiers. During his twenty four hours at Paris he saw nothing of that beautiful but revolutionary city, only what he was able to glimpse from the diligence.[10] Although Froude was very much the late product of a very Oxbridge sentimental Jacobitism,[11] yet he could have been happy in any European city, preferably Paris itself or Florence in the days of Savanorola.[12]

Hurrell Froude was a personality about whom it was impossible to be neutral. Before the storm broke in July 1833, he was able to write in April that "now that one is a Radical there is no point in being nice".[13] Fearing that it was never in his stars "to be contented",[14] he realised in 1831 that the Church needed a blow-up. Without such a happening it could never right itself.[15] In less emotive language, Froude realised that the position of the Establishment was certainly anomalous. Her rights were there by divine permission alone, as the state had secured by law those endowments which it could not have seized without sacrilege and had encumbered the rightful possession of them by various conditions calculated to bring the Church into bondage. The consequence of this was that the ministers in such an unjust arrangement were not bound to throw themselves into the spirit of such enactments. Rather, they must keep from the snare and guilt of them. All that the external oppressor had a right to ask was a literal acquiescence in such enactments. If they did more than that, they would betray their trust in the Church Catholic of the realm.[16]

For Froude, the contemporary age was hollow. Taking a long view of history, it was possible to behold many instances of wilful sin against a knowledge of the truth and a deliberate preference for the servants of Mammon before the servants of God. But to combine this, wrote Froude, with a hollow artificial respect which "hears the Word of the Most High as a very lovely song, this is a kind of neglect reserved only for days of intellectual cultivation".[17] Indeed, many members of society behaved as if they had never heard of Christ and the Gospel. A deist or a heathen might have behaved equally well.[18] The order of the day was for any self-constituted sect of teachers to guide others only by the power of their own judgements.[19] If any work of art were to have any success in such a cultivated, civilised and refined society, it was necessary to satisfy a sort of splendid excitement which was so prevalent and served as an impediment to the expression of those feelings which stem from the heart.[20]

Minor needs did not interest Froude. Only one principle really mattered, the need of supernaturalism in a society which had once again grown godless since Wesley's time.[21] What, then, was the matter with the source, fountain and mainspring of that supernatural power in society? How could the Church of England be saved?[22] As much as his beloved Becket, Froude felt iniquity all around him. Christ was being robbed of what he had purchased with his own blood. The secular arm was once again raising its ugly head. "Shipwreck awaits us. Lord, save us, we perish".[23]

2.2. "KEBLE IS MY FIRE AND I MAY BE HIS POKER"

Keble's ideas about Church and State have been studied in Chapter 1.[24] Keble's main characteristics were patience, resignation, mystical reverence for the past, especially the Royal Martyr, King Charles I. All this was morally motivated, impressing upon all his hearers the awesome but salutary truth that all things truly came from God, making human actions almost indecent.[25] Any radical ideas would not come easily to such a heart. Froude's influence would have to be dramatic to bear any fruit. In 1826 Froude wrote to his father with much prescience about Keble, "I don't think Keble will do anything, till all of a sudden he starts into everything..."[26] The crisis of the Irish Temporalities Bill gave Froude his perfect excuse to stir up Keble to fever pitch.

Froude's whole understanding of the relationship between Church and State is found in articles which he wrote for *The British Magazine* between 1832 and 1833, posthumously published as a separate pamphlet, *State Interference in Matters Spiritual*.[26] In two areas Froude exerted a profound influence upon Keble's political thought.

2.2.1. Froude's understanding of the Sixteenth Century Settlements

For Froude 1533 was a crucial date for that was the year when Henry VIII abrogated to himself the right of appointing bishops. Froude presented the whole affair with a sense of drama, the King appearing very much as the chief villain of the piece. A Licence under the Great Seal contained the name of the person whom the Dean and Chapter would choose. Lay hands nominated, the clergy elected, the Archbishop confirmed. The King represented the laity, the entire right of nomination was in his hands. The King was thus able to control the clergy who had to acquiesce in his wishes. The King might even supersede his clergy and have recourse to presentations. Even consecration was at the King's favour. The rights of the whole Church of England were surrendered unconditionally to the King.[27] Froude revealed all the powers at the command of his lawyer-like penetrating mind. He was able to scythe through the documentary evidence and like a prosecuting counsel asked the fundamental question; "Is the King, subject to latitudinarian influence, any longer qualified to represent the entire Church of England?"[28]

Matters were modified slightly, wrote Froude, when under Elizabeth the body of the whole realm was represented in Parliament and Convocation. Indeed, this was the purpose of Hooker's idea of visualising Parliament as a lay Synod of communicating members of the Church of England, a Synod which for that very reason could interfere in matters spiritual. This was to be the lay counterpart of the Convocation of the Church of England, composed entirely of her clergy. This was the ideal relationship, as it was the general consent of all which gave laws their form and vigour. The whole Church in free and open consent was able to make its own laws. It represented the people, a feat it was competent to perform. Government in such a relationship depended upon Parliament and Convocation annexed to it, the whole body of the realm consisting of the King and all his subjects. According to the Act of 1592 which empowered magistrates to drive out dissenters, the identity of Church and Commonwealth was assured.[29]

Froude's respect, however, for the Elizabethan settlement was severely limited. His real admiration was for those who advocated the spiritual supremacy of a truly theocratic Church.

Hence his unqualified enthusiasm, most surprisingly, for John Penry and the Puritans who did, at least, have the *ius divinum* on their side! This was precisely what the Church of England had relinquished, considering Ordination, according to Froude's interpretation, to emanate from the Queen herself. Such a notion was odious to Penry and his followers. Utterly mistrusting history in matters of religion, it was only in the Bible that a truly divine institution and a valid priesthood could be found. While the men of the Established Church were smugly involved in civilities to each other, it was left to these poor fellows to seek a creditable basis for their own theocratic Chruch.[30]

Froude's understanding of the sixteenth century settlements was a combination of objective assessment and crude propaganda. On the one hand, he understood perfectly the triangular relationship of Church, Parliament and Convocation in Elizabeth's reign, representing that perfect balance of secular and spiritual forces. There were many disparate aspects to the Elizabaethan settlement. Yet it was a rational whole within a universal framework, permeated by divine reason. Society was maintained as a unity of order precisely to give its members that vision of eternity. It was the precise function of the Church to be the medium of grace in such a relationship. The Sovereign was thus eminently suited to deal with spiritual as well as civil matters, yet was always dependent upon the community as the single source of his authority. The Parliament of England, with Convocation attached, was the seat, the essence of all good government, as it was the body of the whole realm, consisting of the King and all who are subject to him.[31] Froude understood all this but never admired it. It was the Puritans, sectarians though they were, who gained his real respect, as they advocated spiritual supremacy for their own Church. Froude's real problem was that, to his mind, the Elizabaethan settlement smacked of Erastianism. Even the central balancing forces at the heart of the Elizabaethan settlement had to rely heavily upon the fragile will of national sentiment. Even poor Penry and his followers were prepared to withstand the onslaughts of state meddlers in religion, even if they happened to be the clergy of the realm. Better to justify the *ius divinum* even in sectarian language than acquiesce in the compromises of schemers and charlatans!

2.2.2. The Constitutional Situation, 1829–1833

Froude was well aware that a new constitutional system had come into operation since the passing of a trilogy of Acts of Parliament, those of 1828, 1829 and 1832,[32] all of which had removed the grounds on which the Civil Legislature could also be the Ecclesiastical Legislature. In principle, Froude was doubtlessly correct. Yet he exaggerated the changed position of the Church with regard to the state during those five cataclysmic years. In fact, Anglican privilege remained intact for another fifty years and the Church was left as an establishment with a state connection and all the appropriate rights. Indeed, it could be argued that after 1832 when the Church no longer rested upon its old constitutional foundations, it flourished accordingly. Between 1833 and 1845 a thousand churches were built, dioceses were reorganised on the principle of spiritual unity and government and ten colonial churches were founded.[33]

Froude was unaware of all that happened in reality after the constitutional changes. For him the new system was nothing short of revolutionary. It was an usurpation and vitally affected Christ's holy, catholic and apostolic church.[34] Froude was of the opinion that the new Ecclesiastical Polity meant that the old establishment of Church and King was no longer applicable in contemporary England.[35] Many members of Parliament were the avowed enemies of holy Church. First principles might have to be advocated and new foundations laid.[36] There was no point in acquiescing in an otiose situation, let alone speculating impractically or inquiring profitlessly. There was no purpose even in just hoping, waiting or being cautious. Everything had to be sacrificed for the Church of Christ, even peace and good order. Froude was not being a melodramatic adolescent. He felt that a downright revolution had taken place since the Church of England had lost her exclusive supremacy in the councils of the nation. Her internal constitution had been changed irredeemably.[37]

What Froude evisaged was the end of a contractual understanding of ecclesiastical polity. If Hooker were alive, Froude thought, he would be the first to acknowledge the awesome but unavoidable logical fact that the conditions which he justified for state interference now no longer applied. The contract had been cancelled, the relationship annulled, the divorce confirmed.[38] All was efficacious when Parliament was actually a lay Synod of the Church of England. In 1833, Froude thought, it was nothing of the kind. Holy Church had simply not been vigilant enough. The Church had, however, become a robbers' den long before 1828. Bishop Hoadly was singled out by Froude as deserving particular censure in this respect.[39]

With relentless zeal, devastation and commitment, Froude wasted nothing in adding insult to injury. Lay duties had been transferred to the King but this was no Charles I, safeguarding and upholding the rights of holy Church. All that England had now was a puppet King, subject to the whims of infidels and barbarians. Lay people had to resist, as they had so frequently and effectively in the past. If they were silent, however, as the result of conscientious forbearance, all would be well and good. But laymen everywhere were guilty if their silence resulted from negligence or apathy.[40] Froude asked the most controversial question of his brief span of years; "Is the King qualified to represent the laity of the Church of England?"[41] The state, wrote Froude, had the finest possible bargain as its protection of the Church was minimal yet its interference was immense.[42]

Froude was no idle theorist. He was also eminently practical. Having diagnosed the disease, he was not too reticent about possible cures. Abandoning the beloved Anglican sense of compromise and diplomacy, Froude attacked his protagonists with the enthusiasm of a radical reformer. Every form of Protestantism was Erastian since, like Herod and Pontius Pilate, they had been made friends together to carry out a joint warfare against Christianity.[43] What exacerbated the present situation, however, was that Churchmen were actually delighting in it. They advocated it and were tamely submitting to it. "The same process which is going on in England and France is taking its course everywhere else; and the clergy in these Catholic countries seem to have lost their influence, and to submit as tamely to the State, as ever we do in England".[44] The talent of the country believed that the theories of political convenience ruled everything, since the safety of the Established Church came a poor second. That might be so, wrote Froude, but let no Churchman coalesce with such people as allies.[45]

The patient appeared to be dying of a terminal illness. Extreme measures were advocated. The root cause of the cancerous growth was the appointment of bishops. If something radical was not done about this, then there must be a separation in the Church and Froude himself would have been the head separatist. A dying patient had no reason to object to surgery which might be painful and dangerous. Froude spoke with conviction not only about a situation which was external but also because of his own failing health.[46] Everything including endowments, prestige, honour, all except truth, had to be sacrificed to the Church of Christ.[47] It was incumbent upon Churchmen to contemplate the separation of the Church from the alien, heathen state.[48]

The best wine was kept until last. Froude's solution was drastic, exuberant, final. It was nothing less than the repeal of the most pernicious piece of legislation which had ever been passed by Parliament, the Statute of Praemunire. In a land famed for religious liberty, the Bishops had to abuse their consciences and so consecrate people of whom they disapproved. Inability to conform led to drastic consequences, the end to protection by the law, the forfeiture of lands to the King, prison without bail till a ransom was paid and no release until a full renunciation was made. No Church anywhere had ever had her liberty curtailed so dramatically as the Church of England in 1833. Froude's appeal was to men of good will of all denominations and none to repeal these ridiculous, anachronistic laws.[49]

Froude pinpointed with rigorous logic the essential dilemma of the Established Church of England. A National Religion was preached, a diversity of denominations practised. Feeling the spiritual pulse-beat of the Church of England, he felt convinced that its life-blood was being extinguished by the wickedness of Erastianism. Kings of the earth had come home to stay. Worse, they had become the ideological prisoners of infidels. Consequently the Established Church was made the subject of worse harrassment than even that practised by Puritans and Papists. The bishops were state appointments only, glorified civil servants rather than sons of God, let alone successors of the Apostles. The people had to resist, for God was on their side.

2.2.3. The Radical Keble, 1833–1839[50]

Piers Brendon has written about Keble's great indebtedness to Froude, not least in the political sphere, and also Keble's profound spiritual influence over his favourite pupil.[51] Froude's assertions about the sixteenth century settlements and the changed situation between 1829 and 1833 did exert a great influence over Keble, whose articles in *The British Magazine* for March 1833 represent his most subtle, precise and rational argument for the Church and State to rectify their increasingly deteriorating relationship. What is surprising, however, is the general tone of the articles. It is only the letter "K" at the end of each article which convinces the reader that it was Keble himself and not Froude who was responsible for them.

Commenting on Lord Althorp's speech to the House of Commons on 12 February, 1833, attempting to explain the Church Temporalities Bill,[52] Keble confined the thrust of his article in the March issue to the principles of the Bill. All were agreed, wrote Keble, that the greatest changes possible were envisaged in the speech but no principles were set up for allowing such actions. "I think there are too many bishops – and I think we may get rid of them". That was all the rationale behind such catastrophic changes! The means by which Christianity had been presented to the nation for centuries was being destroyed. The spiritual welfare of man was impaired and God was dishonoured.[53]

Echoing Froude, Keble stated that it was only churches which had been founded upon Erastian principles which had to be actively persecuted by legislators, the majority of whom were not even in communion with the Church. Such was not the case with the Church of Scotland, the Church of Rome, the Greek Church. Even Independents would have been upset if their spiritual laws had been made for them by others. Only the Long Parliament had before behaved in such a despicable manner. Keble also pointed out that when the whole Church, consisting of clergy and laity, preponderating respectively in Convocation and Parliament, concurred in spiritual enactments, no conceivable human action could have been wanting to that law. Of course, Keble informed his fellow Churchmen that doubtlessly alienation was not sacrilege when clear political expediency required it. So the politicians might argue, in the Lords, Commons, in speeches and tracts but the truth was the antithesis to such conveniently argued cases. The real danger to the Church of Christ in this Kingdom was irreverence, tending to atheistical self-sufficiency.

Then comes the call to battle, a passage which could have been dictated to Keble by Froude himself; "Whenever the union of Church and State, in itself one of the greatest of blessings, is permanently clogged with such conditions, and fallen under such incurable mismanagement, as to encourage this irreverence, rather than check it, – then it will be the plain wisdom of the church ... to throw away from her those state privileges, which in such a case would prove only snares and manacles; and to excommunicate, as it were, the civil government".[54] In the name of God and his holy Church, men must stop this sacrilege immediately, taking liberty with holy things.

This was Keble at his most radical. Never intemperate, let alone unkind, unfair or unscrupulous, he illustrated in this article the heightening of his political awareness of the dangers facing Christ's holy Church. Once again, she was being robbed, plundered, persecuted with remorseless zeal by atheistic vandals.

How profound, however, would Keble's understanding of the relationship between Church and State have been had not Froude been there to encourage, criticise and provoke? Temperamentally, Keble preferred writing verses for *The Christian Year* than polemical articles in *The British Magazine*. Yet every true conservative is also a radical. William Palmer and his friends,[55] let alone the Ultra-Tories like Lord Eldon, were never influenced by Froude. They thought him rash, intermperate, even absurd.[56] But Keble was the heir of the Non-Jurors who had simply refused to compromise their principles. They had suffered for conscience's sake.[57] Underneath Keble's bland exterior there was always the historical precedent of those who had fought and won a moral and spiritual battle. This was precisely the tradition which distinguished Keble from many Tory upholders of the Establishment.[58] This is why Keble was well aware that the dangers to holy Church did not always reside on the outside but that the chalice was already poisoned within by those who were friends of the Church conceived in purely human terms. Tories may well be High Establishment men but their attitudes were indistinguishable from the worldly, the secular and the unscrupulous. In his poem "Church and King" Keble knew where the stains of sin had left their most indelible mark;

> Alas! our care
> Is not from storms without, but stains that cleave
> Ingrain'd in memory, wandering thoughts profane;
> Or worse, proud thoughts of our instructress meek,
> The duteous Church, Heaven – prompted to that strain.
> Thus, when high mercy for our King we seek,
> Back on our wincing hearts our prayers are blown
> By our own sins, worst foes to England's throne.[59]

The radicalism of Keble was not dramatic like Froude's, but all that was required of the latter was to convert an implicit into an explicit position. It was no small wonder that Palmer and his friends thought Keble too radical.

In 1838 W. E. Gladstone wrote his book, *The State in its Relations with the Church*, a classic summary of a Church which could be established and so national, yet catholic as well.[60] Keble's review of the book in the *British Critic* was a logical development of all the arguments he had used so brilliantly in the heady months of March to July, 1833. Keble felt that Gladstone's book was excellently well meant but lacked penetration, a little reconciling, that is, with Froude's views.[61] If Gladstone had read Froude, there is no obvious evidence that his views had influenced him at all.

In three respects Keble illustrated that he had taken Froude's admonitions to heart. First, Keble emphasised the validity of the voluntary method of parochial government. Gladstone, representing the vast majority of Chruchmen on this vexed issue, could see no justification for such a system, as "it tends to give a preponderating influence, in determining the doctrine which shall be taught to the less qualified class". Keble, however, would have none of this. The Church never walked closer to the spirit of the Gospel than after the days of martyrdom and persecution, voluntary poverty and mortification, "the philosophy of the solitaries", as St Chrysostom called it, were brought forward in their power. Churchmen had no right to despair until such an experiment had been tried in this nation, even in the vast wilderness of London and the manufacturing districts, with or without state countenance. What if endowments were to fail completely? Think of St Paul and his followers at Macedonia, working with their own hands. All this might be Utopian but it was not beyond the realms of possibility.[62]

Secondly, Keble was increasingly critical of the King's prerogative. Preaching about Nursing Fathers and Mothers was one of Keble's favourite themes.[63] This was why the tradition still pertained in many parts of the Christian world of the Sovereign at solemn Coronations wearing a deacon's habit under his robes of state. He was a servant of the Church, whose anointing and blessing he had just received. Yet the ideal was unlike the present reality. There was no joy, fulfilment or devotion but only sin, sacrilege and abandonment of basic duties. The state enforced and the Church alas! consented. All was contrary to the Word of God. The successors of the Apostles were appointed by the Crown. Neither Ambrose nor Basil would ever have allowed the claim.[64] Keble never lost his faith in the Royal Supremacy. Patience, passive obedience, constant and persistent hopes were his precepts. The spirit of Froude, however, was constantly coming to the surface.[65] It did not force Keble to abandon his position but to question and criticise it on all occasions. The apparent abandonment of the King's Coronation Oath and his rightful administration of the Royal Supremacy in defence of the Church's spiritual and doctrinal traditions seemed to confirm Froude's worst premonitions in 1833.

Thirdly, Froude was the least insular of the Tractarians. His reading, travelling and frequent contacts would have made him feel completely at home in the world of medieval literary communication. His outlook was not only spiritually and doctrinally but also geographically Catholic as well. Keble, for his part, never went further than Bournemouth. His geographical isolation, however, did not corrupt his theological viewpoints. On the contrary, Froude instilled into his greatest mentor an aversion to all things purely and simply English. Far from nationality and catholicity being harmonious, as claimed by Gladstone, they were distinctly out of tune with each other. Too much English self-will could lead to a sullen, moody independence. It could also lead to an excessive dependence upon the partial stands of the sixteenth century. An island of the free was no substitute whatsoever for the lack of unity in contemporary Christendom. The days of the General Councils and letters commendatory between Church and Church, the times of uninterrupted order and Catholic consent had vanished.[66] The Church of England in her English independence lacked the Catholic outlook of the Middle Ages. It stood condemned, being party to a state which lived in open sin. The Reformation had made the Church of England independent but the results were insularity, introversion and atrophy.

In 1839 Keble gave three instances of the way in which his consciousness of the relationship between Church and State had been progressively formed by Froude. In reconciling so much of his own thought with Froude's, however, Keble distanced himself from Gladstone and the more traditional views of many High Churchmen.[67]

2.3 "LET US THROW THE Z'S OVERBOARD"

Myths, historical or theological, can be powerful instruments in propagating truths. They can also perpetuate gross exaggerations, even lies. To read Newman's *Difficulties Felt by Anglicans in Catholic Teaching*, let alone the *Apologia*, gives the definite impression that in July 1833, Newman, faced with two distinctive concepts of Church and State, that provided by William Palmer, Hugh James Rose and the so-called *Friends of the Church*[68] and that by Froude, immediately thought the latter infinitely more attractive and pursued that path accordingly.[69] The first six volumes of Newman's published correspondence give a very different picture.

It is essential, first, to assess the exact concept of the Church and State which was advocated by Palmer, Rose and the older school of High Churchmen; secondly, to contrast it with Froude's; finally, to see exactly where Newman himself stood in July 1833, so frequently like a ship in mid-river, as it were, thrown to and fro by utterly opposing winds and currents.

2.3.1. The Concept of the Church and State advocated by the Friends of the Church

It is much too facile to study the Z's, as Froude so disparagingly called the older high and dry school of Churchmen, through the eyes of Newman in the *Apologia*. In fact, Palmer, Rose and the *Friends of the Church* were as concerned about the Church's spiritual welfare as Keble, Newman and Froude. Notwithstanding that their basic concept of Church and State was different, that hardly makes them the villains of the piece. Rose was one of the most gifted men of his age, a fact readily acknowledged by Newman.[70] Palmer was exceedingly learned, if pedantic.[71] Their awareness of the real danger to the Church, however, was acute enough. In the Irish Temporalities Act of 1833, the Church was treated as a slave of the state, devoid of faith, and capable of being moulded into any form at the state's pleasure.[72] The Z's felt, as much as any of the "Apostolicals" that legislation could not cure the ills of the Church; "The real grievances are sensuality and selfishness, indifference, dissent and unbelief – the remedies are the Irish Bill, which is a sacrilege, forced commutation of tithes, equalisation of benefices and abolition of pluralities".[73] In many ways, the older school of High Churchmen wanted all the advantages of state protection and the privilege to resist state encroachment.

On the other hand, the advantages of state control were immense. Permanent provision of the clergy by the state meant that there was no temptation to be popular as under the voluntary system. The clergy were sent to places where the poor otherwise would be unable to support them. In places of crime only an endowed clergy could help. The establishment by law of the Church of England was a blessing of unspeakable magnitude to the country.[74] Tithes must be approved as they were the symbols of outward blessings.[75] On the other hand, when the state threatened the Church, she had no option but to resist, as High Churchmanship was confined to no form of government.[76] According to William Palmer, whose *Narrative* is still a reasonably objective assessment of the Movement, the aims of all those who wished to defend the Church and resist the encroachment of the state were the same. "Although there were some differences of view amongst us", he wrote, "yet all acted together as brothers, convinced that they were agreed in all essentials".[77]

2.3.2. Anathema to Froude

For a few moments in history, Froude and Palmer thought along the same lines. Indeed, Froude in August 1833 was magnanimous enough to write that however the conservatives differed from him in basic essentials, like the state of the clergy in society having to be gentlemen and being able to mix in good society, even so they were not all worldly minded and did agree with him in all practical points and might pull together entirely.[78] Already, however, at the Hadleigh Rectory meeting it was obvious that Froude's views were far too advanced for the gathering.[79]

This was hardly surprising. To understand Froude's concept of the Church in her relationship to the state, it is necessary to study the articles which he wrote for the *British Magazine* on Thomas à Becket, beginning in September 1832. It was in these articles[80] that Froude expressed his immense admiration for the Church of the eleventh and twelfth centuries. "Even among the obsolete records of the Middle Ages", Froude wrote, "the reader may expect to find something, not indeed to enlarge his mind but at any rate to amuse his fancy. And among the characters which they present to him, vain as it would be to look for orators or political economists, he may, nevertheless, trace enough of human feeling and perhaps, occasionally, of human intelligence, to awaken his interest and give zest to his researches.[81]

Froude visualised the Catholic Church of the eleventh and twelfth centuries as one compact machine. The churches of the Continent were cemented together, men of letters talked a common language, people expended large sums of money in keeping up their correspondence and frequently met one another at the great centre of ecclesiastical intelligence, the court of Rome. Priests were promoted from one country to another and a strict system of subordination prevailed, which secured a union of action if not opinion.[82] How different it was in 1832! The poor, so powerful in the twelfth century, were now nothing. Becket washed the feet of the poor and called them "pauperes Christi". Peasants were able to exercise spiritual authority over their own land.[83] The laity, the fulcrum of the Church's power in the twelfth century, were now ignored.[84]

If one ecclesiastical statesman summed up the spirit of the twelfth century for Froude, it was Becket.[85] Froude always admired great men who fought against spiritual wickedness in high places.[86] The exaltation of Becket as hero and saint was part of a powerful phenomenon in the 1830's, that of hero worship generally.[87] As Becket was the hero of an ideal world in the twelfth century, so too in the sixteenth century Cardinal Pole summed up the spirit of faithfulness, loyalty and perseverance.[88] All this, however, did not make Froude some kind of refined writer of the best historical fiction. Idealising only atones for the deficiencies of a dull, unimaginative, utilitarian age. Froude was well aware of the dangers of portraits which were not only unrealistic but also perverted; "The achievements of great men in distant ages," he preached in a sermon for All Saints' Day, 1831, "are always likely to take hold of the mind, and to draw it away from the dull realities of every day life; we invest them with a kind of ideal splendour, the resemblance of which we do not trace in the persons and the affairs amongst which we are actually concerned; and there is always a danger lest a mind which has allowed itself to run on things above its own experience, should picture them to itself so unlike anything that it can now realise as to disconnect them from the world we live in, and the people we associate with".[89] Becket was a hero but his feet were still made of clay and the earth upon which he walked was real and tangible.

Froude's main interest was in the struggle between Church and state from 1163 to 1171.[90] His history of Becket, according to Piers Brendon, was his most important expression of romanticised medievalism and yet was surprisingly accurate.[91] Such an assessment, however, must not disguise the fact that Froude was deeply critical of many later medieval developments in papal policy, seeing the increasingly selfish power of the Roman see in the fourteenth century as undermining the foundations on which it had built its power.[92] Froude's enthusiasm for the eleventh and twelfth centuries must be tempered by his anti-papal assertions about the later Medieval Church.

For Froude, Becket in his martyrdom was the most remarkable man of his times, which was apparent from the sympathy, veneration and attachment that followed him everywhere.[93] Yet this was not the opinion of Protestant scholars whose outlook was contrary to everything Froude cherished and loved.[94] Even in the twelfth century many were unable to judge objectively the vital issues involved.[95] The myth that Becket was utterly insincere in his relationships with the King, for instance,[96] was perpetuated deliberately by Protestant historians who stated that Becket offended all principles of law and reason by refusing the concessions wrought from him by the King. Worst of all, Becket wanted only impunity for offending clergymen.[97]

Becket was an ideal hero because he stood for the epitome of the Church against state control. His was the perfect stance against unlawful, secular interference in every age. For Froude, no layman, then or now, ought to interfere in the affairs of holy Church. The spiritual superiority of the Church, it was for this that Becket lived and died. Grandiloquently Becket wrote for posterity; "I will not conform to the usage of this world when they interfere with the privileges of my divine order. For this I have incurred the displeasure of the King ... deserted by my brethren ... I have offended the whole world ... Never will I covenant with mortal men as to forget my covenant with God and my order".[98] "Libertas Ecclesiae", then and now, was the perennial issue. The Pope explained the situation precisely to Becket; "In your whole conduct ... act with caution, prudence, and circumspection, doing nothing in haste, but all things with gravity and deliberation. In ways consistent with the liberties of the Church, labour to conciliate his Majesty the King of England".[99] That was in 1166. Synonymous with liberty was justice, for which Becket was a martyr. The Archbishop needed no reminding of that when John of Salisbury wrote to him in July 1166; "Whoever suffers in the cause of justice, he is a martyr, a witness of the truth, an asserter of the cause of Christ".[100] Of course, Becket was well aware of the abuses at hand-priests accepting more than one living, money paid to bishops unlawfully, men ordained uncanonically. Little wonder that Nicholas of Rouen wrote to him, "If you love the liberty of the Church, for the sake of God show by your words and actions that the before-mentioned things displease you".[101]

The King had the nobles and the Cistercians on his side. But Henry II had forgotten a very basic commandment, that he was King only by the Church's favour, as Becket was keen to show him; "It is certain that the power of Kings is given them through the Church, but not that of the Church through Kings; your Majesty can have no pretence for compelling the Bishops either to absolve or excommunicate; for summoning the clergy before secular courts; for interfering with tithes or presentations; for prohibiting the trial of perjury in the Bishop's court".[102] In this struggle Becket's allies were not the strong, powerful and influential but the "pauperes Christi". The animosity of the nobles towards Becket induced them to join a party whom they feared and hated, only to overthrow a party which, though they feared it less, hated it more. It was precisely the Church's popularity with the poor which alienated the nobles from it. Here indeed was an unequal struggle, the alliance of the King, the nobility and the Cistercians against Becket and the peasantry. Although the chivalry of England was waged against Becket and his followers, Froude wrote with much pathos that Becket and his "pauperes Christi" were too strong for them.[103]

Froude's protrayal of the Church in the eleventh and twelfth centuries contained all the powerful ingredients of didactic historical tales at its best, or, for Protestant historians, worst. An Archbishop had been martyred for the freedom and justice of the Church Catholic. A King with all his nobles, magnates and heads of religious houses on his side had usurped the spiritual rights of holy Church. Yet the cohesion and unity of society during this period still breathed the air of cameraderie and equality. Such a picture was certainly evocative as it illustrated what the Church had once achieved in her fight for spiritual supremacy and integrity.

The image of the Church in her relationship to the State which was portrayed by Palmer, Rose and the *Friends of the Church* was bound to be anathematised by Froude. On three crucial issues, he thought that their beliefs on the Church and State question were mistaken. First, Froude was utterly opposed to the system of tithes. For him they were immoral. Writing in July 1835, Froude's opinion was that tithes could not be a legal debt and a religious offering at the same time. When the payment began to be enforced by civil authority, the desecration took place. Besides, wrote Froude, look how well other denominations are faring which have adopted a system totally dissimilar to that of tithes. Everything was voluntary. The Wesleyans, let alone the Primitive Church, were cases in point. Even if the voluntary system failed in one place, that was no argument for the convenient expediency that the Establishment was necessary. The only way the masses of Manchester, say, could be reached was for each place to support its own Church.[104]

Secondly, the whole basis of the Established Church was anathema to Froude. His feeling was that since the Reformation the Church had not only become Protestant; equally heretical, it had become respectable. Established ways of evangelising, for instance, had become ineffective. In August 1833, Froude was seriously thinking about reviving a monastic system as the best way of bringing religion into the great towns. Colleges of unmarried priests would not only be cheap, there would also be the blessed precedent of the "pauperes Christi", the watchword of the Church in the time of Becket. All this was infinitely preferable to the present state of ecclesiastical polity with its horrid talk of pampered aristocrats, resident gentlemen and smug parsons. Froude summed up his concept of the Established Church with characteristic candour; "The notion that a priest must be a gentleman is a stupid exclusive protestant fancy, and ought to be exploded".[105]

Thirdly, Froude mistrusted Palmer's Association of *Friends of the Church*. Piers Brendon points out that Froude's opposition was both religious, in that he felt that the Church was the only society that mattered, and political, in that Froude was well aware that the more advanced party would be stifled by the heavyweight tactics of Palmer and his friends.[106]

Froude's admiration for the Church of the eleventh and twelfth centuries meant that he was completely at odds with the Established Church of his day. He seriously thought that the Church of England should be deprived of her basic livelihood. Orthodox means of evangelising the masses had become hopelessly ineffective. Conventional ways of reforming the Church would inevitably fail.

2.3.3. Newman's Position, July 1833

It must be asked how exactly Newman saw himself alongside this bewildering difference of opinion; – the Established Church party, wishing an Association, full of zeal for the rights and privileges of the Church of England and Hurrell Froude, .the young nobody, letting off his radical firecrackers in all directions and actually deriving much enjoyment from the experience.

Newman himself was unsure. Never in a hurry to make up his own mind, he was capable of uttering statements which one side or the other could interpret as a vote of confidence in them. Much has been made of Newman as a radical figure in the opening months of the Oxford Movement.[107] Indeed, in *Tract No. 10* Newman looked forward to the day when the clergy would be stripped of all earthly powers, be no longer considered gentlemen, let alone superior in worldly station.[108] Both Toryism and the Church of England were failing precisely because they had lost the support of the laity, the fulcrum of the Church's power in those happier days associated with the Apostles and the third and fourth centuries.[109] Sounding exactly like Froude, Newman was able to stress the significance of having bishops who were independent of the Crown "which has become but a creature of an infidel Parliament".[110]

Yet Newman never shared Froude's extreme enthusiasm for lay participation. Brendon is correct to stress that too much should not be read into Newman's "support" for the laity. What Newman had read about lay support in the Fathers was confirmed directly by Froude and indirectly by Lamennais.[111] Newman, was, however, never as convinced as Froude about lay participation. Froude had grand ideas about an Anglican Parliament "which might function as a 'lay synod' in the Church but this was only valid through membership in the Church it controlled".[112] To Froude's suggestion that laymen might even be consulted about the appointment of bishops, Newman wrote in *The Suffragan Bishops* that such a move would be "a measure utterly destructive of the Church in the present vagueness of the qualification of Church membership".[113] Newman was unsure how the Church might become more popular[114] but was in no doubt that if the Movement were to succeed, it must become what was anathema to Froude, respectable. Having an almost pathological dread of rebellion, it was Newman's profound hope in July 1833 that the Movement would not be seen as a conspiracy but rather a challenge, supported by the bishops, to the state of the contemporary Church.[115] Never wishing to betray his trust or see the privileges of Christ's Church committed to him diminished, Newman was equally assertive that he would stick to the state as long as he possibly could.[116] Rose might well be a conservative, but who would not be anyhow if he could? Newman would have rejoiced if things could have returned to their old state, provided that discipline be enforced.[117]

It was all very well for Froude to act the part of the young agitator but the Oath of Obedience could very well be turned against them. Taking an oath even to bishops, most of whom saw themselves as anything but successors of the apostles, was as serious a matter for Newman as it was for Palmer, Rose and the *Friends of the Church*. It was certainly not an occasion for flippancy, as Froude seemed to counsel.[118] Constantly an essential part of Newman's programme was that Churchmen must protest against anything directly to separate Church and state, while, of course, thinking it necessary steadily to contemplate the contingency of such an event.[119] Newman did not think that the downfall of the Monarchy would benefit anyone. It would be better if the clergy were to stay out of politics completely.[120] Far from wishing to aggravate the conservative "Z" party, Newman only wanted their good will. It was his belief that the older school of High Churchmen would join them anyway, especially, as appeared likely, the Establishment went under like a sinking ship without trace.[121]

In July and August 1833, Newman was resolved that he could not take one step without some authority to back him, directly or by fair inference.[122] Little wonder that Newman was so pleased with the warm congratulations which he received from Rose on the excellence of his scholarship.[123] Temperamentally, he hated to be rushed. He thought that Froude was in too much of a hurry for anyone's good. Utterly impatient with meetings like that held at Hadleigh Rectory, Froude wished to break with Rose immediately. Newman wrote to Keble in August 1833 that such a break must not happen. Newman sounded benign, almost avuncular, in his counsel; "let us wait the course of events; we shall lose all our influence when times are worse, if we are prematurely violent; things must be kept quiet for a year or two that our position may be ascertained; get up precedents and know our duty".[124] All of which was hardly the stuff of which young revolutionaries are made. Newman realised that in Froude he had an excessively irascible spirit on his hands. Far from threatening to bite Rose, Froude would have been much better advised to read some of the aforesaid's last article in the September 1833 issue of *The British Magazine*. Such boldness of spirit was not material for reproof but praise.[125]

The main difference between Newman and the older school of High Churchmen was over tactics. In September 1833, Newman and Palmer were in agreement about the defence of the true

Church. It was the business of how the Church should be defended that difficulties began. The defence of the Church of Christ, according to Newman and Palmer, who were joint secretaries of a committee at Oxford established explicitly for such a purpose, consisted in stressing the immense benefits of communion with our Lord through the successors of his apostles, the advantages of the doctrine of Apostolic Commission, daily prayer and more frequent communions, resisting any unauthorised changes to the Liturgy and propagating the best means of preserving sound worship and discipline.[126] All this was most laudable, but Palmer loved the idea of committees producing tracts. For Newman that was an impossible idea, since "living movements do not come of committees".[127] To which Palmer countered with the justified complaint that the first Tracts should at least have borne Newman's name, since individual speculation ought to be encouraged provided that it did not lead to Latitudinarianism.[128]

Too much should not be made about Newman's differences with the older school. The contrast, minimal as it was originally, lay in the area of tactics for the battle, not the battle itself. Similarly, Newman's first Tracts were not meant to undermine the authority of the bishops, whose support Newman coveted so zealously. Despite the fact that Newman defied the contemporary notion that the Establishment was founded and supported by the state – "a notion has gone abroad that they (the government) can take away your (the Church's) power",[129] the early Tracts contained nothing new, dynamic, let alone radical.[130]

Far from being a tuneful player of Froude's radical notes in July 1833, Newman moved cautiously towards the best means possible of defending the Church. For all his vacillations and doubts, lack of confidence and prevarication, Newman liked to think that he was his own man. Possessed of an independence of mind, he was diplomatic enough to hope that all parties concerned for the defence of the Church would unite, persevere and triumph. Froude might not bite Rose after all. Palmer and he might settle their little differences over tactics. This was the way Newman's mind worked. Unfortunately, events did not materialise as Newman might have wished. This would not be the first time for Newman to be disappointed by his own prognosis. On three crucial issues between October 1833 and May 1836,

Newman's mind was to be tortured remorselessly. The fact that it was not shattered was only because of the influence of Hurrell Froude, who was neither diplomatic, cautious nor timid.

2.3.4. The Night of 13 November, 1833

Throughout September, October and early November 1833, the tactical battle continued between Newman and Palmer over the whole idea of the Tracts. Palmer had perfectly good reasons, theological, diplomatic and utilitarian for wanting to see the Tracts stopped. According to Newman himself, in a letter sent to Froude, dated 18 September, 1833, Palmer wanted no tracts to be issued without the committee's approval and for men of different tastes to be included. Ironically, Newman agreed with Palmer that men of the highest rank possible should be included in the society, a kind of élitist editorial panel, and that till events settled down a little, the committee should publish no tracts at all, but that any individual could, if he so wished.[131] This involved a battle of personal wills, Newman preferring the individual approach, fearing that a board composition would have been nothing better than tame dull compositions,[132] while Palmer was suspicious of individual inspiration, lest it might have led to Latitudinarianism. It would be wrong to see two clearly drawn sides to the battle, as if the older school of High Churchmen were ensconced in their own serene world, terrified of offending traditional High Church support and a younger radical school bent utterly on becoming a movement from within, upsetting everybody in sight. One school cannot be read according to the dictates of Palmer, let alone another according to those of Froude. Rose, for instance, was always magnanimous, enthusiastic even about the first Tracts.[133]

Newman was never totally convinced. He knew that the cause, *Libertas Ecclesiae*, was utterly just but still felt unsure about the most expedient tactical plan. Yet Froude himself was never in any doubt. He was no Job's comforter; rather, he encouraged Newman to fight. That was just as well. Throughout October and November Newman behaved like a young novice in a monastery, never totally convinced that he had made the right decision. Consequently he was always looking around for moral support. He felt that he could confide his deepest doubts and suspicions in letters only to his closest friends, Keble and Froude. The former had already for effective purposes withdrawn from the Oxford scene, apart from sporadic meetings. Newman had to have more than that. He needed daily consultation. Froude was the ideal companion, forthright, sympathetic, positive. Behind the scenes, however, there was always the powerful if shadowy presence of Palmer, whose influence was immense. The fact that only *Tract No. 5* was issued between 21 September and 29 October was largely his doing.[134] By early November Palmer had had enough of his young brothers in arms. Writing to John William Bowden[135] on 13 November, Newman sensed vividly the atmosphere of doom, the day of reckoning, the parting of the ways; "Palmer backed by Mr Norris etc. etc. is afraid of the tracts and wishes them stopped, and is aiming at an Association". Newman was almost beside himself, "I say let every one employ his talent in his own way – Let there be an Association, if they can do it, and we will be members of it to avoid appearance of Schism – tho' I confess I do not like joining in any thing the Bishops have not publicly sanctioned".[136]

November 13 was a crucial day in Newman's life as he was literally at his wits' end. Lacking confidence and moral support, he wrote his most pathetic letter hitherto to Froude; "I am in the midst of trouble, with no one but such οὐτίδανοι (men of naught) as Rogers to consult with. Palmer musters the z's in great force against the Tracts, and some Evangelicals – He presses, and I am quite ready to admit, a disclaimer (in the shape of a circular) of the Tracts. But he goes further, and wishes us to stop them. In these cases success is the test of sagacity or rashness. The said Tracts give offence I know – but they also do good ... What will be done, I know not – but I want advice sadly. I have no confidence in any one. If I could be sure of 5 or 6 vigorous co-operators in various parts, I would laugh at opposition – but I fear being beaten from the field ... I can make no hand of the z's – I am half out of spirits – but how one outgrows tenderness ... Do give me some advice and encouragement".[137]

Froude's reply decided the course of the Oxford Movement. Without Froude, Newman might well have succumbed to Palmer's threats. The Oxford Movement would have been purely and simply a vote of confidence in the Church's establishment. That is no grievous or heinous sin, of course, but for Froude it was a poisoned chalice to be anthematised. It would have validated the whole spirit of Erastianism. The fact that the Oxford Movement did not take this course is due in large measure to Froude's unequivocal reply to Newman on 20 November. The language was neither temperate, gentlemanly nor restrained; "If old Palmer is determined to be carried away by z dissimulations we must cut him loose ... As to giving up the Tracts the notion is odious ... We must throw the Zs overboard: they are a small and, as my Father says, daily diminishing party. ... "[138]

Newman was never advanced politically, either in the secular or ecclesiastical sphere. In this respect he was totally different to Froude. Newman's concern for the Church was purely theological, spiritual, a matter of duty. He craved for calm reflection, patient resignation, determined, united effort. Froude thought the Church needed to experience a blow-up. On the vital issue whether the Movement would be a committee affair, writing articles, making gentle protests and Establishment conscious or a more stimulating, grass roots, in a word, radical protest, Froude played the part of catalyst, agitator and friend. In December 1833 Newman was writing with a new resolve. He was now "impersuadable" over the Tracts.[139] The mouse had suddenly become a dragon, bullying, goading, challenging. Froude had won his first battle of wills with Newman over the nature of the Movement in its tactical battle with the Z's.

2.3.5. *The Address to the Archbishop*

The whole idea of an Address to the Archbishop appeared sound enough in principle, especially as Archbishop Howley represented much that was still good in the Church of England.[140] If no good could ever have come out of a committee, then here was the living proof of it. There was much divergence of opinion over the exact wording of the Address.[141] Froude's original draft was true to character. It was unequivocal, bold and imaginative. Leaving the more experienced to supply the etiquette at the beginning about the undersigned clergy, the main thrust of Froude's draft was this; "They (the undersigned clergy) do not conceal from themselves the misapplication to which some of the Church's services are exposed by the practical disuse of the Rubrics prefixed to them; and the inefficiency of attempting to act on these Rubrics, without first completing the Ecclesiastical system they presuppose. They venture therefore to express their wish for the speedy completion of this System, and their readiness to cooperate in any measures by which your G (Grace) may think fit to carry it into effect.

"Lastly they take this opportunity of declaring their conviction that measures such as these, affecting the spiritual welfare of the Church ought to originate only with its Spiritual Rulers – and that in such matters they deprecate every kind of extra-Ecclesiastical interference".[142] The whole point of addressing the Archbishop, the successor of Augustine, Anselm and Becket, was to point out that legislation affecting the spiritual welfare of the Church ought to have originated with her spiritual rulers. The battle was *semper eadem*; – no interference from the state in the realm spiritual.

By the time the draft had returned from London, however, the Establishment had behaved in an as autocratic a manner as editorial panels associated with nations without a free press. As far as Froude was concerned, not only was their command of the English language deficient, but also their whole understanding of the struggle between Church and state was dictated by their own subjective, parochially limited experiences. Froude was furious not only with the Establishment, however, but also with Newman, whose political immaturity appalled him. Newman had been nothing short of a spoon, to have allowed essential phrases to be omitted by "the editors". Far from being a declaration of belligerent intent, all that was offered was at best a bland declaration of loyalty, at worst a cowardly evasion of the main issues. There was no mention whatsoever of extra-ecclesiastical interference being unnecessary and presumptuous in spiritual affairs.[143] To underline his annoyance Froude wrote again to Newman on 17 November, castigating him for his pusillanimity. Newman was out of touch with so much public opinion which, in Froude's terms, usually meant how his father felt. That was not such a bad precedent since Archdeacons could be the most effective means of feeling the spiritual pulse of the clergy.[144] The revised draft would simply not have been liked because crucial phrases had been omitted. Froude washed his hands of the whole affair, "I would not have had a hand in the printing of that Address".[145]

Newman revealed himself to be, at best, naive, at worst, selfish.

He emerged from the battle over the Tracts as resolute and determined. Of course, that mattered to him personally. It was a case of pride and vainglory. But over the Address to the Archbishop, Froude considered Newman little better than the Z's, whose minion he had conveniently become. Despite Froude's predictions that the Address would do little good, Newman was convinced that the results would be efficacious. On 29 December, 1833 and New Year's Day, 1834, Newman was still enthusiastic about the Address. It was better than nothing.[146]

Without the crucial wording, "extra-ecclesiastical interference", the Address was diverted from being a powerful and dynamic challenge to the Establishment to a vote of confidence in it. Newman was still sanguine enough to feel that anything addressed to the successor of Augustine would bring spiritual benefits. This revealed his distance from Froude, who was convinced that no good could come out of Canterbury while the appointment of bishops was still in the hands of Erastian statesmen.

The Address was presented on 6 February, 1834, signed by seven thousand clergymen of the realm. The die was cast. *The British Magazine* hailed it as a great victory.[147] For Froude it was not even a Pyrrhic victory. It was, at best, hypocritical cant, at worst a gesture of the highest irrelevance.[148] Newman was wise after, Froude before the event. And Newman knew it. Contingency plans had to be put into operation.[149]

2.3.6. *The Royal Supremacy*

In his fine study of Pusey's understanding of the relationship between Church and state,[150] Dr Nockles mentions the important fact that there was a crucial difference between Keble and Pusey on the one hand and Hurrell Froude on the other over their understanding of the Royal Supremacy.[151] For Keble and Pusey, the Royal Supremacy was not Erastian. This is a very important observation. What Harold Laski wrote about the Royal Supremacy, that it was regarded by all the Tractarians as an Erastian principle, is false.[152] Fortunately Dr Nockles has corrected the misunderstanding.[153] It is essential to illustrate how exactly Keble and Pusey differed from Froude and what profound effects the views of the latter had upon the formation of Newman's political outlook.

In 1639 *God Save the King* was an emotional appeal to the heart, as it was in 1833. For Keble the King represented Christ. He was the Defender of the Faith. Writing in *The British Magazine* for June 1833, Keble was aware that the case of Church Reform was urgent. In fires and floods men are excused for calling about them in a tone otherwise than becoming. One of his practical suggestions was that Churchmen should apply *to the Throne especially* "lest future historians should have to say that the great body of the English clergy allowed their Sovereign to be taken by surprise".[154] Writing to Newman in August 1833, Keble was of the opinion that Appeals to Archbishops were not that effective. It might be better to try an Appeal from the New and Old Churchmen, dwelling especially on the point of Supremacy and the Coronation Oath.[155] This illustrated Keble's life-long conviction that "Kings as well as bishops are in a manner representatives of Jesus Christ on earth; consequently our duties to the one, rightly understood, can never by any possibility clash with our duties to the other".[156] Pusey was equally adamant in his defence of the Royal Supremacy.[157] The 1688 Revolution was sinful, as "it was wholly unjustifiable on the most ordinary principles of Christian morality".[158] "The Church has once disobeyed," wrote Pusey, "and she has suffered".[159] Pusey never appealed to the bishops for a solution. Indeed, he wanted the king to take over the appointment of bishops; "Why sit still and endure the degradation and mischief of political trafficking with the offices of the sanctuary? Why not tell his Majesty that the responsibility of recommending our bishops belong to him individually?"[160]

According to Keble and Pusey, the whole purpose of the Royal Supremacy was to safeguard the inherent rights of the Holy Catholic Church of God. Froude, however, took a very different view of affairs. He was concerned only with what he saw happening in 1833, not what ought to have taken place. The only King whom Froude ever admired was the martyred king, Charles I, whose holy death Froude celebrated with so much panache. Indeed, the whole ethos of the Church of England was the martyred king and the Non-Jurors.[161]

What was true of Charles I, however, could no longer be

applied. Historical precedent was one thing but present reality was another. Already in April 1833 a pertinent question had been asked in *The British Magazine*; "How will the King's Coronation Oath stand up to the Irish Bill, including the spoliation of Church property? ... Can any man have the effrontery to affirm that the Archbishops and clergy, and members in general of the established church, could *understand that the king was at liberty to plunder the church, and turn its revenues to state purposes*, when he solemnly swears – 'to the uttermost of his power, to maintain unto the *bishops* and *clergy* of this realm, and to the *churches* committed to their charge, *all such rights and privileges*, as by law do or shall appertain to them, or any of them?' ... How can men in humbler life withstand the temptation to quibble upon the terms of such an oath, when the king himself is to be exhibited to the nation as rendering utterly vain the solemn covenant of his Coronation Oath, and in practice proclaiming that –

> Oaths are not bound to bear
> That literal sense the words infer;
> But, by the practice of the age,
> Are to be judg'd how far th'engage;
> And, where the sense by custom's checkt,
> Are found void, and of none effect?".[162]

Although these sentiments were not expressed by Froude himself, they stated accurately his own severe misgivings about the Royal Supremacy in 1833. The only Royal Supremacy in 1833, wrote Froude in his articles for *The British Magazine*,[163] was the House of Commons, which was the manager of the holy things, even of God. The king was now dependent upon the will of his Parliament and had to act against his most sacred principles and opinions.[164] No Churchman could any longer look with any confidence to the Coronation Oath. Already in the heady months of the Reform Bill, wrote Froude, the King had been outwitted by Lord Grey with comparative ease; "Lord Grey told the King that he was acting, in consenting to the Reform Bill, legislatively and not executively. It was only in the latter capacity that he was bound in his Coronation Oath. Grey reconciled the King to his conscience by stating that he was only acting legislatively; when this would not do, he had to act executively, a violation of the Coronation Oath. Such is the Supreme Head of the Church".[165]

As much as Keble, Froude could also look to historical precedent. The emperors were guardians of public peace and always respected the freedom of ecclesiastical elections. Froude's maxim was that no bishop could be imposed on an Orthodox Church without the consent of its members.[166] One emperor, Theodosius, misbehaved and had to do public penance for his misdeeds.[167] It was in the fourteenth century, however, wrote Froude, that leaks began to spring in the dike. The rights of the people were usurped by Rome. The clergy could only second papal appointments, or refusing, forfeit any share in the appointments. The usurpations of Roman pontiffs were not on the rights of Kings and Governors but on those of the Church itself. Froude saw the mid-fourteenth century as a crucial turning-point in the affairs of the Church. Now began "the systematic and open aggression of the power of this world against that kingdom which shall not be destroyed". The selfish power of the Roman see tended gradually to undermine the foundations on which it had built its power. It paved the way for the course of unscrupulous aggression which had from that time been pursued by "the kings of the earth". Edward III in 1350 passed an Act guaranteeing the freedom of English elections. All this was fine, wrote Froude, since it severely restricted papal interference. Yet a convenient loophole appeared, since where the Pope had once interfered, the King could conveniently fulfil that role. So began the whole idea of "the Supreme Head of the Church". The climax of the substitution of regal for papal interference was the Statute of Praemunire, passed in 1392 by Richard III. The clergy and people played into the King's hands. They stood idly by.[168]

To Froude's mind, all kings, apart from the royal martyr, Charles I, were of the earth. The Royal Supremacy was essentially Erastian and secular interference in Church affairs was usurpation. Never before had the Church had to look to King or emperor, except to guarantee what the Church had already in complete freedom decided for herself. Froude's radical views on the Royal Supremacy were to influnce profoundly those of Newman.

In January 1834, Newman, as much as Keble, was a staunch believer in the Royal Supremacy. Later in life he reminisced trenchantly about his ideal vision of Church, state and society; "I never expected the system of Laud to return but I do expect the due continuation and development of his principles ... the so-called union of the Church and State as it then existed had been a wonderful and most gracious phenomenon in Church history ... a realization of the Gospel in its highest perfection when both Caesar and St Peter knew and fulfilled their office ... Charles is the King, Laud the Prelate, Oxford the sacred city of this principle".[169] In the early months of the Oxford Movement Newman was still inspired by such glorious reminiscences. In January 1834 he wrote to Rose; "The Coronation Oath has secured the Church its liberties to the utter annulment of all former precedents of tyranny – and that we stand by that Oath as our Law as well as our Sovereign's sanction and acknowledgement of it, and that any power in the State that innovates on the spirit of that Oath tyrannises over us".[170]

Newman felt certain that the Monarch would defend the spiritual rights of the Church, come what may, against Parliament. In this respect Newman showed his close affinity to Keble. Yet beneath the apparent tranquillity there were already ripples of doubt entering Newman's mind regarding the King's position towards the Church. Froude's influence was profound. The continuation of the Tracts, the Address to the Archbishop even, paled into insignificance as the intellectual battle proceeded over the lynchpin of the High Church position in its relationship to the state, the mystical reverence for the Monarch, God's anointed and Christ's representative.

What is the good of influence except to influence people? Froude asked this question of Newman in January 1834.[171] By the beginning of 1834, Froude, who had never been able to enter any one else's mind very easily, became increasingly exasperated with all who disagreed with him. Rose became a constant object of his vituperative onslaughts. Rose was going Z again. It was impossible to imagine a worse fate.[172] Neither did Newman escape the vitriol of Froude's pen. When Newman ascertained quite ingenuously that the Church of England taught the whole truth, Froude asked him, "Why, then, do we need to reform it?" Froude could not resist the temptation of a personal gibe; "Newman," he asked, "are you getting stupid?"[173] Such taunts were only a further sign of that dependence upon each other which had always formed the essential and lasting characteristic of their relationship. Newman's articles on "The Convocation of the Province of Canterbury" for *The British Magazine* between November 1834 and March 1835 did reveal that Froude's constant gibes and taunts were bearing fruit.[174] Henry VIII, of unblessed memory, wrote Newman, was determined to "tie up the hands of the clergy, that they might be unable to oppose his designs". The liberties of the Church were lost for ever. Convocation could only meet with the King's permission. No canons could be promulgated without his authority. At the Glorious Revolution, William III, a prince who had just ceased to be a Presbyterian, completed what Henry had begun.[175] The powers of jurisdiction were immense. The King appointed commissions of divines for diverse purposes. He sent directions to the clergy on the matter of their sermons. He appointed state prayers. He addressed the people, through the clergy, on topics such as the royal supremacy, education, charities, temporalities, ceremonies, and holydays. He also had the most important prerogative of appointing bishops.[176] Yet the essence itself of the Church, wrote Newman, the apostolical element, was not in the King's power; the ministry of the Word and sacraments was given only to those whom God especially chose.[177] According to the thirty seventh Article of Religion, which is part of an Act of Parliament, there was no doubt, according to Newman's interpretation, that the oath of supremacy meant that the king was supreme governor in all spiritual or ecclesiastical things or causes as well as temporal but not in the apostolical rights and powers of the Church.[178]

By March 1835 Newman was at long last beginning to show that radical political acumen for which Froude yearned so much. The appointment of the Ecclesiastical Commission, Newman realised, was a direct blow to the whole idea of the Royal Supremacy. The establishment of the Royal Commission, set up by Peel and issued on 4 February, 1835, to encourage the Church of England to reform itself was, to Newman's mind, "a new precedent in the history of the Church ... There is a talk in different parts of the Kingdom of petitions from the Clergy to strengthen the Premier against the Archbishop![179] The apparent truth was now real. What Froude had forewarned about the Royal Supremacy was actually seen to be no mere theory but actual fact. The spiritual rulers of the realm were no longer responsible to the King, who was Supreme Governor, but to a panel of miserable laymen invested by Parliament with all kinds of heinous authority.[180]

The establishment of the Ecclesiastical Commission was a severe blow to those who actually believed that the King would in all times and at all places have kept to his Coronation Oath and protected the spiritual interests of the Church. Yet it was only a mild storm compared with the whirlwind that was unleashed when Hampden was appointed Regius Professor.[181] Already with the news in prospect – he was not actually appointed till 8 February, 1836 and gazetted on the 17th – Newman was able to write on 3 January to Rose that he felt most melancholy about the whole affair. Newman was already *persona non grata* for expressing so many Church views.[182] He did feel, however, that Providence was making Churchmen choose their sides. Froude could have informed him of that dichotomy, painful but necessary, in the ecclesiastical ranks of humanity in the summer of 1833. Newman had listened to Froude but still hoped that it was not really true. Yearning for a quiet academic life, the blessings of profound peace, no schisms and few errors, Newman was reluctantly called to the front-line of battle. What was so painful was that the appointment of the Regius Divinity Chair was accomplished not only with full royal knowledge but also approval.[183] Even at this late hour, there might be a forlorn chance that a petition to the King might work. The King's attachment to the Church and the interests of religion were well known.[184]

After Froude's death on 26 February, 1836 Newman hoped earnestly, as he informed Keble on 6 March, that it would be granted him to receive Froude's mantle.[185] After so much procrastination and diffidence, Newman realised that the Royal Supremacy, far from benefiting the interests of the Church and University against an infidel Parliament, was inimical to both. It was unashamedly Erastian. Froude had been preaching that Gospel since early 1833. In a letter to Rose, dated 23 May, 1836, Newman expressed his new position. It reads like a confession of faith; "The very title 'Church of England' is an offence for it implies that it holds, not of the Church Catholic but of the State. And this is why I insisted on speaking against King William,

Wake, etc. for this is the system under which we find ourselves, actually not indeed the system of the Prayer Book, but de facto ... The simple difference between their (Hooker, Andrews and Laud) views and those I seem to follow is this – they had a divine right King – we in matter of fact have not. ... The 'Church of England' has never been one reality, except as an Establishment. Viewed internally, it is the battle field of two opposite principles: Socinianism and Catholicism ... What is meant when I am asked whether I love the Church of England?"[186] Froude was dead but Newman had declared that the Royal Supremacy now belonged to the past. With no Royal supremacy to uphold the Church's spiritual rights, with Parliament full of infidels, Newman realised that the Church was now fully dependent upon her own spiritual resources. What he had feared in 1833 was indeed true. The search for doctrinal purity had nothing to hope for from King or Parliament. The integrity of Anglicanism was at stake.[187]

Froude did not live to see Newman's conversion to his own uncompromising, anti-Erastian stance. Newman, however, was totally aware of the reason for the change of heart. Ecclesiastical Commissions, the appointment of controversial persons as Regius professors, later to become bishops, such events are always with us. It was the power of personal influence which was far more intriguing than external phenomena. No man exercised more wilful and occasionally remorseless influence over Newman than Froude. Once the movement had begun, Froude did not waste a syllable in his onslaught of words upon what he saw as Newman's inadequate position. No longer reverencing the system in which he found himself, Newman realised in March 1836 that the integrity of the Church of England was at stake. In Newman's search for doctrinal purity, however, his indebtedness to Froude would not remain unrecorded. What had happened privately must be declared to the University and nation. The span of Froude's life was short, but his reputation had not yet begun.

2.4. THE POLITICAL AND SOCIAL SIGNIFICANCE OF THE REMAINS

Piers Brendon ascribed to Keble and Newman many motives for having *The Remains* published in 1838 and 1839.[188] Newman was concerned that Froude's essential role in the development of his own mind should be recorded for posterity and that Froude should be seen as the embodiment of all that was best in the Tractarian tradition. J. R. Griffin, however, went further than Brendon in asserting that the four volumes of *The Remains* were meant as a party political document, a manifesto that Toryism was a thing of the past.[189]

It is hard to imagine Keble and Newman actually having a political motive for any action in which they were involved. Such a base approach would have been anathema to them. It is more salutary to read *The Remains* as actually containing a political and social message.

Much has been made of Froude's poem, "Farewell to Toryism".[190] Dr Perry Butler, for instance, writes in his *Gladstone, Church, State and Tractarianism* that Froude had sung his farewell to Toryism, Newman had little faith in any political party, Keble, though emotionally committed to the Tory Party, had opposed Peel in 1829 and Pusey felt that the 1830's also ended his Toryism.[191] Dr Nockles, however, has already done much to redress the balance by studying Pusey's exact disillusionment with the Toryism of his day.[192]

Like Keble and Newman, Froude in 1829 was very much in sympathy with opposition to much of what happened that year.[193] Between 1829 and 1833, Froude began to shed many of the characteristics of the old High and Dry Toryism, especially after his encounter with Lamennais.[194] However, this did not make him abandon the Tory cause. As much as Newman, Froude felt that much of the old style Toryism had no power to develop. Equally hollow was the new style progressive Toryism of the Conservative Party. Little wonder that *The Remains* managed to upset most of the old style and progressive Tories.[195] For all his dissatisfaction with the old style and new patterns of Toryism, Froude himself to the end of his days was a rabid Tory, neither of the old school, for he was too High Church for that, dismissing that kind of Toryism with its attachment to the Establishment as Church atrophy,[196] nor of the new Peelite mentality.

Writing to Newman on 26 December, 1834, Froude asked, "If I was dead, why should I be cut off from the privilege of helping out the good cause?"[197] Ironically the good cause was even more powerfully presented after his death than during his life. In political and social terms, *The Remains* repudiated both the Toryism ensconced in its old High and Dry ways and the new progressive Toryism.

2.4.1. *Toryism, Medievalism and Feudalism*

The claim has been made by many scholars that Young England was the Oxford Movement translated by Cambridge from religion into politics. Both were essentially protests against a liberal, utilitarian age.[198] It must be claimed also that the Oxford Movement and Young England shared a complementarity of aims with the revived Ultramontanism in France, for which Lamennais was partly responsible. Men like Frederic Uzanam, the founder of the Society of St Vincent de Paul, the Comte de Melun, the Comte de Falloux and Phillippe Gerbet were examples of conservative social Catholicism in action.[199]

The Oxford Movement was only a part of a much wider phenomenon. The exaltation of medievalism, with its Tory and feudal appendages, held much fascination for writers in the first half of the nineteenth century. Scott, Coleridge, Wordsworth, Cobbett, Southey and Carlyle succeeded in making Victorian England the age of medievalism.[200] If there had been a portrait of Froude as an adult, he would undoubtedly stood in the same gallery of medieval eulogisers. Indeed, Froude was much indebted to Scott, Wordsworth, Southey and Carlyle. With Coleridge there was much affinity.[201] Froude's enthusiasm for Toryism was witnessed in his admiration for an age which had been suitably medieval and feudal,

> The feudal court, the patriarchal sway
> Of Kings, the cheerful homage of a land
> Unskilled in treason, every social band
> That taught to rule with sweetness, and obey
> With dignity.[202]

A similar note was struck by Froude in his letter to Newman on 11 June, 1835; "There is something very indescribable in the effect old sights and smells produce on me here just now after having missed them so long. Also old Dartingon House with its Feudal appendages calls up so many Tory associations as almost to soften one's heart into lamenting the course of events which is to reerect the Church by demolishing so much that is beautiful. ..."[203] Opposed to the shocking Latitudinarianism of so many Tories, then and now,[204] there was another age when Toryism had been seen in its spiritual and political glory. The horrors of modern society had been exchanged for the aesthetic, ephemerally fascinating beauties of a bygone age.

As *The Remains* reflected and partook of the glories of medievalism, so also it encouraged many of the later adherents of the Movement to look to things medieval as an analogue of how the Church ought to be in her relationship with the world. W. G. Ward's reaction was typical of a new outlook within the Oxford Movement.[205] F. W. Faber loved the "rough rude music" of *The Remains* and "the eccentric feats of chivalry".[206] Faber, indebted as he was to Keble and Wordsworth, dedicating books to them,[207] found much in *The Remains* to complement both. Keble, for all his love of the Church of the Fathers was not really at home with Hildebrand, let alone Francis of Assisi while Wordsworth, deeply attracted to the Tractarian cause, never fully gave it complete assent. Indeed, Faber occasionally thought Wordsworth unsound because of his dedication to Milton.[208] Much of what the Medieval Traveller had to say in *Sights and Thoughts in Foreign Churches and among Foreign Peoples* was almost an exact parody of what Froude had expounded in *The Remains*. The Divine Right of Kings could no longer be accepted as a doctrine but a dim feeling which had much emotive power amongst loyalists to the throne but was uncongenial to those who had medieval habits of thought and had already caused much mischief in the Church. The Church was now delivered up to the pestilence of Erastian moderation. The manufacturing towns must be evangelised by monasteries.[209] Faber, as intemperate as Froude, reserved his greatest wrath for the Whigs who were for ever attempting to blacken the good name of all things monastic.[210]

The cross-fertilisation is obvious. Faber was one of the great communicators of the Victorian Age.[211] His connection with Young England, for instance, is already well documented.[212] Whatever books were essential reading on the roster of the Young England men, the spirit of *The Remains* was never far removed.[213] Toryism, medievalism and feudalism were very much in concert in the works of Lord John Manners. Far from giving people lectures in astronomy and geology, let a man who works sixty hours a week relax on National Holy-Days.[214] To the average philanthropists of Victorian England, this was laughable, a mood summed up by George Eliot; "Young England was the aristocratic dilettantism which attempts to restore the good old times by a sort of idyllic masquerading, and to grow feudal fidelity and veneration as we grow turnips, by an artificial system of manure".[215] But, like the aspirations of the Oxford Movement itself, Young England was not all bad. Both movements reflected what John Ruskin called the two essential instincts of humanity, "love of order and the love of kindness" in their relations to other people.[216]

Benjamin Disraeli, the most eminent of the Young England party, showed much interest in *The Remains*. J. A. Froude, brother of Hurrell, literary executor of Carlyle, biographer of Disraeli and Regius Professor of History at Oxford, commented that "Disraeli seemed to think that if Newman had paid more attention to *Coningsby*, the course of things might have been different. Saints had worked with secular politicians at many periods of Christian history; why not the Tractarians with him?"[217] Many of Disraeli's novels, *Coningsby*, *Sybil*, *Tancred* and *Endymion* contained a certain amount of Tractarian spirit.[218] Yet this spirit owed far more to Froude than Keble or Newman, neither of whom was at home with the Middle Ages. *Coningsby*, much of its contents plagiarised by Disraeli from Froude,[219] prepared the way for *Sybil*, castigated at the time for much of its Tractarian spirit, its adulation of monasteries and medieval ways of life.[220] Indeed, the principle of the feudal system was the noblest, the grandest and the most magnificent that ever was conceived by sage or ever produced by patriot.[221] Once the Church was the centre of essential communities. As Aubrey St Lys, Disraeli's idea of a Tractarian priest, explained to Egremeont, "The Church deserted the people; and from that moment the Church has been in danger, and the people degraded. Formerly, religion undertook to satisfy the noble wants of human nature, and by its festivals relieved the painful weariness of toil. The day of rest was consecrated, if not always to elevated thought, at least to sweet and noble sentiments. The Church convened to its solemnities, under its splendid and almost celestial roofs, amid the finest monuments of art that human hands have raised, the whole Christian population; for there, in the presence of God, all were brethren. It shared equally among all its prayer, its incense, and its music; its sacred instructions, and the highest enjoyments that the arts could afford".[222] Yet today's Church by contrast had forgotten her mission to the people. The model of a fine priest was one who left everybody alone. Even in the parish church the frigid spell of Erastian self-complacency fatally prevailed.[223] In *Tancred*, the hero described the mirror of Young England's dreams, "a proud, feudal aristocracy, a conventual establishment ... a free and armed peasantry ... bishops worthy of the Apostles".[224] The reality amongst the bishops, however, was different. They were state appointments only. It would have been difficult to seek successors of the apostles among third-rate hunters after syllables, these mitred nullities.[225]

Froude would have loved all this. Here was one of the great political and social novelists of the age actually reflecting and occasionally plagiarising many of the leading political and ecclesiastical ideas of *The Remains*. Disraeli was convinced from 1833 till 1845 that the Oxford Movement with its medieval programme of a revived Church and its inherent feudal, Tory message published in *The Remains* might still lead to the conversion of England.[226]

2.4.2. The Political and Social Interpretation of the Reformation

Froude's treatment of the Reformation, unlike that of the Middle Ages, was bigoted, subjective and insensitive.[227] Froude was in good company. In 1829 William Cobbett wrote that at the Reformation "this land of meat and beef was changed all of a sudden into a land of dry bread and oatmeal porridge".[228] Froude had always been impressed by Southey's *Colloquies*.[229] Both writers, to use Froude's language, were less and less loyal to the Reformation.[230] There were two reasons why the Reformation was particularly odious to Froude. First, on moral grounds, all the English reformers, Cranmer, Latimer, Ridley, even Jewel, were without exception men of the moment only. They lacked any kind of valid ethos. The Catholicism of so many of their formulae was only a concession to the feelings of the nation.[231] In a striking phrase in the Preface to Part II of *The Remains*, "the persons chiefly instrumental in the Reformation were not a party to be trusted on ecclesiastical and theological questions, nor yet to be imitated in their practical handling of the unspeakably awful matters with which they were concerned".[232] For all his mistaken theological principles, Calvin did at least have the courage to resist Erastianism. Most admirable of all were the Non-Jurors who combined sound theology with right conduct.

Secondly, Froude had political reasons for disliking the Reformers. He was never in any doubt about the source of all contemporary evils. The Reformation set the Rationalist spirit on its modern course. Similarly, the usurpation of Reason was dated from the Reformation. It was the Whigs who had anglicised Rationalism and made it palatable. Indeed, Whiggery was a modern disease. It had taken up all the filth that had been secreted in the fermentation of human thought. All vile deviations had come to be associated with it, Puritanism, Latitudinarianism, Popery and Infidelity.[233] Rationalism's *alter ego* was Erastianism. There was no difference between the Erastian Reformers of the sixteenth century and the apostate Whigs of 1832.[234]

By denigrating the Reformation, *The Remains* shared in a general interpretation of history which was unashamedly Tory. If all evils, expediency, commercialism, Latitudinarianism, Rationalism and Erastianism were attributable directly to the lack of ethos on the part of the Reformers, all this would have been acceptable to contemporary Toryism. All good Tories were loyal Church of England men, claiming the independence and spiritual rights of the Church against the filth of the Erastian, rationalist and unscrupulous Whigs.

The Remains became a useful yardstick by which to measure the potential strengths and weaknesses of Toryism. The Church of England, according to Faber, was not an offshoot of the Reformation event but came into existence under the Norman Kings. Then came the shipwreck at the Reformation on the shallows and sound-holes of Erastianism, followed by the glories of Charles I, Laud and the Non-Jurors. Then came chaos, the gentle Georgian shelving down into a well-written, able, moral and gentlemanly Deism.[235] William Cobbett compared the glories of the monastery with the real and metaphysical ruins of contemporary structures.[236] Disraeli also relied upon Cobbett for much of his material for his trilogy of novels. In 1829 Cobbett had argued that the Reformation had created in a hitherto unified and wealthy society "that state of things which sees but two classes of people in a community, masters and slaves, a very few enjoying the extreme of luxury, and millions, doomed to the extreme of misery".[237] What Disraeli read in Cobbett was confirmed in 1838. Like Froude, Disraeli's enemies were also the Rationalistic, Utilitarian, *laissez-faire*, Whig oligarchy. In *Sybil*, such characteristics were ascribed to the Marney family who were like those in one century plundering the Church to gain the property of the people while in another century changing the dynasty to gain the power of the Crown. This family was nothing less than the descendants of the old gentleman usher of King Henry's plundering Vicar-Generals.[238]

Froude insisted in *The Remains* that all deviations from the ways of godly, sober and holy living emanated from the Reformation. Not only did such an emphasis affect dramatically the course of the Oxford Movement after 1838, giving its young supporters new courage and hope in much affliction and its enemies yet another stick with which they could beat their Protestant drum even louder;[239] but Froude's biased view of the Reformation also underlined a theory which was gaining prevalence in the 1830's and 1840's, that Church and society were indeed one in the Middle Ages when all people were members corporately of the Body of Christ, a polity which had been shattered by the ravages of the hedonistic King and his supporters, the forerunners of rationalist, Erastian, filthy Whigs. There had been bright moments in the centuries of doom; a King, an Archbishop, a layman had attempted to salvage the sinking ship in the seventeenth century. Such a tradition had been maintained by the Non-Jurors. Their only tragedy was that they had not excommunicated other members of the episcopal bench and kept their succession in existence. According to Froude, their failure to do this had meant that there had been no English divines since, only twaddlers.[240]

2.4.3. The Tory Spirit of The Remains

Dr Nockles has written sympathetically of the religious aspects of Keble's Toryism which had such a profound influence upon

Pusey.[241] It was inevitable that Froude, who influenced his mentor so much in the formation of his political ideals, could not help being influenced by Keble in other respects. Throughout their acquaintance Keble stressed the importance of tradition, reverence, conscience and duty. Above all, there was that Tractarian favourite concept, referred to by Thomas Mozley in his *Reminiscences of Oriel College and the Oxford Movement*; "What Froude and others discovered continually was ἦθος, the predominant moral habit or proclivity".[242]

The tone of one's moral character and disposition informed the whole of Froude's political outlook. His Toryism was essentially morally motivated. This outlook was expressed in *The Remains* in a posthumously published letter of 6 December, 1832, advising a friend against the dangers of London; "When you go to London you will be among a parcel of Liberals in religion and politics, and ought to expect to find it infectious. Take care you don't get sucked in. Don't get intimate with people of that sort. Let your intercourse with them be only a matter of business, and take as few kind offices from them as you can, where you have not got it in your power to give a *quid pro quo*".[243]

Other religious aspects of Keble's Toryism influenced Froude. Patience, duty and perseverance, qualities which Dr Nockles sees as pervading a kind of religious Tory outlook, came easily to men like Keble and Pusey.[244] For Froude they were ideals to be grasped in a life of effort, self-denial and occasionally morbid asceticism. But the moral counsels were there in Froude's sermons, published in *The Remains*. "The parts of our duty, which will furnish us with the most intelligible answer, are those to which we cannot possible be urged by any other motive than the knowledge that God requires them of us".[245] Preaching about St John the Baptist as a pattern of patience under discouragements, Froude extolled the virtues of the Baptist as one who showed single-hearted disinterested zeal in a cause, the success of which he was not to witness, or materially to promote.[246] Froude had been too much of Keble's disciple, even if he had not possessed these qualities to the full like his mentor, to cease preaching about them and to yearn for them in his daily struggle against the world, the flesh and the devil.[247]

Throughout his life Froude had loathed the Whigs not only on moral and political but also religious grounds. Froude had always considered William Law, for instance, a far greater spiritual figure than Bishop Hoadly. Indeed, Law's letters to him were the most brilliant and argumentative overthrow of liberalism that Froude had ever read.[248] In 1716 Hoadly had written his *A Preservative against the Principles and Practices of the Non-Jurors both in Church and State*. In a letter to Newman, 19 March, 1834, Froude had written that the reason Convocation had been put down in 1717 was the remonstrance of the Lower House against the Upper to make them censure Hoadly's work, as the Upper House had a very little while before taken part with the Socinianising bishops against the Lower.[249] Hoadly had been part of a Whig conspiracy that had for the last hundred and twenty years brought the Church of England into complete subjection to the State. The Chapter of Salisbury, which had elected the flagrant bishop Hoadly ought to have been revealed as protagonists of lies, deceit and conspiracy against the Church.[250]

The ethos, that is, the moral outlook and disposition, of *The Remains* was directly opposed to the political temper of the high and dry Tories and was anathema to the progressive members of the Conservative Party.[251] Froude had always thought that something infinitely profounder was required than the redundancy of the high and dry Tories without succumbing to the alien idols of a progressive new age. In that sense, Froude was a true conservative and a true radical. Every page of *The Remains* reflected this dual nature of his personality. His mystical reverence for the past, the eleventh and twelfth centuries, Charles I and the Non-Jurors was not an excuse for a reactionary attitude but rather a platform from which the essence of a radical critique of state and society could be formed. His passion for right moral conduct, his hatred of the Whigs and all Liberal manifestations, his utter mistrust of vanity and success, ensured that his was a nature in which the religious, apart from the political aspirations of Toryism, had found a kindred spirit and therein dwelt accordingly.

NOTES

1. *Remains of the Late Reverend Richard Hurrell Froude*, Vol. III, p. 274.

2. H. Laski, *Studies in the Problem of Sovereignty*, pp. 74 ff. The chapter on the Tractarians is full of mistaken notions, e.g. "The central point of the Tractarian attack was upon the Royal Supremacy, since in it was involved the notion that the State was supreme no less in spiritual than in temporal affairs", p. 87. Keble, Pusey and even Newman originally were not opposed to the Royal Supremacy as such, only that the State was not true to its rightful prerogative in caring for the Church as a Nursing Mother or Father. It was only Froude who was consistently opposed to the Royal Supremacy. Laski assumed that what was true of Froude was also applicable to the other Tractarians. For a much sounder assessment of Tractarian attitudes to the Royal Supremacy, see Peter Nockles, "Pusey and the Question of Church and State" in Perry Butler, ed., *Pusey Rediscovered*, pp. 255 ff. J. R. Griffin, *Tractarian Politics* devoted a whole chapter of his unpublished thesis to the political thought of Froude, pp. 75 ff.
3. G. F. A. Best, *Temporal Pillars, Queen Anne's Bounty, the Ecclesiastical Commissioners and the Church of England*, p. 258, compared Froude's contribution with that of Archbishop Whately.
4. Piers Brendon, *Hurrell Froude and the Oxford Movement*, p. 96.
5. W. G. Roe, *Lamennais and England: The Reception of Lamennais's Religious Ideas in England in the Nineteenth Century*.
6. Roe, ibid., pp. 97–8. See also Christopher Dawson, *The Spirit of the Oxford Movement*, p. 61.
7. ibid., p. 98.
8. See, for example, E. B. Pusey, *Councils of the Church from the Council of Jerusalem to the Council of Constantinople*, p. 14; "We need missions among the poor of our towns ... " Yet Pusey was at this time, along with Keble, the most conservative of the Tractarians. See Nockles, op. cit., pp. 276 ff.
9. See Roe, op. cit., p. 105.
10. *Apo.*, p. 42.
11. For Froude's sentimental Jacobitism, see H. C. G. Matthew, "Edward Bouverie Pusey: From Scholar to Tractarian", *The Jl. of Theol. Studies* Vol. XXII, p. 105.
12. Dawson, op. cit., p. 68; Brendon, op. cit., p. 138.
13. *Remains*, Vol. I, p. 308.
14. ibid., p. 177.
15. ibid., p. 250.
16. ibid., p. xiv.
17. *Remains*, Vol. II, p. 197.
18. ibid., p. 203.
19. ibid., p. 239.
20. ibid., p. 314.

21. L. I. Guiney, *Hurrell Froude, Memoranda and Comments*, p. 119.
22. *Letters of the Revd J. B. Mozley* (ed. by Anne Mozley), p. 102.
23. *The British Magazine*, Vol. III, April 1833, p. 411.
24. Chapter 1, pp. 59–65.
25. See Nockles, op. cit., pp. 276 ff.
26. This work did form an important part of *The Remains*, "Remarks on State Interference in Matters Spiritual", Vol. III, pp. 196 ff. The copy used in this study is the reprint of the work in pamphlet form, "State Interference in Matters Spiritual", A Reprint from a work entitled *Remains of Richard Hurrell Froude*, with a preface by William J. E. Bennett, Vicar of Frome Selwood.
27. Froude's understanding of the Reformation and its social and political implications is treated in 2.4.2.
28. *State Interference*, pp. 39–45.
29. ibid., pp. 10–18. The 1592 Act was not repealed until 1688 but even then its founding principle was allowed to survive. From 1688 the Church was no longer coterminous with the Commonwealth but Parliament still represented the Church. Royal appointments could only be made to communicants. But, wrote Froude, the Church was not vigilant. In the fifth year of George I, elections into corporate offices could be given to non-communicants. In the ninth year of George II an Act was passed indemnifying all those who, though not communicants, held offices restricted to communicants. In 1828 the Test and Corporation Act was repealed; in 1829 Roman Catholics were given the vote; the 1832 Act gave a concluding blow to the ancient system. In 1833 Parliament was no longer a lay Synod of the Church of England. The conditions under which Hooker had allowed state interference were thus cancelled.
30. *Remains*, Vol. I, p. 326.
31. For the relevant studies of Hooker's understanding of the Elizabethan Settlement, see Chapter 1, fn. 124.
32. *L. & D.*, Vol. V, p. 18, Letter to Newman, January 1835. Froude was referring to page 10 of Pusey's *Tract No. XVIII* on Fasting.
33. See, for example, H. E. Manning, *A Charge delivered at the Ordinary Visitation of the Archdeaconry of Chichester in July 1845*, pp. 50 ff. Charles Smyth, *The Church and the Nation, Six Studies in the Anglican Tradition*, pp. 167 ff. was of the opinion that the Church of England was saved not by John Keble and the Tractarians but by Sir Robert Peel and Bishop Blomfield of London. On this aspect of co-operation between Church and State, see P. J. Welch, "Blomfield and Peel: A Study in the Co-operation between Church and State", *The Jl. of Ecc. History*, Vol. XII, pp. 71 ff. Owen Chadwick, *The Victorian Church*, Pt. I, pp. 126–141, is not so impressed by this co-operation between Church and

State, witnessed to especially in the work of the Ecclesiastical Commission. Other vital factors were also responsible for the change of mood; public opinion, the press, Nonconformist rivalry and conscience, moral fibre of the middle classes and Evangelical and Puseyite zeal.
34. *State Interference*, op. cit., pp. 2–3.
35. ibid.
36. ibid., p. 3.
37. ibid., pp. 6–7.
38. ibid., pp. 10–11. See also Archdeacon Froude's agreement with his son's position.
39. ibid., pp. 17, 35. "Church influence was undermined before our times with a Grafton or Shelbourne in the Cabinet, Hoadly to the bench". Cf. also R. I. Wilberforce, *A Sketch of the History of Erastianism*, pp. 61, 66; "The Church, as a supernatural power, was got rid of by the theology of Hoadly". It is strange how Newman, Froude and Wilberforce constantly spelt Bishop Hoadly's name as Hoadley.
40. ibid., pp. 37–8.
41. ibid., p. 44.
42. ibid., pp. 58–9.
43. *Remains*, Vol. III, p. 394.
44. ibid., Vol. I, p. 296.
45. ibid., Vol. I, p. 144.
46. ibid., p. 370.
47. *State Interference*, p. 6.
48. *Remains*, Vol. I, p. 323; Letter to Newman, August 1833, "My subject is the duty of contemplating the contingency of a separation between Church and State".
49. *State Interference*, pp. 47–56. There was much irony in Froude's appeal, as he would gladly have excommunicated all those who were outside the Church of England. For reactions to Froude's ideas, see Brendon, op. cit., p. 130. See also *L. & D.*, Vol. IV, p. 90. Keble was realistically aware of the constitutional dilemma how the Church could be separated from the State, only giving up her temporal advantages without incurring the penalties of Praemunire. See John Keble, *The State in its Relations with the Church*, op. cit., pp. 45–6.
50. For a study of this aspect of Keble's political thought, see J. R. Griffin, "John Keble, Radical", *The Anglican Theological Review*, Vol. LIX; "The Radical Phase of the Oxford Movement", *The Jl. of Ecc. History*, Vol. XXVII.
51. Brendon, op. cit., pp. 41–86.
52. See Owen Chadwick, *The Victorian Church*, Pt. I, p. 57.

53. *The British Magazine*, Vol. III, March 1833, pp. 367–9.
54. ibid., pp. 374–7.
55. see section 2.6.
56. On Lord Eldon and his type of Conservatism, see Nockles, op. cit., p. 276.
57. For Keble's Non-Juror and Jacobite background, see H. C. G. Matthew, op. cit., p. 105. On the Non-Jurors in general, see L. M. Hawkins, *Allegiance in Church and State, The Problem of the Non-Jurors*, pp. 167 ff.; H. Laski, *Political Thought in England from Locke to Bentham*, pp. 66 ff.; W. K. Lowther Clark, *Eighteenth Century Piety*, pp. 3 ff.; W. L. Mathieson, *English Church Reform, 1815–1840*, pp. 7–10; N. Sykes, *Church and State in England in the Eighteenth Century*, pp. 285–290; J. H. Overton, *The Non-Jurors, Their Lives, Principles and Writings*.
58. On the difference between the two traditions, see Nockles, op. cit., pp. 258–260.
59. "Church and King" in *The Christian Year, Lyra Innocentium and Other Poems*, pp. 430–431.
60. See A. R. Vidler, *The Orb and the Cross*, pp. 23 ff; Perry Butler, op. cit., pp. 7 ff.
61. Brendon, op. cit., p. 145.
62. See Keble, *The State in its Relations with the Church*, pp. 35–37.
63. e.g. "Kings to be honoured for their Office Sake"; cf. Chapter 1, fns. 142–145.
64. Keble, *The State in its Relations*, pp. 29, 43.
65. For Froude's attitude to the Royal Supremacy and his influence over Newman, see 2.3.6.
66. Keble, *The State in its Relations*, p. 49.
67. See Brendon, op. cit., p. 146 for Gladstone's favourable response to Keble's review, actually quoting Keble in his fourth edition.
68. See 2.6.
69. *Apo.*, p. 47. Newman referred to Palmer as a representative of safe, sound and sensible men in the Church of England.
70. ibid., pp. 44–47. For an eulogistic account of Rose's contribution to the Oxford Movement, see Dean Burgon, *Lives of Twelve Good Men*, pp. 62 ff. For a critique of Burgon, see J. H. Rigg, *Oxford High Anglicanism and its Chief Leaders*, pp. 43 ff.
71. J. H. Newman, *Ess. Crit. and Hist.*, Vol. I, p. 181 referred to Fr Perrone's great praise of Palmer as a theologian. In many respects, the two men were very similar. See Owen Chadwick, *Newman*, p. 13 on Perrone.
72. William Palmer, "Altered Position of the State", *Narrative*, pp. 34 ff.
73. H. J. Rose in *The British Magazine*, Vol. IV, August 1833, p. 98.

74. ibid., December 1832, p. 337; January 1834, p. 96.
75. ibid., July 1833, p. 91.
76. ibid., September 1833, p. 337.
77. William Palmer, op. cit., pp. 46–7.
78. *Remains*, Vol. I, p. 320.
79. For the Hadleigh Rectory meeting, see Owen Chadwick, *The Victorian Church*, Pt. I, pp. 70–71; Brendon, op. cit., pp. 128–129.
80. Later published as Vol. IV of *The Remains* in 1839.
81. *The British Magazine*, Vol. II, 1 September, 1832, p. 233.
82. ibid., Vol. III, February 1833, p. 149.
83. ibid., pp. 143, 146.
84. *Remains*, Vol. III, pp. 207–208.
85. For Newman's comments on Froude's articles in *The British Magazine*, see L. & C., Vol. II, p. 234.
86. R. H. Froude, "The Duty of Aiming at the Highest Excellence", *Remains*, Vol. II, p. 138.
87. See W. Houghton, *The Victorian Frame of Mind*, p. 343 for the Victorian Age embodying all the characteristics of hero worship.
88. *Remains*, Vol. I, p. 254. "The person whom I like best of all I have about is Cardinal Pole. He seems a hero of an ideal world, a union of chivalrous and Catholic feeling, like what one hopes to find people before reading about them".
89. ibid., Vol. II, p. 137.
90. *The British Magazine*, Vol. II, September 1832, pp. 334–335. Froude gave all his reliable sources for his life of Becket. Particular interest was expressed in the four hundred and thirty five letters written by Becket which passed between the principal men in Europe, relating to the Church and State struggle, 1163–1171.
91. Brendon, op. cit., p. 29.
92. See Section 2.11.
93. *Remains*, Vol. IV, p. 532.
94. *The British Magazine*, Vol. II, September 1832, p. 237. Froude wrote that it was possible to elicit from the material the view generally adopted by staunch Protestants. Lord Lyttleton interpreted the evidence of Henry II appointing Becket to Canterbury as the King being empowered to govern ecclesiastical and civil affairs to his own satisfaction. Yet two pages of the evidence Lyttleton did not bother to translate. According to Froude, Becket was very unwilling to become Archbishop, knowing that somehow or other he would have had to displease either God or the King.
95. *The British Magazine*, Vol. III, January 1833, pp. 33 ff. on Becket's election being opposed by many clergy and laity. The letter of Gilbert Foliot, consecrated Lord Bishop of London, 28 April, 1163,

showed that Becket had lost the King's confidence. Although Gilbert was one of the most venerable monks in the land and aspired to Canterbury on the death of Theobold, he was hardly the person to judge Becket's conduct impartially. His celebrated letter was an *ex-parte* statement, vindicating purely his own conduct in the affair.

96. ibid., Vol. II, pp. 454 ff; Vol. III, pp. 38 ff.
97. ibid., Vol. III, pp. 155 ff.
98. ibid., Vol. III, p. 402.
99. ibid., Vol. IV, p. 260.
100. ibid., Vol. V, p. 15.
101. ibid., Vol. III, p. 156.
102. ibid., Vol. IV, p. 380.
103. ibid., Vol. III, pp. 144–148.
104. *Remains*, Vol. I, pp. 414, 434.
105. ibid., pp. 322, 323, 329, 374.
106. Brendon, op. cit., p. 135.
107. Griffin, op. cit., pp. 110 ff.
108. *Tract No. 10*, p. 5.
109. For a discussion of Newman's views on the laity, see Chapter 3.5.5.
110. *L. & D.*, Vol. III, p. 293. The letter was dated 17 April, 1833.
111. See Chapter 3.5.
112. *Remains*, Vol. III, p. 196.
113. *The Suffragan Bishops* was reprinted in *V.M.*, Vol. II, pp. 55 ff.
114. *L. & D.*, Vol. IV, p. 28. The letter to C. P. Golightly was dated 11 August, 1833; "We wish to make the Church more popular than it is – how is, of course, a question".
115. *L. & C.*, Vol. I, p. 479.
116. *L. & D.*, Vol. IV, p. 9. Letter of 6 July, 1833.
117. ibid., p. 17. Letter to Froude, 1 August, 1833.
118. ibid., pp. 17–18. Letter to Froude, 1 August, 1833.
119. ibid., p. 28. Letter to Golightly was dated 11/13 August, 1833.
120. *L. & C.*, Vol. I, p. 450; *Tract No. 2*, p. 1.
121. *L. & C.*, Vol. II, p. 7.
122. *L. & D.*, Vol. III, p. 74. Letter to Rose, 25 July, 1832; "I have not confidence in myself sufficient to warrant an attack upon others".
123. *L. & D.*, Vol. III, p. 8. Letter from Rose to Newman; 22 January, 1832, congratulating him on Sermon IV of the *U.S.* Newman dedicated Vol. II of *PPS* to Rose. See *Apo.*, p. 515.
124. *L. & D.*, Vol. IV, pp. 20–21.
125. ibid., pp. 52–3.
126. ibid., p. 42.
127. *Apo.*, p. 46.

128. For Palmer's ideas about committees and his objections to Newman, see his *Narrative* op. cit., pp. 56–57.
129. O. J. Brose, *Church and Parliament, The Reshaping of the Church of England*, p. 30.
130. Mathieson, op. cit., pp. 10–11, on those High Churchmen who had written on themes similar to Newman's a generation before, especially Archdeacon Daubenny on Apostolic Succession.
131. *L. & D.*, Vol. IV, p. 52.
132. Newman expressed this fear in a letter to Keble, 24 September, 1833. See *L. & D.*, Vol. IV, p. 55.
133. See Rose's letter to Newman, 18 October, 1833; "Your Tracts are most admirable". *L. & D.*, Vol. IV, p. 62.
134. Mathieson, op. cit., p. 89.
135. *L. & D.*, Vol. IV, p. 98. Letter to J. W. Bowden. Bowden (1798–1844) was a leading Tractarian, contributing Tracts 5, 29, 30, 56 and possibly 58.
136. ibid.
137. ibid., p. 100.
138. *L. & D.*, Vol. IV, p. 112. Letter of 20 November, 1833.
139. ibid., p. 140. Letter of 15 December, 1833.
140. William Howley (1766–1848) was always an extreme Tory and defender of Church privilege. See F. L. Cross and E. A. Livingstone, eds., *The Oxford Dictionary of the Christian Church*, p. 671.
141. Chadwick, op. cit., pp. 175 ff.
142. *L. & D.*, Vol. IV, p. 89. Letter from Froude to Newman, November 1833.
143. ibid., p. 91 for the draft as it returned from London. It had been re-written three times. Ibid., p. 104 for Froude's re-joinder to Newman.
144. See Charles Smyth, *The Church and the Nation, Six Studies in the Anglican Tradition*, p. 167 for the view that the first half of the nineteenth century was the golden age of the Archdeacon.
145. *L. & D.*, Vol. IV, p. 104 for Archdeacon Froude's reaction; ibid., p. 112 for Froude's annoyance with Newman, 17 November, 1833.
146. ibid., p. 151.
147. *The British Magazine*, Vol. V, pp. 365–368; "The document is one which must give the warmest satisfaction to all true friends of the Church, and the greatest annoyance to its enemies".
148. Froude's reaction to the Lay Declaration to the Archbishop, headed by Joshua Watson, was similar. See Palmer, op. cit., p. 15.
149. *L. & D.*, Vol. IV, pp. 189–190; Letter to Bowden, "The very fact of addressing the Archbishop is enough . . . " yet later in the same letter, "I would do nothing to disturb existing relations, but it is

hard if we may not prepare for contingencies – and doubtless in proportion as the relations are altered by the civil power, it is the duty of the Church to demand corresponding alterations in its favour".
150. Nockles, op. cit., pp. 280 ff.
151. ibid.
152. Laski, op. cit., p. 87 wrote that "the central point of the Tractarian attack was upon the Royal Supremacy". This oversimplifies the real position.
153. Nockles, pp. 280 ff.
154. "The nation without the King would be but a deformed monster", Henry Valentine, *God Save the King* (1639), quoted by R. Eccleshall, *Order and Reason in Politics*, op. cit., p. 77. See also *The British Magazine*, Vol. III, p. 734.
155. *L. & D.*, Vol. IV, p. 23.
156. Keble, *The State in its Relations* ... op. cit., p. 15.
157. Nockles, op. cit., pp. 274, 288, 289.
158. E. B. Pusey, *Churches in London*, p. 42.
159. ibid., p. 76.
160. ibid., p. 25.
161. *Remains*, Vol. I, p. 308. See also Froude's remark to Newman on Keble's Glorious Accession Sermon, "Why not publish it as a Tract?" *L. & D.*, Vol. V, p. 98.
162. *The British Magazine*, Vol. III, p. 395.
163. Posthumously published as a pamphlet, *State Interference*.
164. *State Interference*, p. 20.
165. ibid., pp. 20–22.
166. ibid., p. 26.
167. ibid., p. 31.
168. ibid., pp. 29–33.
169. J. H. Newman, *D. & A.*, p. 22.
170. *L. & D.*, Vol. IV, p. 164. 3 January, 1834, Letter to Rose.
171. *L. & D.*, Vol. V, p. 20. January 1835, Froude to Newman.
172. *L. & D.*, Vol. IV, p. 254. 8 April, 1834, Froude to Newman.
173. *L. & D.*, Vol. V, p. 7. 23 November, 1834, Froude to Newman.
174. J. H. Newman, "The Convocation of the Province of Canterbury", *The British Magazine*, Vol. VI, pp. 517–524, 637–647; Vol. VII, pp. 33–41, 145–154, 259–268.
175. ibid., Vol. VII, pp. 151–154.
176. ibid., p. 263.
177. ibid., p. 264.
178. ibid., p. 265.
179. *L. & D.*, Vol. V, 5 February, 1835, Letter of Newman to Bowden.
180. For Froude's views, see pp. 134 ff.

181. For the historical details about Tractarian objections to Hampden, see Chadwick, op. cit., pp. 112–121.
182. *L. & D.*, Vol. V, p. 193.
183. ibid., p. 210. The date was 23 January, 1836.
184. ibid., pp. 231–232. Newman's letter to Rose, 12 February, 1836, exressing grave doubts about Hampden's appointment.
185. *L. & D.*, Vol. V, p. 253, 6 March, 1836, Letter to Keble.
186. ibid., Letter to Rose, pp. 301–302.
187. How Newman was able to grapple with these issues, see Chapter 3.5.
188. Piers Brendon, "Newman, Keble and Froude's Remains". *The English Historical Review*, No. CCCXLV, pp. 697 ff. Brendon makes two specific points. First, Newman was so concerned about the details of his own religious development that *The Remains* became "a stage in the history of my own mind" (Oratory papers, 2 February, 1836) pp. 709–710. Secondly, Newman and Keble wished to present Froude as a Tractarian saint, symbolising all that was glorious in that tradition, "The revelation of one of God's angels in disguise", *PPS*, Vol. IV, Sermon XIV, p. 248. Brendon's argument is convincing. See *L. & D.*, Vol. VI, p. 145, 6 October, 1837, Letter of Newman to Bowden, "The journals do certainly portray a saint".
189. Griffin, op. cit., pp. 99–100.
190. The poem, first published in *The British Magazine*, Vol. VII, had as its title, "The Exchange". In *The Remains*, it had a title, "Farewell to Toryism", Vol. II, p. 429. Sometimes it was referred to as "Farewell to Feudalism".
191. Perry Butler, op. cit., p. 102.
192. Nockles, op. cit., pp. 276 ff.
193. Brendon, *Hurrell Froude and the Oxford Movement*, p. 30. For Newman's opposition to the events of 1829, see Chapter 3.2.
194. ibid., pp. 120–121. Before publication Newman had expressed his fear to Bowden, *L. & D.*, Vol. VI, p. 177.
195. For the reaction of the Episcopal bench to *The Remains* and Tractarian theology in general, see Brendon, op. cit., p. 191; W. Bricknell, ed., *The Judgement of the Bishops upon Tractarian Theology*. For the public response, see Newman, *Diffs*. pp. 33–36. Most Tractarians were treated with suspicion after 1839. See B. A. Smith, *Dean Church, the Anglican Response to Newman*, pp. 203, ff. See also G. Tracy in his introduction to *L. & D.*, Vol. VI, p. xviii. Fausett made a vicious attack upon *The Remains* at Oxford, ibid., p. 276. Lord Morpeth was very critical in the Commons, though Gladstone defended *The Remains*, ibid., p. 276.

Note also the critique of Edward Churton, ibid., pp. 324, 334. A High Churchman, he was not unsympathetic towards the Tractarians. Yet his criticisms echoed the sentiments of many; "*The Remains* have sadly encumbered a plain good cause"; Letter to Newman, 18 September, 1838, ibid., p. 324.
196. For Frederic Rogers's comment to Newman that Froude in August 1833 was too High Church to be a Tory, see Brendon, op. cit., p. 121.
197. *Remains*, Vol. I, p. 388.
198. See, for instance, J. E. Baker, *The Novel and the Oxford Movement*, pp. 45–53; Robert Blake, *Disraeli*, p. 171.
199. See A. R. Vidler, *A Century of Social Catholicism, 1820–1920*, pp. 21 ff, 64–67.
200. On Scott, see J. H. Raleigh, "What Scott meant to the Victorians", *Victorian Studies*, Vol. VII, pp. 7–34; Alice Chandler, "Sir Walter Scott and the Medieval Revival", *Nineteenth Century Fiction*, Vol. XIX, pp. 315–322. On Wordsworth, see Chapter on Keble, fn. 34. William Cobbett's main work was *A History of the Protestant Reformation*, 2 Vols.; on Cobbett, see G. H. D. Cole, *The Life of William Cobbett*; Raymond Williams, *Cobbett*. Robert Southey's main works were *The Book of the Church*; *Essays Moral and Political*, 2 Vols. On Southey, see G. Carnall, *Robert Southey and His Age; The Development of a Conservative Mind*; S. W. Gilley, "Nationality and Liberty, Protestant and Catholic: Robert Southey's Book of the Church" in S. Mews, ed., *Studies in Church History*, Vol. 18, *Religion and National Identity*, pp. 409–432. For Thomas Carlyle, see his *Past and Present*, ed. by A. M. D. Hughes; J. A. Froude, ed., *Reminiscences of Thomas Carlyle*.
201. Brendon, op. cit., pp. 26–37, 101–102.
202. "Farewell to Toryism", op. cit.
203. *L. & D.*, Vol. V, p. 78.
204. *Remains*, Vol. I, p. 15.
205. G. Prevost, ed., *Autobiography of Isaac Williams*, p. 85; Brendon, op. cit., pp. 185–186. W. Ward, *W. G. Ward and the Oxford Movement*, pp. 81 ff.
206. F. W. Faber, *The Cherwell Water-Lily and Other Poems*, p. 157. On Faber, see Ronald Chapman, *Father Faber*; Raleigh Addington, *Faber, Priest and Poet, Selected Letters by Frederick William Faber, DD, from 1833 to 1863*.
207. See Chapman, op. cit., pp. 42 ff. B. W. Martin, "Wordsworth, Faber and Keble, Commentary on a Triangular Relationship", *Review of English Studies*, Vol. XXVI, pp. 436–442. Faber dedicated *Sights and Thoughts in Foreign Churches and among Foreign Peoples* to Wordsworth "in affectionate remembrance of

much personal kindness, and many thoughtful contributions on the rites, prerogatives, and doctrines of Holy Church". In 1842 he dedicated *The Styrian Lake and Other Poems* to Keble. "To the author of 'The Christian Year' this volume is with his kind permission respectfully inscribed with the hope that age may bring to kindred aspirations a poetic utterance unworldly as his own".
208. "England has no need of Milton: how can a country have need of anything, policy, courage, talent or anything else which is unblessed of God?" Faber wrote this from Florence, 18 August, 1843. See J. E. Bowden, *Life and Letters of Frederick William Faber, DD*, p. 175. See also Chapman, op. cit., p. 69 about some of Faber's misgivings about Wordsworth. Faber occasionally disapproved of Wordsworth's pantheism. See Addington, op. cit., p. 61.
209. *Sights and Thoughts*, op. cit., pp. 211, 291, 361.
210. Faber, writing from a Benedictine Monastery, Ad Montes, 25 July, 1841, mentioned the Whig historians who referred to the monks as "lazy, the drones of monasteries". "If they were here," wrote Faber, "they would soon discover how the monasteries have been the backbone of the poorest communities". See Bowden, op. cit., p. 139.
211. On Faber's genius as a writer of hymns and his ability to communicate the profoundest theological truths to the uneducated, see S. W. Gilley, "Vulgar Piety and the Brompton Oratory, 1850–1856," *Durham University Journal*, December 1981, pp. 15–21.
212. C. Whibley, *Lord John Manners and his Friends* is still the best account of Young England.
213. For the general reading material of a Young England member, see Robert Blake, *The Conservative Party from Peel to Churchill*, p. 55.
214. The similarities between Froude's "Farewell to Toryism" and many of the sentiments expressed by Lord John Manners are clear. See Lord John Manners, *England's Trust and Other Poems*, p. 16; *A Plea for National Holy-Days*, p. 1. Young England appeared attractive to many young clergymen with Tractarian sympathies. See, e.g. Robert Gray, *Cardinal Manning, A Biography*, p. 89.
215. George Eliot, "The Natural History of German Life", *Westminster Review* (July 1856), p. 55.
216. See Alexander Baillie-Cochrane, "In the Days of the Dandies III: the Young England Party", *Blackwood's Magazine*, Vol. XLVI, pp. 314 ff. for a different opinion from that expressed by George Eliot.
217. Christopher Dawson, op. cit. expressed the opinion that Disraeli was very familiar with *The Remains*, p. 95, fn. 1. Not only was

Disraeli's diatribe against Toryism and Erastianism in *Coningsby*, Book VII, Chapter II thoroughly Froudian in character but he used the arguments and even the actual words of Froude's *Remarks on State Interference*; cf. *Remains* III, pp. 198–207 with *Coningsby*, pp. 376–379.
On Disraeli's part in Young England, see Robert Blake, *Disraeli*, pp. 167–190; W. F. Moneypenny, *The Life of Benjamin Disraeli, Earl of Beaconsfield*, Vol. II, pp. 164 ff. On Disraeli as a novelist, see T. Braun, *Disraeli the Novelist*, pp. 75 ff; L. Cazamin, *The Social Novel in England, 1830–1850, Dickens, Disraeli, Mrs Gaskell, Kingsely*, pp. 186 ff; V. Cunningham, *Everywhere spoken Against, Dissent in the Victorian Novel*, pp. 102 ff.; D. R. Schwarz, *Disraeli's Fiction*, pp. 86 ff., S. M. Smith, *The Other Nation, The Poor in English Novels of the 1840's and 1850's*, pp. 70–74, 115. ff, 178 ff. "From what other novelist do we learn so much about the Oxford Movement?". See Walter Houghton, *The Victorian Frame of Mind*, p. 153. The comparison between Newman and Disraeli was made by J. A. Froude, *Lord Beaconsfield*, p. 108.

218. *Coningsby, or The New Generation*; *Sybil, or The Two Nations*; *Tancred, or The New Crusade*; *Endymion*.
219. See C. Dawson, op. cit.
220. R. W. Stewart, *Disraeli's Novels Reviewed*, p. 207.
221. B. Disraeli, Earl of Beaconsfield, *Selected Speeches of the late Rt. Hon. the Earl of Beaconsfield*, ed., T. E. Kebbel, 2 Vols., Vol. 1, p. 50.
222. *Sybil*, p. 113. Aubrey St Lys was generally regarded as Faber. See M. B. Reckitt, *From Maurice to Temple, A Century of the Social Movement in the Church of England*, p. 57.
223. *Sybil*, pp. 47, 55, 109.
224. *Tancred*, p. 338.
225. ibid., Book II, Chapter IV.
226. Newman's secession dealt a grievous blow to Disraeli. See Blake, op. cit., p. 207. Although Disraeli lost his enthusiasm for the Tractarian Movement after 1845, and more especially after the 1848 Continental Revolutions, he always considered himself a devout Church of England member. While Gladstone was prepared to make alliances with Nonconformists to secure political power, Disraeli loathed dissent, seeing it no better than irreligion, both testifying to the absence of the Church of England, "the main remedial agency in our present state". See Cunningham, op. cit., p. 102. For Gladstone's alliance with Nonconformists, see G. I. T. Machin, "Gladstone and Nonconformity in the 1860's; The formation of an Alliance", *The Hist. Jl.*, Vol. XVII; D. W. Bebbington, "Gladstone and the Nonconformists: a religious

Affinity in Politics", Derek Baker, ed., *Studies in Church History*, Vol. 12, *Church, Society and Politics*, pp. 369–382.
227. W. J. Baker, "Hurrell Froude and the Reformers", *The Jl. of Ecc. Hist.*, Vol. XXI, pp. 243–260.
228. Cobbett, *A History of the Protestant Reformation*, Vol. I, p. 165.
229. Brendon, op. cit., p. 101.
230. *Remains*, Vol. I, p. 336.
231. ibid., pp. 251–252. Letter to Newman, 29 July, 1832.
232. Preface to Part II, Vols. III and IV of *The Remains*. Reference to Calvin, see *Remains*, Vol. III, p. 386.
233. *Remains*, Vol. I, p. 389.
234. *Remains*, Vol. I, p. 340. Letter to Newman, 25 January, 1834.
235. Bowden, op. cit. Letter from Faber, 25 November, 1841.
236. Cobbett, op. cit., Vol. I, v, p. 155.
237. ibid., p. 149.
238. *Sybil*, p. 12.
239. W. J. Baker, op. cit., pp. 254–255.
240. *Remains*, Vol. I, pp. 355, 394–395, 438.
241. Nockles, op. cit., pp. 276 ff.
242. T. Mozley, *Reminiscences Chiefly of Oriel College and the Oxford Movement*, I, pp. 211–12.
243. *Remains*, Vol. I, pp. 258–259.
244. Nockles, op. cit., pp. 277 ff.
245. *Remains*, Vol. II, p. 9.
246. ibid., pp. 218–223.
247. Keble showed the same characteristics in his *The State in its Relations with the Church*, p. 16 when he counselled resignation and obedience, a heavy heart, protest against lax notions, irreverent proceedings and a time of passive resistance.
248. *Remains*, Vol. I, p. 355.
249. *L. & D.*, Vol. IV, p. 215.
250. ibid.
251. For the Liberal progressive approach, see Chapters 3.2. and 3.7.

3
J. H. NEWMAN
"To Make Trial of the Age"[1]

3.1. INTRODUCTION

To study Newman's understanding of the Church in relationship to State and society is to encounter, using his own terminology, a night battle of words, concepts and ideas.[2] Newman can either be all things to all men or a pitiful irrelevance, arousing only at worst, derision, at best, sympathy. The opinion of F. D. Maurice, appealing to the Tractarian spirit in general, that the leaders of the Oxford Movement opposed to the spirit of the present age that of a former age,[3] has been claimed to be very true of Newman himself. Consequently, the idea has evolved that there is little to interest the student of Church and society, the value of civilisation, the rise and fall of nations or the reform of social evils in Newman's thought. In Newman, wrote Keith Feiling, there was no political creed as such.[4]

Even so, for many Newman appeared to be the epitome of the Conservative spirit. D. J. de Laura claimed that Newman was the most Conservative since Burke.[5] According to Anthony Quinton, Newman's detachment from the greatest social changes for a quarter of a millenium made Newman the last of the old Conservatives who did not have to take account of the new social order.[6] A selected edition of Newman's writings could add considerable weight to his own boast that he was too much of a Tory for "these smart times".[7] Newman felt adamant that he had nothing new to say. He did not wish to be original and had no love for reforms.[8] "If the English Church is to bear upon a new course", he wrote, "then I must witness against it".[9] Newman claimed enthusiastically that one of the great glories of the Prayer Book was that it was no modern production[10] while there was no need for originality, as divine wisdom was infinitely preferable.[11] However, other scholars, like J. D. Holmes, have seen in Newman a different spirit. Politically and socially, Newman was far more enlightened than a mere conservative thinker.[12] On many occasions Newman was bitterly hostile to the contemporary Conservative spirit.[13] The evidence for his rejection of Peelite Conservatism is overwhelming.[14]

Much has also been made of the mystery of Newman.[15] There were many incompatible strands in his writings. "Strength is consistency," wrote Newman.[16] That was certainly appropriate for one who felt that "mistiness is the mother of wisdom".[17] Yet Newman was hardly consistent himself, a fact of which he seemed aware. "I am become neither Whig nor Tory", he once claimed.[18] On the one hand, he could write, "I can be a Reformer"[19] or "to be stationary is to lose ground, and to repose is to fail"[20] while, on the other hand, he claimed, "Show me that I am an innovator and I will be silent".[21]

Newman was a conservative, and yet a revolutionary.[22] Only one Reformation really mattered, the return to Christ.[23] It could be claimed that he considered all sides of most questions.[24] Although he apparently had no interest in movements[25] and believed that protests wasted time,[26] yet he had compassion for the whole world.[27] Even if he had nothing to say, C. S. Dessain claimed that he was the Augustine of the modern world.[28] Newman had to do with matters of ultimate concern.[29] In the light of so many trials, he discovered the birth-pangs of a new Creation.[30] Having to defend the Christian life, Newman showed the need to understand his adversaries and their new weapons.[31] He had "to reassert what is old and illumine what is new".[32]

Newman, who only wrote in matters of crisis,[33] realised that the talent of the day was against the Church.[34] The temper of the age,[35] which indulged in a restless and intemperate desire of novelty and change, was to do with the growth of secular knowledge, the march of mind.[36] In such a world, Newman was realistic about man's condition.[37] At worst, Newman could have been a bore, an irrelevance, the epitome of a disaffected intelligentsia.[38] At best, he could become profound, vital and dynamic, a prophet who believed that events had to be interpreted theologically.[39]

3.2. ROMAN CATHOLIC EMANCIPATION, 1829

In the *Apologia*,[40] Newman stated that his action against Peel over Catholic Emancipation was on academic and not on ecclesiastical or political grounds. This was rather disingenuous on Newman's part, especially as he had the most specific moral charge against Peel, that the Home Secretary's action was directly contrary to what Newman's conscience dictated.

Newman was the Doctor of Conscience. Throughout his life, he believed passionately that Conscience was the natural law, an impression of the divine light in man, a participation of the eternal law in the rational creature, apprehended in the minds of individual men.[41] Anglicans, Wesleyans, the various Presbyterian sects in Scotland and Catholics were all agreed that Conscience was the Voice of God, not the creation of man.[42] Newman's life-long commitment was not to Utility but Conscience,[43] "the aboriginal Vicar of Christ, a prophet in its informations, a monarch in its peremptoriness, a priest in its blessings and anathemas".[44] Newman always distinguished two aspects of conscience. On the one hand, it was a moral sense which supplied men with "the elements of morals", particular judgements about what men must or must not do, "such as may be developed by the intellect into an ethical code". On the other hand, Newman conceived Conscience as a sense of duty which enforced those prescriptions. It was on this latter aspect, Conscience as "a sanction of right conduct", that Newman mainly relied. This aspect of Conscience, he suggested, "does not repose on itself, but vaguely reaches forward to something beyond self, and dimly discovers a sanction higher than self for its decisions, as is evidenced in that keen sense of obligation and responsibility which informs them". Any person, wrote Newman, who recognised his own conduct as immoral, "has a lively sense of responsibility and guilt, though the act be no offence against society, – of distress and apprehension, even though it may be of present service to him, – of compunction and regret, though in itself it be most pleasurable, – of confusion of face, though it may have no witnesses". Such affections, Newman wrote, "are correlative with persons". "If, as is the case, we feel responsibility, are ashamed, are frightened, at transgressing the voice of conscience, this implies that there is One to whom we are responsible, before whom we are ashamed, whose claims upon us we fear". Similarly the enjoyment of a good conscience implied a person in whose approval we were happy. "These feelings in us are such as require for their exciting cause an intelligent being". Yet Newman felt there was no earthly person who could systematically fill this role. Conscience, therefore, had to be related to a supernatural and divine person: "and thus the phenomena of Conscience, as a dictate, avail to impress the imagination with the picture of a Supreme Governor, a Judge, holy, just, powerful, all-seeing, retributive, and (are) the creative principle of religion, as the Moral Sense is the principle of ethics".[45]

Newman was aware that the great difficulty for the Christian was to combine the internal divine informants, Conscience, Reason and Natural Religion with the external agencies, the Church and the Scriptures. Far too many Christians were eager to dispense with either the former or the latter. The Roman Catholic removed Reason, Scripture and Antiquity and relied mainly upon Church authority. The Calvinist relied on Reason, Scripture, and Criticism, disparaging the Church, Tradition and Antiquity. The Latitudinarian relied on Reason, with Scripture in subordination. The mystic relied on the heart, the Politician took the National faith as sufficient, the man of the world acted by common sense while the popular Religionist considered the authorised version of Scripture to be all in all.[46] Yet Newman realised that there was a truly Catholic Christian position regarding the voice of Conscience and that of the Church. The development of one's conscience, Newman wrote, was not automatic. It needed to be elicited and cherished: "Our parents and teachers are our first informants concerning the next world; and they elicit and cherish the innate sense of right and wrong which acts as a guide co-ordinately with them. By degrees they resign their place to the religious communion, or Church, in which we find ourselves, while the inward habits of truth and holiness which the moral sense has begun to form, react upon that inward monitor, enlarge its range, and make its dictates articulate, decisive and various".[47] If the individual chose to put himself in the context of the community of the Church where the vision of Christ, as presented in the Church's Scriptures, could not merely correct his perceptions but challenge him to lift them to an higher plane, then the individual conscience could consequently be enlarged much further in its range. The result was immense joy for the Christian as he saw the continuity of God's purposes and his moral vision enlarged and confirmed by the teaching of Christ: "There is, perhaps, no greater satisfaction to the Christian than that which arises from his perceiving that the Revealed system is rooted deep in the natural course of things, of which it is merely the result and completion; that his Saviour has interpreted for him the faint or broken accents of Nature; and that in them, so interpreted, he has, as if in some old prophecy, at once the evidence and the lasting memorial of the truths of the Gospel".[48]

Beyond the individual and the Church, however, Newman saw the anti-Christian world, which was conceived in essentially Johannine terms.[49] For Newman, the world was reality apart from God. Man on his own had no life, no hope. Unlike the material and natural world which was so vigorous and reproductive amidst all its changes, man lacked this power of revivification. Without help from somewhere beyond him, "man ... tends to dissolution from the moment he begins to be ... he is ... as a bubble that breaks, and as water poured out upon the earth ... as night folows day ... so surely are failure, and overthrow, and annihilation, the issue of this natural virtue".[50]

It was always a case of the school of this world against Christ and his Church, especially as "the world sweeps by in long procession: – its principalities and powers, its Babel of languages, the astrologers of Chaldea, the horse and its rider and the chariots of Egypt, Baal and Ashtoreth and their false worship; and those who witness, feel its fascination; they flock after it; with a strange fancy, they ape its gestures, and dote upon its mummeries ... ".[51] The Christian owed this world no allegiance, no service, especially as it died, never to rise again. It had no claim over men, as it could neither harm nor do them any good.[52] This world was full of vanity and falsely enlightened teachers. It was base and miserable.[53] It was Newman's conviction that this world, worse as it was than the Dark Ages,[54] was as unbelieving as when Christ came. Newman asked his congregation, "Does there not seem too great cause to fear that this nation, in spite of its having been baptised into the Cross of Christ, is in so unholy a state, that, did Christ come among us as He came among the Jews, we should, except a small remnant, reject Him as well as they?"[55] Men were of this world only, since the present and future were their only concern. Such a world was less than human. It was not glorious, as it knew nothing of the saints in light. It had no faith and was unaware of the cause of the righteous in bygone ages. It was content with things as they were.[56] People had lost any consciousness of transcendence, eternity, infinity. They squabbled like philosophers and lived like the world.[57] Full of an ardent political temper, men became indifferent even to common sense.[58] As the average layman was but a worldly statesman, there was little wonder that there was always war between the Church and the secular power.[59] What sort of pride had those people who changed everything according to the season? They were truly Satanic, thoroughly corrupt, imitators of the heretic Arians.[60]

The anti-Christian world was increasingly successful in its assault on the traditional social and political order of Christendom, which had been created by the Church. Newman realised that in 1829 Christianity was still the law of the land. Indeed, reviling the ordinances of the Church of England was a crime of a much grosser nature than the other of non-conformity, since it carried with it the utmost indecency, arrogance and ingratitude. Acts like the Test and Corporation Acts did, at least, give a tone to society, to all classes and to the publications which represented public opinion.[61] Yet such a Christian polity was being betrayed by the contemporary Peelite Conservatism, which was supposedly committed to the defence of that order. Newman's opposition to Peel was based on two principles. First, Peel had changed sides. Far from defending the Christian Confessional state, the tradition of fifteen hundred years, Peel actually betrayed the whole tradition of the Tory Party. As far as Newman was concerned, Peel was simply not being Conservative enough. The Home Secretary favoured the emancipation of Roman Catholics purely on the grounds of political expediency.[62] No one was more aware of the profound change than Peel himself.[63] For Newman, Emancipation was the symptom of an ever virulent Liberalism, a systematic hatred of the Church borne by Romanists.[64] The campaign to prevent Peel's re-election certainly excited Newman. The Member of Parliament for Oxford must not represent the University again![65] It was obvious to Newman that the Liberal lawyers were for Peel. All decent men, like College tutors and resident Fellows, however, were utterly opposed to Peel, who was unworthy.[66] The fact that Keble added his modest voice against Peel was to Newman like "some beautiful and sublime poetical incident and quite touching".[67]

Secondly, Newman objected to Peel and the Conservative government for attempting to dictate a change of policy involving religion in Oxford, still the exclusive preserve of the Church of England with her incomparable medieval motto, "Dominus illuminatio mea".[68] After Peel's defeat on 28 February, 1829, Newman wrote the following day to his mother, "We have achieved a glorious Victory ... We have proved the independence of the Church and of Oxford. So rarely is either of the two in opposition to Government, that not once in fifty years can independent principle be shown; yet in these times, when its existence has been generally doubted, the moral power we shall gain by it cannot be overestimated".[69] Throughout the campaign, it was a question of the insolence of the so-called "talent" of the University against the smaller Colleges of inferior ability. For Newman it was a matter of principle. The University, let alone the Church, would never change according to the whims of any government minister. The Conservatives in power were mere sucking pigs in comparison with the accumulated traditions of Oxford over the centuries.

Newman's behaviour throughout was never inconsistent. It was a matter of conscience, nurtured by the teaching of the Church, against a wicked and fallen world, epitomised by politicians who were prepared to sacrifice the traditions of an ancient Christian polity. The Conservatives had accommodated their principles to the spirit of the age. Newman seriously believed that the influence of the Church and the University was being threatened. In the first public event with which he had been concerned, Newman felt that he had done his duty to preserve the integrity of Church and University.[70]

3.3. THE 1832 REFORM BILL

In the *Apologia*, Newman wrote that the expulsion of the Bourbons in 1830 was an act of unchristian disobedience towards those with divine right of inheritance.[71] His opposition to the Reform Bill was total.[72] Newman, as in 1829, had theological reasons for his sense of profound disquiet with the events of the world. So great was his annoyance after the passing of the Bill that he would have excommunicated Lord Grey and other reformers.[73] The 1830 Revolution in France and the 1832 Act offended Newman's sense of reserve, a theological principle with political overtones.

Newman's unique contribution to the understanding of the doctrine of Reserve has already been well researched.[74] Newman always felt indignant towards those who behaved in an unreserved manner. Many contemporary politicians, at home and abroad, were no better than the Arian heretics, who had shown no reverence for traditions.[75] In the world there was always an incessant din. Nothing attracted attention but that which cried aloud.[76] The pleasures of immediate excitement had to be scrutinised most carefully.[77] Rome's great weakness was that it laid excessive store by public display.[78]

Opposed to all the superficial nonsense of political reform was the glorious example of St Basil who had much reserve and sedateness of manner.[79] It was no coincidence that God spoke quietly to the world. When God came in the flesh, "He was in the world, and the world was made by Him, and the world knew Him not". Nor did He strive nor cry, nor lift up His voice in the streets. "So it is now", preached Newman, "He is still here; He still whispers to us, He still makes signs to us. But His voice is so low, and the world's din is so loud, and His signs are so covert and the world is so restless, that it is difficult to determine when He addresses us, and what He says".[80] It was hardly surprising that Newman felt he could never have been a demagogue.[81] It was far more expedient to trust the minorities who, like Christ, worked quietly, as a few highly endowed men would always rescue the world.[82]

A reserved attitude towards life was echoed in respect, reverence for traditions, usages and customs in society. Only a mind which was totally aware of the power of historical traditions could have written the following sentiments: "In every nation will be found ... a certain assemblage of beliefs, convictions, rules, usages, traditions, proverbs and principles; some political, some social, some moral: and these tending toward some definite form of government and 'modus vivendi', or polity, as their natural scope ... This, then, is the constitution of a state: securing, as it does, the national unity by at once strengthening and controlling its governing power. It is sometimes more than law; it is the embodiment of special ideas perhaps which have been held by a race for ages, which are of immemorial usage, which have fixed themselves in its innermost heart, which are in its eyes sacred to it, and have practically the force of eternal truths, whether they be such or not".[83] Martin J. Svaglic has suggested that Newman's political thought in this period was a blend of the conservatism of Burke and the Non-Jurors.[84] Like Burke, Newman's presumption was in favour of the inherited and established system of laws and institutions, reflecting at a stroke the collective wisdom of the community. "Living in these republican times", Newman had to make a stand against further innovations in the Constitution.[85]

As God spoke quietly to his world, so also the reaction to the divine revelation would only be felt in the hearts of the few.[86] Newman's championship of the old unreformed order of society had within it a profound reverence for the idea of accumulated wisdom over the centuries. He was certain about what the protagonists of the pre-1832 system were attempting to achieve; "The anti-reformers of that day", he wrote as he reminisced later in life, "took their stand upon antiquity and prescription; they professed to transmit what they had received. They cried out with the old barons, 'Nolumus leges Angliae mutari'; ... It was not with them a question of abstract perfection or of popular belief, but of things as they were. They considered that a reform was 'in rerum natura' impossible. The Constitution was a fact, not an idea; a substance, not a circumstance. It had grown into its existing shape in the course of centuries; it partook of the past; and if the past could be recalled or undone, then could it be changed? It did not admit of alteration, for the better or the worse, of reform or improvement, any more than you could change some tortuously branded gnarled, mistletoed, and ivy-crowned oak. You might destroy it; you might destroy its identity; but you must either take it or leave it, as it were. It was not certainly the pattern result of the laws of ideal perfection; its methods and provisions were roundabout, cumbrous, provokingly tiresome, dilatory, but still it effected its ends, in its own way, and did its work well, however paradoxically ... and herein was good government, which is the end of political institutions ... the existing state of things ought not perhaps to work well, but it did".[87]

Newman's reflections in later life echoed what he felt about the passing of the Reform Act in 1832. In November 1832, Newman preached a sermon before the University of Oxford with the title, "Human Responsibility, as Independent of Circumstances". His sentiments were an accurate expression of what he thought about Lord Grey and the Reformers. The structure of society does indeed pass through different stages, and philosophers of the day commonly infer unwarrantably from this that "what has been, and is, ought to be" as if "because at certain eras this or that class of society gains the ascendancy, therefore it lawfully gains it". The truth is that "the usurpation of an invader, and the development, as it is called, of popular power, are alike facts, and alike sins, in the sight of Him who forbids us to oppose constituted authority".[88]

3.4. THE HISTORY OF THE ARIANS (1833)

Newman's first published work in 1833 was an accurate summary of his method as an historian. This method had an important bearing upon his whole understanding of the Church in relationship to the State and society. Newman was suspicious of mere history, which always tended to reflect knowledge or intellectualism for its own sake. Newman was not an historian like Dollinger, for instance.[89] Rather, he attempted to endow the record of the past with his own personal understanding of it. This does not mean that Newman lacked a proper historical perspective or that in himself the historian was always at the mercy of the theologian.[90] History was the sphere in which faith was told, revealed and enacted. Faith had to be historical, otherwise it was mere fideism. Indeed, Newman felt that "ignorance of our historical position is one of the great evils of the day",[91] as it was the fashion of the times to reduce sacred history to a mere record.[92] History was never intended to be like scientific truth in the modern sense. Only personal faith could achieve that.[93] This was one reason why Newman always appealed to the whole experience of his readers.[94] History was viewed through divinely enlightened eyes.[95] His *History of the Arians* was splendid not only because it was serious history but it was also essentially personal. It was not a question of either serious history or personal opinions but both.[96] Newman imposed his own pattern in this work. The result was not propagandist historicism but history with a personal appeal. Although all his works were doubtlessly autobiographical,[97] they also contained the most fascinating kind of history.

With the passion, commitment and enthusiasm of a professional story teller, Newman's reading of history taught him many lessons. First, God does rule providentially. This was not a personal opinion but a matter of certitude.[98] Newman saw the whole panorama of the world's events, as every moment was measured by eternity.[99] Since Providence created nothing in vain, God was always there behind this fleeting world. Everything that took place in the material order was economically connected with God's providential plans.[100] Newman had no sense of the history of the worst events except through the eyes of the man of faith.[101] Writing of the religion of Anti-christ, Newman reminded his hearers that it was sufficient that "the all-watchful eye and the all-ordaining hand of God is still over the world, and that the seeds sown in prophecy above two thousand years since, are not dead, but from time to time, by blade and tender shoot, give earnest to the future harvest".[102] This was the cardinal sin of the Arians, to deny the fundamental reality that "of all the ages the Word is King and Maker" which made no sense of any claim that "there was once when the Everlasting was not".[103] This was why Newman laid so much emphasis on the idea that

> the world has cycles in its course
> The same bad round fulfil.[104]

Society might shatter all things but it would inevitably perish before God himself. It had happened before and would doubtlessly happen again.[105]

Secondly, history had its own interpretative power. Newman

was never concerned simply with facts. There had to be an interpretative hypothesis to account for them as they stood on the dusty pages of time. That account had to be satisfactory.[106] This could only mean that God had chosen as his supreme instrument the One, Holy, Catholic and Apostolic Church in his dealings with the world. Christianity was no ordinary history but the only realm where God had chosen to guide his Church.[107] All things seemed to hang together around the vitality, health and perseverance of the Church throughout the ages, for if she failed, then so did everything else.[108] The Church was a divine society, founded by our Lord, and existed to this day with its government vested "in the very dynasty which His Apostles began".[109] Not only was it a reality that the vast catholic body was the holy Church throughout all the world but also that it was independent of time and space.[110] Everything was in and for the Church.[111] The Church need not fear excessively even in times of the direst trials as she was there to rule. Newman quoted enthusiastically Alexander Knox in his *Remains*;[112] "My persuasion of the radical excellence of the Church of England does not suffer me to doubt that she is to be an illustrious agent in bringing the mystical kingdom of Christ to its ultimate perfection".[113] Similarly Newman claimed that although men might reverence old lineage, noble birth and royal ancestry, "yet the royal dynasty of the Apostles is far older than all the kingly families which are now on the earth".[114]

Thirdly, the study of history taught Newman where exactly the end of all things would be. He grappled with what has been called "the ultimate theological problem of the nineteenth century Church", that Christians could be certain about their beliefs with history only being able to provide a probable but never certain base.[115] Yet the Church in history and beyond it could rescue the Christian believer, not from the rigours, trials and vicissitudes of historical research but from entering upon a journey which had no happy ending. Within the Church, history did not cease to be history but transcended its human, fallible limitations. It ceased to be a purely earthly discipline. Since the Church had nothing less than divine authority, especially as only supernatural prowess could have the certainty to handle human nature, man did not need to concern himself with building temples made of human hands or reforming societies which had a limied life-span. For Newman, there were no ideal goals. Movements in history did not perform such convenient miracles. Far from emphasising secular progress,[116] Newman was keen to point out that each period in time was precisely that chosen by God to work out his will for each human individual. This work did not cease when political reforms were passed, only when the Divine City was built. If truth belonged to every age, then the end, omega, final point moved into the sphere of eschatology.[117] What was eternally significant was not human victories, which were essentially frail and finite but the victory of Christ and his Church, which was sailing triumphantly towards the new World.[118]

Fourthly, Newman learned from his reading of history that the movement towards God was away from society. Like St Athanasius,[119] Newman had the courage to stand within the divine dispensation and realise exactly where he stood in relation to his own past, present and future. Like St Augustine, Newman preferred the Hebraic to the Greek view of human affairs.[120] The paradoxes and difficulties of history were good for man as they led him firmly towards God.[121] If there were universal guiding principles in history, then no age was better than another[122] and each society was equally distant from God's eternity.[123] Newman was neither unduly pessimistic nor optimistic. He had learned that within the dispensation of God's providence the one cardinal truth needed to be emphasised, the irreconcilable opposition between the Church and the world. Of course, if truth belonged to every age, the present age had no more or less than any other which had made its pilgrimage towards God. It was the Heavenly City which interested Newman as it had fascinated St Augustine. "Historical facts support St Augustine's view of things", he wrote; "God showed visibly, not only provided secretly, that the Church should be the salvation of the city. The fierce conqueror, Alaric, who first came against it, exhorted his troops, 'to respect the Churches of the Apostles St Peter and St Paul, as holy and inviolable sanctuaries' ... fifty years afterwards, when Attila was advancing against the city ... St Leo formed one of a deputation of three, who went out to meet him, and was successful in arresting his purpose. A few years afterwards, Genseric ... appeared before the defenceless city. The same fearless prelate went out to meet him at the head of his clergy ... gained a promise that the unresisting multitude should be spared, the buildings protected from fear, and the captives from torture". Even from the worst possible enemies, the Christian Church was always there, not on the periphery of life but at the centre, in the midst of the conflict, protecting even the guilty city from the barbarian hordes. "What a wonderful rule of God's providence is herein displayed," commented Newman. This was a daily event.[124]

The Church gloriously survived the conflicts of the centuries. That was her destiny throughout time. But as God was her beginning, so too all things pointed towards Him. As Newman semed constantly aware of his own mortality,[125] so the age was passing away, as "earth and sky are ever failing; Christ is ever coming; Christians are ever lifting up their hands and looking out, and therefore it is the evening. We may not set our hearts on things present. ... "[126] In the world, there were always those who scoffed at religion, who advocated wicked measures, defended injustice, cruelty, sacrilege, infidelity and did not comprehend that God saw and heard the sins of many in contemporary England.[127] In the world, there was mortality, hopelessness, finitude. It was only with God, in and for God, that man could survive his fate and become an instrument in God's providential dealings with humanity.

3.5. CHURCH AND SOCIETY, 1833–1837

3.5.1. *The Church of the Fathers*

The Fathers, especially those of Alexandria, formed the whole background to Newman's understanding of the Church.[128] If Antiquity ever ran counter to the contemporary Church in important matters, then the Christian was bound to follow Antiquity.[129] For his main inspiration, Newman constantly looked to his *alter ego* of the fourth century, royal-hearted Athanasius.[130]

As an academic, Newman was too well aware of the inconsistencies, failings and tensions of a mere romantic appeal to some bygone, heroic and golden age. There was the constant temptation to overcome faith completely by sight. The attempt to revive what was past was as absurd as seeking to raise what was literally dead. For many the appeal to the Fathers was pure romance, especially as the constitution of the Church was utterly different in contemporary England from what it was then. Episcopacy had changed. Bishops were similar to those of the Early Church in name only. The notion of the Apostolic Succession had become a fond thing.[131] Others treated the Fathers with disrespect. "Is our own age," asked Newman, "its character, tastes, opinions, habits, to be the only admissible or tolerated standard of what is good?".[132]

The contemporary Church could not imitate the Fathers for imitation's sake, since "some persons are apt to think that when Antiquity is talked about, that it implies an actual return to the exact forms of opinion and modes of feeling which prevailed in those earlier times as a fact; and they forthwith begin to talk about the nineteenth century, and the impossibility of our retrograding, and the folly and disadvantage of a too narrow standard, and the fallacy of thinking that whatever is ancient is, as such, an object of imitation".[133] Newman was not an antiquarian fanatic but believed that some essential points needed to be considered carefully in the present climate. The reception of such points had to be considered a natural development. The Fathers had been more mystical in their theological use of Scriptural texts. Persecuted, the Fathers had a higher moral state of mind for such mystical interpretations. Realistically speaking, it was impossible for the Church of the modern age to move back in time to that of the Fathers.[134]

If there could be no servile imitation of the past, it was still possible to think in terms of reproduction, representation, reenactment. This was an essentially theological task. It had to be historically based, otherwise it would have been no better than Greek myths. To reproduce in the present was to study vigorously the past, which would become a living reality, a valid experience. Such a system, thought Newman, might well prove superior to the age, even though it harmonised with it. Something higher was in prospect.[135]

When Newman studied the Church of the Fathers, he was not involved in contemplating mere historical documents. What he saw was the Church of the nineteenth century as it ought to be. He constantly referred to the real Church behind the existing one, "a system indeed which will take time and suffering to bring us to adopt, but still a firm foundation".[136] "What would the Fathers have done?" became Newman's increasingly urgent question of the hour.[137] Athanasius and Basil were not figures of the past only. They increasingly came to the rescue. That was essential, especially as the Archbishop of Canterbury, though a man of the highest principle and a willing martyr as well, lacked the boldness of the old Catholic Prelates. Indeed, "if he had but the little finger of Athanasius, he would do us all the good in the world".[138] Newman's research of the patristic period had confirmed his vital yearning for a real Church, at once visible where Christ could be encountered validly and publicly. His enthusiasm was most explicit when he realised that in his time a more primitive spirit was abroad.[139]

"It is the Incarnation of the Son of God rather than any doctrine drawn from a partial view of Scripture (however true and momentous it may be) which is the article of a standing or falling Church".[140] For Newman the Incarnation was the incomparable centre-point of time and eternity. That was the pivot around which the history of nations revolved. However, this event could not stand alone, isolated and remote. The centrality of Christ had to bear fruit in the Christian Church, where Christ had come so close to humanity that men could not gaze on Him or discern Him. It was in the Incarnation, wrote Newman, that Christ took possession of His purchased inheritance.[141] Yet the Church in her historical pilgrimage through the centuries had never experienced the reality of the incarnate Lord more powerfully than in the age of the Fathers. It was there that the Church was as near Christ as she could possibly be. In her collective holiness the Primitive Church "may be considered to make as near an approach to the pattern in Christ as fallen man ever will attain; being, in fact, a Revelation in some sort of that Blessed Spirit in a bodily shape".[142]

Newman's question, "In what sense does our Christianity resemble that of the Fathers?"[143] was not only that of the Church historian but also of the prophet bent on making the past and present bind together philosophically. Writers who were regardless of the constitutional relation of the past towards the present "could not be expected to recognize the philosophical bond which connects one age with another, the correspondence of certain periods in the recurring cycle of human affairs, and the instruction thence derivable for our political conduct. Accordingly, far from feeling reverence for an institution which has, in one shape or another, existed in the country for at least 1200 years, they have not allowed it to avail itself of its antiquity even as a guide, but have considered it as a mere subject for external interference and for ingenious experiment".[144] Primitive Christianity had to be restored not because Newman was a myopic reactionary, fancifully attempting the impossible, but because the Church of the Fathers was the fullest, most perfect icon of God.[145] Not only was God in Christ in the Church, wrote Newman, but also the Church was fully in Christ in God. The Church was the Universe of Christ, for it was only in the Church, born of the incarnate Son of God and Son of Man, that humanity, fallen, corrupt and mortal, could find its true destiny.

For Newman the Church had to remain on the foundation of the Apostles and hold fast the traditions of the Fathers. Only then would all strife and rivalry cease and the futile questions of the heretics be condemned, The Truth would shine again in the hearts of all. The end, wrote Newman, would be truly spiritual, so that there might be confessed in every Church, One Lord, one faith, one baptism, in Christ.[146] "If we claim to be the Church, let us act like the Church, and we shall become the Church".[147] Every Christian was bound by the necessity of going to the Apostles, and not to contemporary teachers and oracles. It was only at the feet of the Apostles, in their blessed company, that men would discover the knowledge of their duty as individuals and members of the Christian Church.[148] The effect of such constant teaching was summed up well by Tom Mozley; "All the Fathers and Church Councils were to be marshalled in Anglican costume and marched before us as we sat at our firesides".[149]

3.5.2. *The Episcopal and Prophetic Traditions and the Individual*

In 1834 Newman became involved in a discussion regarding the idea of "fundamental articles" with the Abbé Jager. There was nothing new in an Anglican attempting to justify the integrity of his position to a Roman Catholic. Laud, Stillingfleet, Hall and Jewel in their time had treated the same question at some length in earlier controversies with Roman Catholics.[150] "The main principle", Newman was at pains to point out to the Abbé, "which we of the Anglican Church maintain is this: that Scripture is the ultimate basis of proof, the place of final appeal, in respect of all fundamental doctrines".[151] By "fundamental doctrine" Newman explicitly noted that he had in mind "such doctrines as are necessary for Church Communion".[152] He was in fact referring to "the Articles of the Creed". Indeed, in a second letter to the Abbé Newman went so far as to reduce the foundational doctrine of the Church to its simplest expression in the Confession of Peter, "Thou art the Christ, the Son of the Living God".[153] The articles of the Apostles' and Nicene Creeds had developed from this basic source. Newman tried to show that these alone as the fundamentals of the faith were indeed historical. Like Hooker, Newman was able to quote Irenaeus and Tertullian to show the reasonableness of his position; "To be simple and precise in fundamentals is a socially charitable arrangement, so that all classes might profess the same faith in the same terms, the totality be easily memorable, and minds be saved from perplexity".[154] It was at this point, however, that Newman added a qualification to his position. Although the creed in which the fundamentals of Christianity consisted in simple and precise words, yet its meaning was "incomprehensible in its depth and indefinite in its extent".[155] It was nothing less but the property of faith to "wish to conceive rightly of sacred doctrine, so far as it can be conceived at all, and to look towards the Church for guidance how to conceive it".[156]

The Abbé, however, was singularly unimpressed by Newman's arguments. What kind of Church was it, he asked, to which people looked for guidance, and which for the sake of the wise and simple alike claimed to give certain guidance on matters said to be fundamental, but which could actually err on the prior question of what was fundamental?[157] But it was not the Abbé who had exposed the Achilles's heel of Newman's argument most but Hurrell Froude who had been following the debate with his usual consummate zeal. In a letter to Newman on 17 July, 1835, Froude revealed the idiosyncratic element in Newman's argument by imagining a debate between the Abbé and Newman about the rule of faith in fundamentals. Newman denied the Abbé's assertion that the Eucharist was fundamental because it could not be proved from Scripture. No doctrine was fundamental which could not be proved from Scripture. What if the Abbé could show that the Christian of the second and third centuries regarded the doctrine of the Eucharist was fundamental, was the assertion that it could not be proved from scripture enough? That would not have been enough, retorted Newman, but it could not be proved. Then, the Abbé in Froude's imaginative discourse made the point which not only revealed the weakness of Newman's own position but also that of Anglicanism; "Then you admit your reason for not thinking this Doctrine fundamental is not that it is not proved by Scripture but that it was not held such by the early Christians".[158] If it was not enough to show that a doctrine which could not be proved from Scripture was not fundamental, was it enough to show that a doctrine which could be proved from Scripture had to be fundamental? According to Froude, the Abbé could only conclude that Newman's test of fundamentality was one which, complied with, did not prove doctrines fundamental and which, not being complied with, did not prove them fundamental.[159]

Newman's response to Froude on 20 July was significant because it tentatively contained the seeds of what was to be one of his main arguments in the *Lectures on the Prophetical Office of the Church*, the distinction between the prophetic and episcopal traditions. The prophetic tradition, according to Newman, was "the system taught, interpretative, supplementary, illustrative (applicative), of the Scripture doctrine, the reception of which was the privilege of the Christian when admitted, not a condition of his admission into the Church". But there was also another Tradition, called apostolic or episcopal, which was necessary for Communion. This Tradition was strictly handed on from one person to another. It was definite, official and exact. The fundamentals of this Tradition were contained in the Apostles' Creed.[160]

In his *Lectures on the Prophetical Office of the Church* Newman attempted to point out that the episcopal tradition did indeed contain the fundamentals of the faith, as it was delineated and recognized in Scripture itself, where it was called the Hypotyposis, or "outline of sound words" and in the Fathers.[161] Yet to assert dogmatically that all the fundamentals of the faith were contained in the episcopal tradition was inadequate. There was nothing in the Creeds about Original Sin, justification by faith, election or the sacraments. Newman's definition of the prophetic tradition was nothing less than his own idiosyncratic interpretation of the fundamentals and non-fundamentals of the faith. The adaptation of his own Anglican position was forced upon him by the valid objections not only of his Roman Catholic antagonists but also of Hurrell Froude. Newman was convinced that the prophetic tradition was as apostolic as the episcopal, since it existed in the bosom of the Church itself. Indeed, it pervaded the Church like an atmosphere. It was "partly written, partly unwritten, partly the interpretation, partly the supplement of Scripture, partly preserved in intellectual expressions, partly latent in the spirit and temper of Christians; poured to and fro in closets and upon the housetops, in liturgies, in controversial works, in obscure fragments, in sermons, in popular prejudices, in local customs".[162] It was unnecessary to draw too sharp a distinction between the two traditions. In the presence of such divine mysteries, the Christian must either believe or simply acquiesce in what was handed on to him. The duty of each individual Christian was active faith, whether it was apprehension or submission, since individuals themselves could never distinguish what they spiritually perceived from what they merely accepted upon authority.[163]

Individuals fascinated Newman. That was only natural for someone who believed that living movements did not come from commitees, no great work was done by a system and systems rose out of individual exertions. Luther was an individual. There was only one Homer, Cicero and Caesar, one Constantine or Charlemagne, one Paul and John, one Athanasius, Augustine or Thomas, one Patrick, Martin and Boniface, one Anthony, Jerome and Chrysostom.[164] As misfortunes multiplied in this mortal world, so too the individual Christian perceived that there were but two beings in the whole universe, his own soul and the God who made it.[165] It is in the light of Newman's profound reverence for each individual's capability of a personal, vivid and intimate relationship with God that it is possible to understand his sermon, "Personal Influence, the Means of Propagating the Truth". Even in the face of unwilling minds, the truth has been upheld in the world "not as a system, not by books, not by argument, nor by temporal power, but by the personal influnce" of the teachers and patterns of it.[166]

Newman advocated a Church which was certain in her fundamentals, bound to the episcopal and prophetic traditions to enable the truth to become a reality in the hearts of men. He was equally concerned about the integrity of each individual personality. The difficult task at hand was to enable the individual to find his place in the episcopal and prophetic traditions of the Church. The exercise of private judgement was a matter which was of particular interest to Newman in the *Lectures on the Prophetical Office of the Church*. Without private judgement, Newman wrote, there was no responsibility. A man's own mind, and nothing else, was the cause of his believing or not believing, and of his acting or not acting upon his belief.[167] Christians should not be denied the religious use of Private Judgement. Scripture might still be read without schismatic interpretations. There might be minor differences about issues without disagreement about fundamentals. With more primitive simplicity and rational freedom, Private Judgement might give as much certainty as the doctrine of Infallibility.[168] Newman was adamant that it was every individual's prerogative to maintain and defend the Creed. Indeed, the humblest and meanest among Christians had as much stake in defending the Faith and as much right to it as any Bishop or Archbishop.[169] Newman quoted Vincent of Lerins who tacitly allowed the use of Private Judgement in lesser matters, that is, "the necessity and duty of judging on our own responsibility piously and cautiously, provided our conclusions be not pertinaciously urged, for then our Judgement is no longer private in any unexceptionable sense of the word".[170]

For Newman, the use of Private Judgement in lesser matters meant those issues which had not been determined already by "Church authority".[171] In matters of inferior moment, both the Church and the individual had room to exercise their own powers. The individual could judge for himself and the Church could give her judgement.[172] According to Newman, the Church was a witness and keeper of Catholic Tradition and so invested with authority. She was a witness to the fact that such and such a doctrine, or such a sense of Scripture, had ever been received from the Apostles. Far from undertaking to determine the sense of Scripture, the Church had no immediate power over it but alleged and submitted to that doctrine which was ancient and

Catholic. In that sense, neither individual, nor Bishop, nor Convocation, nor Council could venture to decline the Catholic interpretation of its sacred mysteries. Scripture by necessity infringed upon an individual's private judgement and demanded assent. It threatened if individuals refused it. Scripture, when illuminated by the "Catholic Religion", or the Catholic Religion when fortified by Scripture, might either of them be called "the Gospel committed to the Church, dispensed to the individual".[173] In a memorable phrase, Newman held that the real task of private judgement in fundamental matters of doctrine was to determine "what and where is the Church".[174]

For all his advocacy of Private Judgement, then, Newman was also equally keen to limit its range, making it subordinate to the Christian's duty to accept what he had been told by authority. Newman also believed that individual souls were in need of guidance. Writing in *The Arians*, Newman referred to the doctrinal office of the Church as "the most momentous and fearful that can come upon mortal man, and never to be undertaken except by the collective illumination of the Heads of the Church".[175] According to the 20th Article, the Church has "authority in controversies of faith". Newman interpreted this not as the Church enforcing truth at all costs but rather possessing a power which individuals did not have. The fact that certain doctrines were necessary to be believed for salvation and that they were minutely and precisely described meant that there was no room left for Private Judgement. Even in the very first ages of the Church, before it could grow into a well-organised and well-disciplined body, authority as a useful guide for individuals was at work. At that time "Prophets or Doctors are the interpreters of the revelation; they unfold and define its mysteries, they illuminate its documents, they harmonize its contents, they apply its promises".[176] The words of the Church Catholic in England were not the accidental out-pouring of any period in history but "the joint and accordant testimony of that innumerable company of Saints, whom we are bound to follow".[177] To follow the Prayer Book was infinitely more rewarding than following preachers, who were but individuals.[178] However gifted an individual might be, nothing was more powerful than the collective Church, where what was wanting in one member could be supplied by another. Of course, men possessed of much holiness, clearness of intellectual vision, or the immediate power of the Holy Ghost, could penetrate the inner meaning of the sacred text without any recourse to tradition, authority of doctors and theology. Yet, added Newman ironically, "it is difficult to prove that the individual has performed what the Church has never attempted".[179]

In his understanding of the relationship of the individual with the Church in her episcopal and prophetic traditions, Newman combined the use of Private Judgement which was not flagrantly Protestant with the structures of the authority of the Church which was neither Roman, infallible nor authoritarian.

In his study of Newman's understanding of the Church's relationship to society, John Coulson wrote that "a Church which does not care to be socially plausible, in a changing industrial society, soon moves to the margins".[180] For Newman the Church had to have a social soul and authority was its social bond. An individual only really came to God in Christ when he became a member of the Church of Christ. It was there that he became a social whole.[181] The social orientation of the Church was not at man's disposal to be eliminated at his will. To be in Christ was a social principle. The Church was not merely a philosophy or a book but actually set up a society.[182] The Church was the collective conscience of humanity, establishing the *koinonia* where the individual could find true fulfilment.[183]

In an age when Christians needed something definite to lean upon,[184] Christianity for Newman became dogmatic and social.[185] After all, the Fathers never gave their own views,[186] as theirs was the collective wisdom of centuries. The doctrine of the Trinity was permanently valid because it was the belief of the Catholic Church of the fourth and fifth centuries, verifiable by its collective witness over the centuries.[187] Newman was certain that it was in the dogmatic, social and prophetic structure of the Body of Christ that nineteenth century man, like man in every age, was to acquire his full status, not only as an individual, infinitely precious and unique, but also as a living member of a real, vital organism. Listening to the orthodox tradition of the Church over the first six centuries, man became more than an individual in any anonymous world. He was a spirit-filled person, identifiable as socially justified and redeemed.

3.5.3. The Church's Relationship to Society

In his sermon, "The World our Enemy", Newman explained how he conceived the Church's exact relationship to society; "The Church so far from being literally, and in fact, separate from the wicked world, is within it. The Church is a body, gathered together in the world, and in a process of separation from it ... All Christians are in the world, and of the world, so far as sin still has dominion over them ... Though then ... the Church is one thing, and the world is another, yet in present matter of fact, the Church is of the world, not separate from it".[188] Newman's position was that the Christian ought never to go out of the world, let alone abandon his duties in the world. Rather, he must redeem the time.[189] On this crucial issue, to spiritualise, to redeem the age in which Christians lived, Newman was at one with the Fathers, echoing the sentiments of one of the most beautiful writings of the second century, the *Epistle to Diognetus*.[190]

The Church's task was always to sanctify and yet to suffer with the world. The Church shared the sufferings of the world and yet lightened them.[191] The system of the Church was superior to that of the world. Although the Church was in the world, her primary purpose in every age was essentially the salvation of souls.[192] The Church's task was to redeem humanity and not reform society.[193] Newman always provided theological reasons for his position. Christian subjects had to be trained for the Kingdom, since their prerogative consisted in the possession, not of exclusive knowledge and spiritual aid, but of high and particular gifts.[194] The world had to be changed into the Kingdom of Heaven[195] as social and political reforms could not change man's essential nature.[196]

This was Newman's most significant contribution to the perennial debate on the relationship between Church and society.[197] Resisting the temptation to socialise Christianity let alone Christianise Socialism, Newman's way was that of the individual saint in the *koinonia* of the One, Holy, Catholic and Apostolic Church. The Church's task, the salvation of souls, would lead to the redemption of humanity, Newman argued, by the creation of saints. Reformers were frequently more attractive figures than saints. Inevitably, reformers tended to improve man's social conditions, expand his learning and deepen his sense of benevolence. Yet reformers could not save man's soul. That was the prerogative of the saint. Newman preached that holiness was the end of all things.[198] The saint, the holy person, was frequently hidden from society;

> Hid are the saints of God: –
> Uncertified by high angelic sign;
> Nor raiment soft, nor empire's golden rod
>   Marks them divine.
> Theirs but the unbought air, earth's parent sod
>   And the sun's smile benigh: –
> Christ rears His throne within the sacred heart,
> From the haughty world apart.[199]

In the world saints were frequently degraded. To the world they were a complete mystery since "the true light of the world offends more men than it attracts; and its divine origin is shown, not in its marked effects on the mass of mankind, but in its surprising power of elevating the moral character where it is received in spirit and in truth. Its scattered saints, in all ranks of life, speak of it to the thoughtful inquirer; but to the world at large, its remarkable continuance on the earth is its witness – its pertinacity of existence, confronting, as it has in turn, every variety of opinion, and triumphing over them all".[200] Newman's emphasis was essentially personal. Accepting God's grace, men could make their own the redemption of Christ and so redeem humanity. Yet the results wers not in men's hands but God's. The way of the saint was totally different to that of the reformer. No affectation, no pretence, no ambition, no singularity, that was the lot of the Christian. Indeed, although he was a sober, discreet, grave, moderate, mild and not unusual member of society, yet the Christian might at first sight be taken for an ordinary man.[201] The world, however, did not understand where the power of the Christian lay. The world could do nothing against such persons, against that Truth which was their birthright, that Cause which was theirs, as of all the saints in the past.[202] Christians might seem like other men but they had crowns on their heads.[203]

Consequently the world's wisdom was overthrown and the faint light of the Truth dawned continually brighter.[204] For all their otherworldliness, the effect of heroic Christian deeds was there for all to behold. The marks of their activities were indeed invisible as they were essentially men who did not make much noise in the world.[205] The sons of the Church only hid their true beauty from the world for a while[206] but their opinions made their way slowly but surely.[207] In this way the spirit of the age had to be directed.[208] Although some Christians were silent in the world's annals,[209] yet their secret was their purity of heart. Christianity was in the world to do nothing less than to raise up images of Christ; "Such is the result of Christian teaching", Newman preached, "namely, to elicit, foster, mature the seeds of heaven which lie hid in the earth, to multiply (if it may be said) images of Christ, which, though they be few, are worth all else that is among men, and are an ample recompense and 'a crown of rejoicing for Apostles and Evangelists' in the presence of our Lord Jesus Christ at His Coming".[210]

Opposed to the busy and restless Christian, Newman gives us images of the perfect character who had the potential, by God's grace, to redeem the world. Such a Christian was otherworldly, spiritual and detached yet also dynamic, radical and world-conquering. Newman attempted in his writings of 1833–1837 to substitute the saintliness of the Church of the Fathers with her beatitudes and attachment to God in Christ without distractions for the contemporary Church of worldliness, human power and social reform.

3.5.4. Newman's Social Conscience

It is precisely in the context of Newman's Apostolic Christian, the saint, that his understanding of social problems must be firmly set. "Times are changed, I grant; but without going on to the question of the obligation now of such a profession of the Gospel as I have been describing, do persuade yourselves, I entreat you, to contemplate the picture. Do not shut your eyes, do not revolt from it, do not fret under it, but look at it. Bear to look at the Christianity of the Bible; bear to contemplate the idea of a Christian, traced by inspiration, without gloss, or comment, or tradition of man. Bear to have read to you a number of texts; texts which might be multiplied sevenfold ... prevail on yourselves to realize the idea of a Scriptural Christian, and the fact that the first Christians really answered to it. Study what a Bible Christian is; be silent over it; pray for grace to comprehend it, to accept it".[211] Newman's idea of society was concerned solely with the maintenance and propagation of spiritual values. What mattered fundamentally was not to change the material condition of mankind, but to minister primarily to their spiritual needs in the local situation. As a young Curate in the parish of St Clement's in Oxford, Newman in 1824 visited every family "going from house to house, asking the names, numbers, trades " of the parishioners and to help raise the £6,000 required to build a new church in the parish.[212] In July 1832 his concern about the outbreak of cholera in the St Ebbes, St Aldate's, the Jail region of Oxford and the failure of some obstinate parishioners actually to destroy the bad furniture of a cholera victim illustrates the personal charitable approach of the devoted Cure of Souls.[213]

A concern for the spiritual welfare of individuals, however, never blinded Newman to what he regarded as some of the social evils of the 1830's. Centralization was the new creed of active legislators. Newman's views about this new trend were expressed clearly in a letter to Hugh James Rose in October 1834. State control was raising its ugly head, he wrote, and, in the name of efficiency, was substituting for the parochial unit where the poor, the young and the sacred fabric itself were in the care of the clergyman, a centralized bureaucracy with its own magistrates and police officers. It would only be a matter of time before the clergy themselves were organised along such secular principles.[214]

Newman was also well aware that evil in society was not the exclusive work of those whom he branded as "Socialists, Red Republicans, Anarchists and Rebels".[215] As editor of the *British Critic* in 1839 Newman criticised two of the Chartist leaders for inciting violence but, as befitted a writer who was once asked to be a leader writer for *The Times*,[216] Newman's balanced judgement of the events of the day demanded that he was even more critical of the Whigs and the millowners for directing economic discontents into political channels. The violence of the masses always abhorred Newman but the calculating political selfishness of the new industrial order was equally horrific. Newman's discernment of the signs of the times saw social threats to the Church not only from the violent masses but also from the unscrupulous, nascent capitalist classes.[217]

Far from being apathetic, ensconced firmly in his ivory tower existence, Newman did care about the social problems of his day. It was merely that his perspective was always eternal; "after restlessness comes rest, peace, joy – our eternal portion, if we be worthy – the sight of the blessed three, the holy one; the three that bear witness in heaven; in light unapproachable".[218] This might appear a selfish approach today, a charge which Newman himself was aware of; "They that are can heal others; but in my case it was, 'Physician, heal thyself'. My own soul was my first concern, and it seemed an absurdity to my reason to be converted in partnership. I wished to go to the Lord by myself, and in my own way, or rather his way".[219]

The Christian had to put off hopes of earthly good. Indeed, he must even be sick of "flattery and the world's praise, see the emptiness of temporal greatness, and be watchful against self-indulgence; these are but the beginnings of religion; these are but the preparation of heart, which religious earnestness implies".[220] This theme was pursued with the utmost moral severity; "The Catholic Church holds it better for the sun and moon to drop from heaven, for the earth to fail, and for all the many millions on it to die of starvation in extremest agony, as far as temporal affliction goes, than that one soul, I will not say should be lost, but should commit one single venial sin, should tell one wilful untruth, or should steal one poor farthing without excuse".[221]

Newman's standpoint was that the Faith, once delivered to the saints, ever to remain in the world, the treasure and life of the Church was "the engrafted word, which is able to save our souls".[222] This was Newman's mission in life and everything else was seen in its eternal shadow. A visible Church existed in the world for one primary purpose only, "that souls will be saved".[223] The essential purpose of all work was the salvation of souls.[224] To be saved Christians must have tender hearts till they became their gardens.[225]

All the social reforms ever devised could not secure man's permanent, eternal happiness. Only a complete change of heart could effect the supreme destiny for which man had been redeemed. Good works alone were essentially Pelagian.[226] For Newman it was more effective to be a soldier in Christ's army than perform social reforms.[227]

3.5.5. The Church of the People

Newman's understanding of the Church as a popular power in the 1830's must be placed in its proper theological context. Of course, Newman stressed the importance of the poor, since Christ's Kingdom belonged to them.[228] In a famous passage in the *University Sermons*, Newman reminded his congregation, "If children, if the poor, if the busy, can have true Faith, yet cannot weigh evidence, evidence is not the simple foundation on which Faith is built".[229] In the Early Church such was the faith of the uneducated man that society could be transcended. Such faith was not less philosophically correct, nor less acceptable to God for the simple reason that "it does not happen to be conceived in those precise statements which presuppose the action of the mind on its own sentiments and notions".[230]

Knowledge and the training that books gave lacked the power to unloose one sinner from the bonds of Satan while there were others who thought that the poor were irreligious because they had no education, as if much knowledge was a necessary step for right practice.[231] Newman believed that an unlettered peasant could stand for the whole truth[232] while the widow and the fatherless were the strength of the Church.[233] There was nothing to hinder the poorest man from living the life on an Angel, "in all the unearthly contemplative blessedness of a Saint in glory, except so far as sin interferes with it. I mean, it is sin", claimed Newman, "and not poverty which is the hindrance".[234]

Newman's writings and correspondence between 1833 and 1836 also reflect his general desire to make the Church of England more popular. Writing to Golightly in August 1833, after mentioning the Apostolical Succession and the exclusive privilege of Bishops and Priests to consecrate the Bread and Wine, Newman stated that "the Church must become more popular than it is".[235] In a letter to Rose on 10 April, 1836, Newman wished "to encourage Churchmen to look boldly at the possibility of the Churches being made to dwell in the affections of the people at large. At present it is too much a Church for the Aristocracy, and the poor through the Aristocracy".[236] The Church had to come to the people, who were the fulcrum of her power. The Church had to rest not on the great but the multitude.[237] Newman was certain that the Church could be popular without being subservient to them. When Ambrose was threatened with the spoliation of the Church, he argued for resistance in terms which were easily understandable to the people. Although the people reacted angrily, with inevitable violence and tumult, Newman still believed that the multitude of men, always zealous, should be so for religious reasons rather than flow and ebb under the irrational influences of the world.[238] The Church was never more powerful than during this period of her history. The Church of Ambrose and Athanasius always influenced not the few but the many.[239]

Yet Newman's enthusiasm for the Church as a popular power must be treated with circumspection. He certainly had no concept of the laity having any voice in the formulation of Christian doctrine. The laity did, of course, attend the synods of the Early Church but their power was severely restricted.[240] At Nicaea, the laity attended[241] and Communion was not denied them, provided they had formulated no doctrinal novelties of their own.[242] There is no indication in any of Newman's writings during the 1830's that the laity actually had an active voice in the formulation of Christian doctrine. It was the clergy, and others in station, who had to be questioned as to their doctrinal views, but for the mass of the laity "it is enough if they do not set up counterstatements of their own, as imply that they have systematized, and that erroneously".[243] Indeed, Newman was suspicious of lay power in the actual formulation of Creeds and doctrines. He warned his readers explicitly, "When was it you ever heard ... that in a question of faith laymen should be judges of a bishop? What! have courtly manners so bent our backs that we have forgotten the rights of the priesthood that I should of myself put into another's hands what God has bestowed upon me? Once grant that a layman may set a bishop right and see what will follow".[244]

Newman's position concerning the Church as a popular power was that the laity had no actual voice in the formulation of Christian doctrine. Their reaction, however, was considered crucial, as to whether a doctrine was actually orthodox or not. No heresy had caused greater consternation in the Early Church than Arianism. It was "by the faithful people," wrote Newman, "under the lead of Athanasius and the Egyptian bishops, and in some places supported by their Bishops or priests, that the worst of heresies was withstood and stamped out of the sacred territory".[245]

The reaction of the laity to Christian doctrines was consistent with Newman's prevalent emphasis upon actual Creeds being formulated by a small élite of theologians. Newman was well aware of the dangers of an uneducated laity, especially if the Scriptures were rashly taken from the Church's custody and committed to public opinion, men who had not cultivated the internal moral sense. It was for this reason that Newman advocated the idea of an endowed class for the cultivation of learning and for diffusing its results among the community. The masses needed to be educated according to the principles of true Catholicity, since "the few can never mean the many; and to be called without being chosen cannot but be a misery ... Let us then set at nought the judgement of the many, whether about truth and falsehood, or about ourselves, and let us go by the judgement of that line of Saints, from the Apostles' times downwards, who were ever spoken against in their generation, ever honoured afterwards ... ever protesting against the many, ever agreeing with each other".[246] Newman has been aptly compared with Origen who likewise appealed to the People of God, especially the poor and illiterate, in general principles of Christian salvation but who was also a fierce advocate of the idea that the actual formulation of Christian doctrine was the preserve of the few entrusted to do so.[247]

For all his admiration of the role of the faithful in the history of the Church, especially during the Arian crisis of the fourth century, Newman was always sceptical about the masses in general. "How careless the many are!" was his reaction to seeing outbursts of religious enthusiasm with the crowds kissing the foot of a poor representation of the statue of St Peter.[248] It was Newman's constant fear that so many Christians were wandering through life like sheep without a shepherd. They were busy themselves in human schemes, following strange guides, taken captive by new opinions, becoming the sport of chance. They were full of anxiety, perplexity, jealousy and alarm. All this was because the multitudes did not seek the one body and the one spirit and the one hope of their calling.[249] The uneducated masses of society, tossed to and fro by every blast of theological or political jargon, were a fearsome sight.

The masses had not heeded the basic lesson that rebellion was always contrary to God's will. Despite his profound influence upon the Oxford Movement, Lamennais's greatest weakness was that he had not realised that rebellion was always a sin. Like Jeroboam, he could not bear to wait God's time. Worst of all, his views meant conflict, speaking more like a politician than a man of God. Conflict could never be God's will. Lamennais was certainly not a prophet or guardian of the truth, as he belonged to a party which talked loudly and strangely.[250]

Newman had no illusions concerning the role of the Church of England if democracy were let loose upon the people. The Church was the providential instrument for re-adjusting society and must check the rabble of the towns. If people were not entirely vigilant, wrote Newman, democracy might get in between two venerable institutions, the Church and the King.[251] There was, however, one guarantee of safety, which was the episcopal form, ever repressive as it was of democratic tendencies and in the hands of a loyal Church.[252] Newman asked his readers whether England really wished to be democratic. France in 1833 was such an appalling phenomenon that Newman dared not think of her.[253] The reason was obvious. Liberty and equality were adored as divinities and democracy was a monster.[254]

Newman's views during the period 1833–1837 about the Church as a popular power were consistent. Athanasius or Ambrose would have expressed exactly the same sentiments. The faithful People of God had a crucial, if passive, role to play in the formulation of Christian Creeds and doctrines, as their reaction was a vital test as to whether the statements of theologians were orthodox or not. But Newman wished to argue in his writings of the 1830's that the actual formulation of Christian doctrine was the exclusive responsibility of the few. Only with such an arrangement could sound Catholic Order be maintained, which was always the best witness to unity and decency. The order of the Church, where the voice of the laity was constantly heeded, was the soundest antidote to the leaderless masses, tossed to and fro by the latest theological and political jargon. Little wonder that Newman saw democracy as Anti-Christ.[255] Reminisicing later in life, Newman was able to write; "I have no wish for reforms and should be sorry to create in the minds of your readers any sentiment favourable either to democracy or absolutism. I have no liking for the tyranny whether of autocrat or mob; no taste for being whirled off to Siberia, or tarred and feathered in the Far West, by the enemies of my religion. May I live and die under the mild sway of a polity which certainly represses ... the blind fanaticism of a certain portion of my countrymen".[256]

3.6. "THE TAMWORTH READING ROOM" (1841)

3.6.1. Peelite Conservatism

The Tractarians never forgave Sir Robert Peel for his support of Roman Catholic Emancipation in 1829. To the majority of Churchmen, however, the return to office of Peel and the Conservatives in 1841 was reassuring. The *British Critic* refused to believe that Peel would bring any benefits to the Church, since from beginning to end the career of the Prime Minister had been one of shifts and expedients. Above all else, Peel had been unfaithful to the everlasting Catholic Church.[257] Peel was particularly proud of his boast that Conservative principles meant that "there would always be in this country an established religion, fostered and encouraged by the state; and that established religion shall maintain the doctrines of the Protestant Reformed faith".[258]

During the whole of his Anglican ministry, Newman was convinced that the Conservative Party always took care of Number One.[259] The average Conservative was always at the top of the tree and never meant to come down. He supported the Establishment, not because it was for the good of society but that he did rather well as a result of it. A religion had to be defended not for its own sake but for its externals.[260] Newman was also aware that the Conservative Party had been influenced by the Benthamite spirit. To the end of his life, Bentham addressed politicians as if they wre his favourite pupils.[261] Although Peel was ostensibly no Benthamite, yet he passed a mass of Benthamite legislation.[262] It was the philosophy of Utilitarianism which provided the sanction for what Newman considered to be complacent selfishness in an age of progress. Most men, though unaware, were full of the Benthamite spirit.

Although Peel was a better man in Newman's opinion that Bentham,[263] yet Peel's legislation, his attitude towards man's place in society, his views on knowledge and benevolence, religion and the Church reflected much of the prevailing Benthamite spirit. The younger Tractarians looked forward to the demise of this kind of Conservatism.[264] Newman's writings in *The Times*, which became known as "The Tamworth Reading Room", encapsulate most fully his critique of the Conservative Party. Not only were his articles unpopular with Peel and his friends,[265] but they also represent a penetrating analysis of the values advocated by the then Prime Minister for modern man.[266]

3.6.2. Faith and Reason

Newman's letters to *The Times* in 1841 were occasioned by an address which Peel had delivered on the occasion of the establishment of a public reading room at Tamworth. In these letters, Newman attacked the whole Liberal theory of Education which had been popularised by its chief apostle and Peel's Home Secretary, Lord Brougham. To understand the nature of Newman's attack, it is necessary to bear in mind Newman's sermon, preached on the Feast of the Epiphany, 1839, on "Faith and Reason, Contrasted as Habits of Mind".[267] Newman wished to distinguish between two kinds of proof, that which did all the work of convincing by itself and the other which could convince only if it was completed and interpreted by something in the individual, namely the correct antecedent knowledge and moral disposition. It was the former which was so frequently the exclusive right of Reason, that habit of deciding about religious questions with the off-hand random judgements which were suggested by secular principles. Inevitably, this meant the faculty of Reason exercising itself by *a posteriori* or evidential methods.[268] It was precisely this approach which reduced the intellect, itself capable of so much achievement, to mere ratiocination, divorced from insights into moral truth and the perfection of the spiritual part of their nature. Newman wished to argue that the deepest level of the intellect transcended ratiocination and had an intuitive grasp of what it understood.[269]

To Newman faith was "the reasoning of a divinely enlightened mind", an act of the whole man, and not merely of his reasoning powers. It was "a simple lifting of the mind to the Unseen God, without conscious reasoning or formal argument. ... Those who believe in Christ, believe because they know Him to be the Good Shepherd; and they know Him by His voice; and they know His voice because they are His sheep ... The divinely enlightened mind sees in Christ the very Object whom it desires to love and worship".[270] Faith was a grace, a gift, higher than reason. It was not based on evidence, which only came in later to protect it. "A judge does not make men honest", wrote Newman, "but acquits and vindicates them: in like manner, Reason need not be the origin of Faith, as Faith exists in the very persons believing, though it does test and verify it". Further, "if the children, if the poor, if the busy can have true Faith, yet cannot weigh evidence, evidence is not the simple foundation on which Faith is built".[271]

What, then, prevented faith from being mere superstition?[272] Newman replied, "a right state of heart". Right faith was the faith of a mind whose disposition, whose conscience was right. "Does a child", asked Newman, "trust his parents because he has proved to himself they are such, and that they are able and desirous to do him good or from the instinct of affection?"[273] Faith is the acceptance of truths as a duty, under a sense of personal responsibility. This acceptance, claimed Newman, was mainly swayed by antecedent considerations, especially that of the likelihood of a Revelation. Thus, Faith was in accordance with Reason to the extent that, "taken together with the antecedent probability that Revelation will reveal Himself to mankind, such evidence of the fact, as is otherwise deficient, may be enough for conviction, even in the judgement of reason". Then, too, men might and did have implicit reasons for their faith, which they were incapable of developing.[274]

3.6.3. The Man of Business and the Religious Man

It was the vision of man, his place in society and his eternal destiny, which was at the heart of Newman's articles in *The Times*. Although Peel had a better style and loftier tone than Bentham who lacked poetry,[275] yet he resembled the political philosopher in his insatiable desire to create the New Model Man, taking his place amongst his fellows and commanding their respect. In the courts of the ungodly, the new scientific power was praised without ceasing. The concern of the age, however, only reflected what was intrinsic in all that Bentham ever wrote, that every age must be measured by its knowledge of facts[276] and that the business part of man was his greatest concern.[277] Newman realised the temptation of this kind of language, as it was "education, periodical literature, railroad travelling, ventilation, drainage, and the arts of life, when fully carried out," which served to make a population happy and moral.[278] Such knowledge was incomparably intoxicating,[279] serving its ends even on man's death-bed.[280]

Newman's vision of man was axiomatically opposed to the Utilitarianism of the modern Conservative Party. His advocacy of essential Christian principles was anathema to the contemporary spirit. Newman was convinced that even superstition was better than illumination, especially if it led to greater faith.[281] The affections and the will had to be trained.[282] Basic facts were insufficient, especially as the whole idea of a theology of grace attacked the basic assumption that such knowledge led to moral improvement.[283] Opposed to the idea that morality could actually be converted into a science, based upon facts and applicable only to real things which had definite relations and a common measure,[284] Newman argued that the intellectual was always subordinate to the religious affections.[285] The essence of religion was "the submission of the reason and heart to a positive system, the acquiescence in doctrines which cannot be proved or explained".[286] All of which meant that it was better in perplexity to be silent and believe, than to disbelieve on account of perplexity.[287]

Wisdom was all very well, wrote Newman, but many became wiser without necessarily becoming better. "Is a man better by knowing more?" asked Newman mischievously.[288] What was crucial in the debate was the method of achieving goodness. Citizens of the Kingdom were more useful than those who belonged to Stoic Republics.[289] It was a shallow philosophy which based ethical systems on a few intellectual truths. The educated conscience by an implicit act of reasoning could detect moral truth wherever it was hidden.[290] This was vital since Newman did not want to be converted by a smart syllogism. It was vain to overcome men's reasons without also touching their hearts.[291]

According to Newman, the Knowledge school was worldly and mortal. It lacked the transcendental dimension, for it had no metaphysical attributes. It was incapable of raising man above himself, since it left him in his original state of sin. It was unable to transform men into their eternal destiny of communion with the saints.[292] Benthamite philosophy was concerned only with expedients. Pills after dinner were the remedy for a broken heart.[293] The cardinal sin of the age was to bring human chaos into the divine order of things. If poetry were to be the essence of all things, then people would become frivolous and sentimental. If argument, then there would be unamiable longheadedness. If science, then scepticism would ensue. There was only one infallible method for the Christian life, that was to put Faith first and Knowledge second.[294] Far from being anti-intellectual, Newman proposed a method which truly appealed to the heart and mind, but to the heart first, for the beauty of virtue itself could not move the heart, while it remained an abstraction.[295] Only when virtue was "seen and heard" could it become personal and so influence the human personality.

3.6.4. The Dessication of Modern Man

What Newman encountered in Benthamite philosophy was an attempt to turn man into a person of calculus only. Newman asked, "What is a mystery in doctrine, but a difficulty in explaining it? Why should Revelation address itself to the intellect, except so far as intellect is necessary for conveying and fixing its truths on the heart? Why are we not content to take and use what is given us, without asking questions?"[296] Such a question was sheer nonsense for the man full not of the Holy but Benthamite spirit. All that mattered, claimed Newman, was facts which made an instant appeal to the intellect. Man was only as good as the facts he could master.

It was Newman's conviction that intellectual knowledge by itself was inimical to true religion. Intellectualism was capable of producing a philosophy of life in place of Revelation. Of course, in the human body the brain was vital but what of the heart and lungs?[297] Christianity had never emphasised the kind of man at the cost of minimising his other faculties.[298] The glory of Christianity was that it alone could change the whole man. Knowledge could not heal a wounded heart, let alone raise the dead.[299] Newman was always trying to join together what man had put assunder.[300] By drawing many things into one, the human personality became an indivisible whole. As Newman's concern was with the whole Church, so too in social matters his interest was in the whole man. Every human action had a moral, spiritual and emotional concern. It was only the moral aspect which interested the Benthamites, claimed Newman.

In his Baptism man was originally made whole.[301] This meant that each man would employ all his faculties, albeit unconsciously. In the act of pure living, the heart, the passions, the senses, the emotions as well as the mind were involved. Onesidedness was not only mistaken, it was also sinful. As Bentham had attempted to turn wholes into parts, abstractions into things,[302] Newman's concern was to gather all things into one, in the totality of the Holy, Catholic and Apostolic Church and in the unique individuality of each human personality.

3.6.5. One-dimensional Man

"Can I believe as if I saw?"[303] Such a question, of passing interest only to Peel, was anathema to Bentham. One only sees what one sees, an observation which Bentham never tired of expounding. For contemporary man, claimed the Utilitarians, motives were reduced to scientific knowledge, history only showed how men blundered in the pre-scientific period and the heroic was silly, leading to sentimentalism and emotionalism.[304] Newman seized upon this attitude in a ferocious battle of words; "Is not this the error, the common and fatal error, of the world, to think itself a judge of Religious Truth without preparation of heart? ... the powers of the intellect, acuteness, sagacity, subtlety, and depth, are thought the guides into Truth".[305] One of the saddest features of the day was that men had succumbed to the temptation of regarding the pursuit of truth only as a syllogistic process.[306] A new phenomenon had appeared on the scene. Note him carefully, warned Newman, since his mistress was logic which made but a sorry rhetoric with the multitudes.[307] Theology had become the School of Evidences and theologians mere textuaries.[308]

To have true belief, Newman claimed that appropriate feelings had first to be cultivated. Peel was no romantic since he had no imagination.[309] He was an example of the worldly, mechanical and stereotyped man. For Newman, imagination was of the essence. "How can a man believe, give his assent to anything without this fundamental faculty? Every faculty has its place, especially the imagination, a wonderful means of apprehending the truth".[310] After all, claimed Newman, it was not religious preaching, let alone administrative powers, which converted the first Christians. It was rather the power of actually seeing the image of Christ in their midst. It was precisely there that Revelation met Christians with simple and distinct facts and actions, not painful inductions from existing phenomena, generalised laws, let alone metaphysical conjectures, but Jesus and the Resurrection.[311]

Man had to have one quality or attribute, however, before all his faculties, including the imagination, came into being. He had to have feeling. For Newman feeling and contemplating were on a more refined plane than that of reasoning.[312] Man could imagine only because he was prepared to do so. One could not imagine anything if one was prepared only to reason. That was why seeing, feeling and contemplating were of the essence of the imagination. Newman expressed these sentiments succinctly; "Strictly speaking, it is not imagination that causes action; but hope and fear, likes and dislikes, appetite, passion, affection, the stirrings of selfishness and self-love. What imagination does for us is to find a means of stimulating those motive powers; and it does so by providing a supply of objects strong enough to stimulate them". Actions were always the result of much imaginative power in that the object of the imagination acts upon man's affections.[313]

What Newman wrote about in "The Tamworth Reading Room" encapsulated the nature of his protest against a society inebriated with the attractions of the Utilitarian spirit. Yet in spite of this philosophy, claimed Newman, men still had hearts. That is why the emphasis had to be on a hearty, congenial belief.[314] Rather than defacing the Faith with arbitrary philosophy, it was more important to safeguard it with a right state of the heart. After all, it was holiness above all else which gave faith eyes.[315] It was pointless to cultivate the intellect without disciplining the heart,[316] which was reached not through Reason but the imagination.[317] In his protest Newman showed that he was very much a man of his age in that he understood the ideas and ideals of his contemporaries without sharing their aims but rather exposing and condemning them for their inadequacies and aberrations. As Newman said at the end of his sermon, "Unreal Words"; "It is not an easy thing to learn that new language which Christ has brought us. He has interpreted all things for us in a new way; he has brought us a religion which sheds a new light on all that happens ... God is great, man is weak; he stands between heaven and hell; Christ is his Saviour; Christ has suffered for him. The Holy Ghost sanctifies him; repentance purifies him, faith justifies, works save. These are solemn truths, which need not be actually spoken, except in the way of creed or teaching; but which must be laid up in the heart. That a thing is true, is no reason that it should be said, but that it should be done; that it should be acted upon; that it should be made our own inwardly".[317]

3.7. CHANGE, DEVELOPMENT AND PROGRESS, 1841–1845

Newman's opposition to political Liberalism was obvious throughout the 1830's. In 1831 he wrote that most people one met were Liberals, and in saying that, he believed, one was saying almost as bad of them as could be said of anyone.[318] His opposition to the 1832 Reform Bill was based upon the firm conviction that Whigs were vermin. Yet theological Liberalism was an even more insidious phenomenon. It was nothing less than "false liberty of thought, or the exercise of thought upon matters, in which from the constitution of the human mind, thought cannot be brought to any successful issue, and therefore is out of place ... Liberalism then is the mistake of subjecting to human judgement those revealed doctrines which are in their nature beyond and independent of it, and of claiming to determine on intrinsic grounds the truth and value of propositions which rest for their reception simply on the external authority of the Divine Word".[319]

Typical of this Liberal spirit was Henry Hart Milman, one of the most distinguished historians of his age.[320] In his *History of the Jews* of 1829, Milman caused much offence by minimizing the supernatural element in the Old Testament miracles. In telling how the bitter waters of Marah were made sweet by the branch of a tree, Milman added the comment, "whether from the natural virtue of the plant seems uncertain".[321] In general, Milman emphasised the natural means by which a miracle was accomplished rather than the Supernatural Agent by whom these means were employed. On 31 August, 1829 Newman wrote to Pusey about Milman's interpretation of the Old Testament; "I suppose M. has aimed at 2 things – to exhibit the internal evidence of the truth of the history viewed as a human (compo)sition and to give a philosophical view of the second causes etc. which were concerned in the Jewish system; – and to pre-occupy a subject which certain other persons might treat in a worse spirit. To judge by the work itself, I should have said it was written by a Socinian who either thought the whole Mosaic system merely providential or almost entirely so – or conceived the record to be the human and traditionary account of a miraculous history, and therefore full of exaggeration ... Perhaps M. intends his human accounting for things as ironical, forcing the mind to a supernatural cause; if so, in this conceited and flippant and shallow age his attempt is very unfortunate – the philosophy of the day will swallow a camel".[322] On 28 October, 1830 Newman wrote to S. L. Pope along similar lines; "It seems to me that the great evil of M's work lies, not in the *matter of the history*, but in the prophane *spirit* in which it is written. In *most* of his positions I agree with him but abhor the irreverent scoffing Gibbon-like tone of the composition".[323] According to Newman, *The History of the Jews* was written in a supercilious liberalistic spirit which liked to be philosophical and above the world.

When Milman wrote his *History of Christianity* in 1840, Newman reviewed it in the *British Critic*.[324] It was not the historical method employed by Milman but the spirit in which the historical research had been carried out which was rejected by Newman.[325] Newman's charge against Milman was that, by attempting to view Christianity "as a secular fact, to the exclusion of all theological truth",[326] he had adopted a perilously reductionist viewpoint. Milman's book was dangerous because viewing Christianity as an external political fact, he had gone very far indeed towards viewing it as nothing more.[327] Newman did not wish to deny that the history of the Church could be seen as a "fact in the world's history". What was important to stress was the great truth, "what is historically human can be doctrinally divine".[328] A true historian, as Newman considered himself to be[329] had to take account not only of the outside but also the inside of the events in question. Christianity was infinitely more than researching for pure facts. Newman considered the Liberal attitude towards history as hypocritical, since its adherence to a kind of neutrality was impossible. The facts of Christianity are inextricably bound to the principles which are their life, wrote Newman. Milman inevitably made a theory of the facts which he recorded.[331] The end result was catastrophic. Milman's view of Christianity was no better than anatomists who treated man according to their science and became materialists, physical experimentalists teaching pantheism or atheism, political economists making wealth the measure of all things and denying the social uses of religion or the professors of any science denying the existence of any world of thought but their own.[332] The history of the Church was viewed on the side of the world.[333] It was the sign of an acute and practised intellect to pare down as closely as possible the supernatural facts of Christianity, the multiplying bread, the raising Lazarus, or the Resurrection.[334]

Ironically, Newman's own reading of Church History was arbitrary to the Liberal Anglicans who considered his whole theological understanding of the relationship between history and theology totally unhistorical.[335] In reality, Newman's opposition to the Liberal spirit was based upon his conviction that it was the essential task of the Church to correct, censure and destroy all those anti-Christian forces at work in the world. The Liberal Anglicans, on the other hand, felt that what Newman declared to be anti-dogmatic principles were the essence of religion.

It was not only the spirit of Milman's historical method, however, which Newman considered deficient. Those of a Liberal theological disposition loved to pick and choose their doctrines, retaining some as relevant, while rejecting the rest. He instanced those who concentrated exclusively on the one truth that God is love. "In consequence", Newman claimed, "they are led on to deny, first, the doctrine of eternal punishment, as being inconsistent with this notion of Infinite Love; next, resolving such expressions as the 'wrath of God' into a figure of speech, they deny the Atonement, viewed as a real conciliation of an offended God to His creatures".[336]

In the eighth of his *University Sermons*, Newman severely criticised the Liberal denial of a man's individual responsibility for evil; "This is the theory; and hence it is argued that it is our wisdom to submit to a power which is greater than ourselves, and which can neither be circumvented nor persuaded; as if the Christian dare take any guide of conscience except the role of duty, or might prefer expediency (if it be such) to principle. Nothing, for instance, is more common than to hear men speak of the growing intelligence of the present age, and to insist upon the Church's supplying its wants; the previous question being entirely left out of view, whether those wants are healthy and legitimate, or unreasonable, – whether real or imaginary, – whether they ought to be repressed or gratified ... But, surely, our first duty is, not to resolve on satisfying a demand at any price, but to determine whether it be innocent. If so, well, but if not, let what will happen".[337]

Of all the eighteen propositions of Liberalism which Newman listed in the *Apologia*, none was more invidious than the seventh: "Christianity is necessarily modified by the growth of civilization, and the exigencies of times".[338] In 1829, Milman had spelt out the implications of this "accommodation" principle in his *History of the Jews*. The Divine Spirit in manifesting itself through the Jewish people necessarily accommodated itself to their particular stage of development. It showed itself as barbarous when they were barbarous, as ignorant when they were ignorant, and had to wait upon their refinement to become the civilized religion of later times. In his *History of Christianity* Milman endeavoured "to trace all the *modifications* of Christianity, by which it accommodated itself to the spirit of successive ages; and by this apparently almost skilful, but in fact necessary, condescension to the predominant state of moral culture, of which itself formed a constituent element, maintained its uninterrupted dominion. It is the author's object, *the difficulty of which he himself fully appreciates*, to portray the genius of the Christianity of each successive age, in connexion with that of the age itself; *entirely to discard all polemic views*; to mark the origin and progress of all the subordinate diversities of belief; their origin in the circumstances of the place and time at which they appeared; their progress from their adaptation to the prevailing state of opinion or sentiment: rather than to confute error or to establish truth; in short, to exhibit the reciprocal influence of civilization on Christianity, of Christianity on civilization".[339] In short,

Christianity must advance with the advancement of human nature and intellectual culture is that advancement. Newman claimed that Revelation for the Liberals meant a single, entire, solitary act, or nearly so, introducing a certain message. Christianity was simply some one tenet or certain principles given out at one time in their fulness, without gradual accretion before Christ's coming or elucidation afterwards.[340]

Milman's Liberal understanding of the Annunciation spelt the end of supernatural happenings. The followers of Hume and Bentham found that the incidents surrounding the Angel Gabriel being sent from God to a Virgin were irreconcilable with men's actual experience. Supernatural events did not accord with the more subtle and fastidious intelligence of the present times. It was impossible, claimed Milman, for an inquiring and reasoning age to receive such supernatural facts as historical verities. For Newman, the Liberals were denying that what was historically human could also be doctrinally divine. They confused the outward process with the secret providence and argued as if instruments in nature precluded the operation of grace. "When they once arrive", wrote Newman, "at a cause or source in the secular course of things, it is enough; and thus, while Angels melt into impressions, Catholic truths are resolved into the dogmas of Plato or Zoroaster".[341] The Liberals wished to cast off all that they found in Pharisee or heathen. For Newman, the Church, like Aaron's rod, devoured the serpents of the magicians.[342]

The logic of Milman's accommodation principle implied that Christianity was not a religion but a past event which exerted a great influence on the course of the world. It simply gave a tone and direction to religion, government, philosophy, literature and manners. Like the discovery of printing or the steam-engine, it was a great boon to the world. It was only in its effects that it was capable of any continuity, like the shock of an earthquake or the impulsive force which commenced the motions of the planets.[343]

In his review of Milman's work, Newman proposed his own theory about the way the Church had made her pilgrimage among the schools of the world. Beginning in Chaldea, she encountered Canaanites and Egyptians and then went to Egypt, till she rested in her own land. She encountered the merchants of Tyre, the wisdom of the East and the luxury of Sheba. Carried away to Babylon, she then wandered to the schools of Greece.

Wherever she went, claimed Newman, she was always the mind and voice of the Most High, "'Sitting in the midst of the doctors, both hearing them and asking them questions'; claiming to herself what they said rightly, correcting their errors, supplying their defects, completing their beginnings, expanding their surmises, and thus gradually be means of them enlarging the range and refining the sense of her own teaching".[344]

It was in the *Essay on Development* of 1845 that Newman propounded fully his whole theory about change and development. Although he did doubtlessly write it to satisfy his own mind,[345] yet the whole tenor of the work was, albeit unconsciously, a riposte to the whole Liberal understanding of the accommodation principle. Its essential thesis was that religious development was according to the same sort of cultural and historical influences which defined the process of change in all things. Revealed truth was transmitted through human agency in the historical Church. The intellectual patterns and real events of each successive age, however mysterious the pattern, moulded and transformed men's perceptions of the original deposit of faith. The difficulty is to ascertain exactly what Newman meant by change. There is no doubt that Newman was always highly suspicious of any unnecessary political or social change. Writing in January 1840 on "The Catholicity of the Anglican Church", he had referred to the Roman Church "pandering to the spirit of rebellion, the lust of change, the unthankfulness of the irreligious, and the enviousness of the needy. We see its grave theologians connecting their names with men who are convicted by the common sense of mankind of something very like perjury, and its leaders in alliance with a political party notorious in the *orbis terrarum* as a sort of standard in every place for liberalism and infidelity".[346] The only change of which Newman approved was spiritual. "Holiness rather than peace", "Growth the only evidence of life" was one of the master themes of Newman's philosophy of mind.[347] Newman was convinced that growth in holiness was a necessary condition of growth in the knowledge of God.[348]

Newman claimed that doctrinal truths could never be learned in a hurry. Rather, they were for the sober and the watchful, attainable only by slow degrees, with dependence on the Giver of Wisdom and with strict obedience to the light which has already been granted.[349] If this was the case, even in greatest turmoil, the Church would always rise again and all things would once more be in their place, since "doctrine is where it was, and usage, and precedence, and principle, and policy; there may be changes, but they are consolidations or adaptations; all is unequivocal and determinate, with an identity with which there is no disputing".[350] In the course of human history an idea might change but only in order "to remain the same".[351] That is why Newman wished to see the correspondence between development, doctrine and principle. A development, as such, if it was faithful, must retain both the doctrine and the principle with which is started. A Church might have doctrine but if its principle had not developed accordingly, it would either be lifeless like the Greek Church or a sham like an Established Church.[352]

For the Liberal Anglican historians like Milman, to regard the history of Christian belief and practice as a process of development implied necessarily a progressivist view of Church history. The latter stages were bound to be a profound improvement upon the earlier. "One religion, and that *one* because it is the truth", said Milman "and that religion in its original purity, as taught in the New Testament, will co-exist and be co-extensive with the progress of knowledge".[353] Any sentiment which seemed to express that the contemporary Church was more perfect than the Church during the preceding centuries was anathema to Newman. He simply did not believe in progress.[354] Doctrinal or personal change, as such, was good, especially if it was gradual. Societies, like ideas, did change over the centuries. Development ensued but Newman's understanding of it was totally different from the Liberal Anglican idea of progress. An innovation might epitomise progress but that was utterly dissimilar to sound development. Changes could be made but firmer footing was required than mere abstract fitness, alleged scripturalness or adoption by the ancients. If this was the only foundation, then such changes could be called innovations Changes which sprang from existing institutions, however, could be called developments. These could be recommended unreservedly. That was precisely what Our Lord did, claimed Newman; instead of substituting Christianity for Judaism by a violent revolution, Judaism was allowed to develop graciously into Christianity.[355]

The Church of God, like Christianity, had developed dramatically over the centuries. Such developments were proved to have been in the contemplation of the Divine Author.[356] Unless there was complementarity in the growth of holiness, however, it was exceedingly doubtful whether the contemporary Church was in any sense "better" than its earlier counterparts.[357] Indeed, Newman remained adamant that the Church of the Fathers possessed a degree of sanctity never again attained in its subsequent history.[358]

To the Liberal Anglicans, Newman's whole theory of development was unhistorical. Indeed, it was exasperating in its historical perversity.[359] The feeling was mutual. To Newman, the Liberals with their adulation of progress, knowledge, civilisation and the march of mind, wished to rid Christianity of its supernatural element. Carping at the Fathers and denying Tradition, declaiming against mysticism and scoffing at the miracles of the Church, they were reflecting the predominant spirit of orthodox Protestantism.[360] This Liberal attitude was a profound religious error which was to be dreaded. Truth and falsehood had been set before men for the trial of their hearts. Men could choose the Liberal way or the dogmatical principle, which alone had strength; "'if thou criest after knowledge, and liftest up thy voice for understanding, if thou seekest her as silver, and searchest for her as for hid treasure, then shalt thou understand the fear of the Lord, and find the knowledge of God'".[361] The Liberal Anglicans seriously believed that statements about Christian truth could be modified to suit the spirit of the age in which they were made. Thus, the Church would become relevant to the needs of society. Newman, on the contrary, believed that the revealed message was given once and for all by God, to be more and more fully grasped as time went on. For the Liberals, Christian dogmas had no absolute truth and were valid only for the period in which they were made. For Newman dogma was "supernatural truths irrevocably committed to human language, imperfect because it is human, but definitive and necessary because given from above".[362]

3.8. CHURCH, STATE AND SOCIETY: THE IMPERIAL IMAGE OF THE CHURCH, 1837–1845

1836 was a crucial turning-point for Newman's understanding of the Church in her relationship with the State. Although Hurrell Froude had died in February 1836, his anti-Erastian spirit lived on ever more fiercely within Newman's own soul. Convinced by April 1836 that the Royal Supremacy was Erastian,[363] Newman devoted an increasing amount of time to the Catholicity and Apostolicity of the Church of England. Indeed, Paul Misner has written that "the battle for Newman's soul was fought out on the terrain of apostolicity and catholicity of the Church".[364] That meant asking how precisely the Church of England stood in relation to the Church of Rome. Till that was done, wrote Newman in the *Apologia*, "we could not move a step in comfort".[365] It was being claimed on all sides in 1836 that the Tracts and the writings of the Fathers would lead Newman and his fellow Tractarians to become Catholics, before they were aware of it. Evangelicals thought that the Popery of the Movement would have to be put down. The situation was urgent, especially as Monsignore Wiseman had in 1836 delivered Lectures in London on the doctrines of Catholicism and created a distinct impression that the Tractarians had for their opponents in the controversy not only their brethren but also their hereditary foes.[366] The external pressures were echoed in Newman's own soul. The time had come to find an intellectual basis in reason for his belief.[367]

As Misner has shown, much of the central idea of the *Lectures on the Prophetical Office of the Church* of 1837 had already appeared in "Home Thoughts Abroad", composed about 1833 or 1834 but not published in *The British Magazine* till 1836.[368] The State was plainly unworthy to look after the principles of the Church. Who would, then, save the Church of England in her Catholicity and Apostolicity? For all Froude's insistence, under the guise of Ambrose in the articles, that only the Church of Rome was truly Catholic, Newman was certain, speaking through his mouthpiece Cyril, that the foundations and doctrines of the Church of England were as truly Apostolic and Catholic as Rome's.[369] A distinction had to be made between Popery and Catholicity.

The *Lectures* were published in 1837. Answering Froude's provocative question, "Was it not the lesser of two evils if a foreign Church usurped the power of nominating bishops from the local ecclesiastical authority, rather than delivering it into the hands of the civil power?", Newman insisted that the Church of England was essentially Catholic against the obvious perversions of Popery, especially after the Council of Trent, like the veneration of images, the honour paid to the Virgin Mary and the saints, the doctrine of purgatory and prayers for the dead.[370] In contrast to the imposition of a yoke upon the faithful after the manner of Rome, the true Catholic Church made her way by love, having that confidence in the truth of her doctrine and in the sovereignty of truth.[371] The accents of the Church Catholic and Apostolic, claimed Newman, were manifest enough in England. The Daily Prayer, the Occasional Offices, the Order of the sacraments, the Ordination Services and the Prayer Book itself were not the invention of this Reformer or that but the witness of all saints from the beginning.[372] Yet the Church of Rome remained a false prophet. Her denying the cup to the laity, her idolatrous worship of the Blessed Virgin Mary, her Image-worship, her recklessness in anathematizing and her schismatical and overbearing spirit were all novelties.[373] Throughout the *Lectures* Newman attempted to prove the Catholicity and Apostolicity of the Church of England against the usurpations and deviations of the Church of Rome.

Newman's quest for the Catholicity of the Church of England was seriously hindered, however, during the Long Vacation of 1839, some seventy eight days spent in the doctrinal study of the Monophysite heresy. Christendom of the sixteenth and nineteenth centuries were reflected in the fifth. Newman realised that he was a Monophysite[374] with Rome in the same position as she was in the nineteenth century and the Protestants as Eutychians. The foundations of Newman's *Via Media* received another blow with Wiseman's article on the "Anglican Claim". What was relevant about this article was the comparison of the Donatists with the Anglicans. Augustine's words, "Securus judicat orbis terrarum", cited by Wiseman, kept ringing in Newman's ears.[375] Augustine had insisted against the Donatists the validity of the testimony given by the whole Church, the Church spread over the face of the earth, against all local schisms or heretical sects.

Augustine had decided against Antiquity, "that the deliberate judgement, in which the whole Church at length rests and acquiesces, is an infallible prescription and a final sentence against such portions of it as protest and secede".[376] Newman knew that the four words which Augustine had used against the Donatists damned Anglicans as well. Many in the Church of England had relied historically on Ignatius of Antioch and Cyprian for their theory of the essentially diocesan establishment which they had inherited. Yet such a claim was countered by Augustine's insistence that the unity of the Church could only apply unambiguously to the universal Church. The theory of the *Via Media*, claimed Newman, had been pulverized.[377] The shadow of a hand was upon the wall. As an argument for Anglicanism, the "Prophetical Office", wrote Newman, "had come to pieces".[378]

A theologian who has been intellectually unnerved by the arguments of others can either succumb to their logic or stand his ground and make a final defence. In "The Catholicity of the Anglican Church", an article which he wrote for the *British Critic* of January 1840, Newman chose the latter course of action. Newman was seriously concerned about the Roman Catholic charge against the Church of England, that she lacked Catholicity. It was obvious that the Church of England was indeed separated from the rest of Christendom. It was not so evident alas! that the faith of Rome was an addition to the primitive.[379] To the Anglican claim of Antiquity and Apostolic witness, the Roman Catholics countered with Catholicity and universal consent.[380] Newman tried to impress his readers that intercommunion was not necessary to unity, the absence of unity did not at once involve a state of schism and the grace of the ordinances was not necessarily suspended in a state of schism.[381]

Newman insisted that the essence of the Church consisted in her descent from the Apostles. Each diocese was a perfect independent Church, sufficient for itself. The unity of Christians did not lie in mutual understanding or common activities but in what they were and had in common, the possession of the Succession, the Episcopal form, the Apostolic faith and the use of the Sacraments.[382] Inevitably the Church was complete in one bishopric. According to the Gospel system, all bishops were shadows and organs of the same divine reality. Their communion with one another was totally dependent upon their communion with God rather than common action with each other. Each bishop was the ultimate centre of unity. Schism consisted in setting up one altar against another or introducing one Church into the heart of another.[383] One bishop was only superior to another in rank, not in real power. Logically the Bishop of Rome was not the centre of unity, except as having a primacy of order.[384] Papal supremacy, like the Royal Supremacy, was a matter of expedience, custom or piety. It was not a point *de fide*, resting on duty or revelation but merely on specific engagement.[385]

In the Church of the Fathers, Ingatius and Cyprian spoke of bishops "in high language". The former especially warned his brethren against schism, for if the bishop is Christ's representative, "the effect of separating from the bishop is thus simply shown to be a separating from Christ".[386] Considering the latter, Newman was well aware that the question between Anglicans and Romanists was whether the Church is the local Church everywhere or whether "it is the literal and actual extended communion of all Christians everywhere viewed as one body under the supremacy of the Pope".[387] The best proof, claimed Newman, that St Peter's authority at Rome was not the papal power was Cyprian's own controversy with Pope Stephen on the subject of heretical baptism. Had Cyprian accounted Stephen to be the one Bishop in the Church, he never would have spoken of Stephen's "Obstinatio", let alone his "audacia et insolentia". The "supremacy of Peter" clearly did not mean the power of the Pope but only of the Bishop of Rome.[388]

Newman knew, however, that Ignatius and Cyprian were not the only authorities on the relationship of the diocese with the universal Church. Augustine believed that the principle of unity lay, not in each individual bishop, but in the body of the Church. The union of Church with Church was not a mere accident but the essence of ecclesiastical unity. The famous assage in Cyprian's *De Unitate*, "Tear the ray from the sun's substance, unity will not admit this division of light; break the branch from the tręe, it will not bud when broken; cut off the channel from the spring, the channel will dry up", which was interpreted by Anglican divines as applying only to the episcopal and diocesan unit, Augustine interpreted of the body of the universal Church.

The universal Church, Augustine maintained, was right in a quarrel with a particular Church. The universal Church, diffused through all countries, included the idea of active communion.[389] The conclusion was obvious. The contemporary Church, according to the logic of the Augustinian argument, was indeed cut off from the Catholic body.[390]

In replying, Newman kept to what he regarded as the one essential note of the Catholicity of the Church of England, that the possession of the Apostolic Succession was as much a *sine qua non* of the Church's essence as intercommunion.[391] After all, why should Augustine's maxim about the authority of the "orbis terrarum" be any more valid than Lactantius's claim, "That is the true Catholic Church *in qua est confessio et paenitentia*" or Jerome's "ecclesia ibi est, ubi *fides est*"?[392] Throughout history, Newman maintained, heretical and schismatical bodies were formed upon a certain doctrine, or began with certain leaders. No one ever referred to the Church of England as a body of Cranmerites or Jewellists. This fact differentiated the Church of England from Lutherans, Calvinists, Socinians or Wesleyans.[393] The authentic Notes of the Church of England were real enough, "the note of possession, the note of freedom from party titles, the note of life, a tough life and vigorous". In addition, the Church of England had ancient descent, unbroken continuance, agreement in doctrine with the ancient Church.[394] The contrast with the Church of Rome could not have been more marked, whose agents were "smiling and nodding and ducking to attract attention, as gipsies make up to truant boys, holding out tales for the nursery, and pretty pictures, and gold gingerbread, and physic concealed in jam, and sugar-plums for good children".[395]

The ink was hardly dry on Newman's article before the ghost came a second time.[396] In stressing the Ignatian-Cyprianic conception of communion and schism, Newman knew that he was treading on thin ice. Wiseman had indeed got the better of him in his article, "The Anglican Claim of Apostolical Succession".[397] He had truly fixed on Newman's weak point, a fact Newman was ready to acknowledge in a letter to J. W. Bowden on 5 January, 1840.[398] In the Summer of 1841, Newman began in earnest his researches on Athanasius. He now saw clearly in the history of Arianism that "the pure Arians were the Protestants, the semi-Arians were the Anglicans, and that Rome now was what it was then".[399] Once again, the *Via Media* was discredited. The significance of Athanasius for dismantling the *Via Media* is immense. Newman's historical conversion to Roman Catholicism, Father George Dragas maintains, was "a concrete way of affirming the vision of the Church which Newman found in the Fathers, the vision which demands the union of all people into one communion".[400] When Newman had written his *History of the Arians* nine years before, he had seen the controversy through the eyes of the Anglican divines. Then he had only looked through a glass darkly. Now he saw the reality face to face, the picture of the Church in communion with Rome making the decrees and only the heretics resisting.[401] Now he saw the Arian history as a complete whole rather than in parts.

What Newman discovered for himself privately seemed to be confirmed publicly by the action of the bishops in condeming *Tract XC*,[402] behaving more like Semi-Arians than the successors of the Apostles. The final blow came with the establishment of the Jerusalem Bishopric. The Church of England, whose Notes of authenticity Newman had written about with such scrupulousness eighteen months before, was actually courting intercommunion with Protestant Prussia. Newman feared that the Church of England since the sixteenth century had "never been a Church all along".[403]

The background to Newman's understanding of the Church as an imperial power, a theme of so many of his sermons in 1841 and 1842, is found not only in his interpretation of the Catholicity or otherwise of the Church of England but also in the Protestant interpretation of prophecies attached to the Church of Rome as Antichrist, an essential component of the *Via Media*.[404] It is impossible to understand Newman's emphasis on the Church as an imperial power without a thorough grasp of the developing role played in Newman's thought by the Antichristian theme and its relationship to the Church of Rome. In a recent study, Dr Sheridan Gilley has illustrated the fascination which this theme had for Newman, who wrote in the *Apologia* that the anti-Roman interpretations of Antichrist prophecies stained his imagination until 1843, although they had lost their grip on his intellect earlier.[405]

As Gilley has shown, Newman never lost his rigorist Evangelical extremism which was firmly rooted in his conversion, a fact of which he was still more conscious, even half a century later, than his hands and feet.[406] This Evangelical outlook manifested itself in an otherworldliness which "foresaw, and branded as apostasy, our modern preoccupation with politics".[407] It was precisely in this world-denying temper that Newman delighted in Bishop Thomas Newton's *Discourses on the Prophecies*, and was firmly convinced that the Pope was the Antichrist predicted by Daniel, St Paul and St John.[408] In 1840, Newman referred to Newton as "the main source, we suppose, of that anti-Roman opinion on the subject of Antichrist, now afloat among us, as far as men have an opinion".[409]

In his exegetical notes of 1822 on Chapter 6 of Revelation, one of the most difficult Scriptural passages to interpret with its references to the four horsemen of the Apocalypse and the "great day of God's wrath"; in his Advent sermons of 1824–1825 when he dated the Roman Antichrist from the days of Gregory the Great and in his critical review of 1825 of Edward Cooper's *The Crisis*, Newman was thoroughly preoccupied with the argument from prophecy about Antichrist.[410] By his own admission in the *Apologia*, Newman spoke of the Roman Church as "being bound up with 'the cause of Antichrist', as being one of the 'many antichrists' foretold by St John, as being influnced by 'the spirit of Antichrist', and as having something 'very Antichristian' or 'unchristian' about her".[411] Such an emphasis was consistent, wrote Newman, with Bernard Gilpin's notion that it was the idea of Rome as Antichrist which justified the Reformation. Popery was not merely a collection of erroneous doctrines but the very embodiment of Antichristianity, the living substance and essence of all those texts which predicted the Antichrist to come.[412]

Newman's position, however, began to change after 1827. In *The Christian Year*, Keble told his readers to treat Rome gently while Hurrell Froude was sharply critical of Newman's anti-Roman polemic and did much to rub the idea out of his mind.[413] In his unpublished Advent Sermons of 1830, Newman referred to that "scoffing unbelief", a part of the liberal progressivist mentality and self-trust rooted in the false English pride "in our own greatness as a nation" as a definite sign of the end of the world.[414] Similarly, in his published Sermons of that period, "The Religion of the Day", "Watching" and "Waiting for Christ", an otherworldly adventism was much in evidence. A subtle but profound development had taken place in the whole nature of the Antichrist prophecies. The infidelity of political Liberalism, not Popery, was now the Antichrist of the age.[415]

Writing from Rome on 14 March, 1833 to George Ryder, Newman saw in the ruins of the city the survival of the monstrous Fourth Beast of Daniel: "Here we see the only remnant of the 4 great Enemies of God – Babylon, Persia and Macedon have left scarce a trace behind them – the last and most terrible beast lies before us as a subject for our contemplation, in al the visibleness of its plagues".[416] But Newman was not referring to the Church of Rome but the pagan city of Rome, an "offshoot" of the "hateful Roman power, the 4th Beast of Daniel's Vision".[417] This was an important differentiation in Newman's mind, for the Church was not the city, and the city was the Beast and not the Church. For all Newman's objections to the Pope's foot being kissed, "considering how much is said in Scripture", he wrote to his mother on 25 March, "about the necessity of him that is greatest being as the least, nor do I even tolerate him being carried in on high",[418] yet the Roman Church was still a Church with the marks of Christ upon her: "I could only say in very perplexity my own words. How shall I name thee, Light of the wide west, or heinous error-seat?"[419] Newman could not see his way out of it.

It was in 1835, in his four lectures on "The Patristical Idea of Antichrist", preached as Advent sermons and published in 1838 as *Tract No. 83*, that Newman gave serious consideration to whether the Church of Rome was Antichrist or not. The four sermons were perfectly consistent with those he had preached in 1830 in identifying Antichrist as the Liberal spirit which was everywhere apparent, that "apostasy to infidel doctrines, perhaps the most flagitious and blasphemous which the world has ever seen". The attempt to educate without religion, to build societies on mere principles of utility, to make numbers and not truth the ground of maintaining this or that creed, all this was the especial Shadow of Antichrist. During the French Revolution, men had exalted the reprobate state into a kind of God, called it LIBERTY and literally worshipped it as a divinity.[420]

Similarly, wrote Newman, the ancient Fathers had predicted that Antichrist would come out of the Roman Empire upon its destruction, as that Empire would in its last days divide itself into ten parts and the enemy would come up suddenly out of it upon those ten and perhaps subdue all of them. It was no coincidence, asserted Newman, that Hippolytus had claimed that the ten states would be democracies. These predictions were seen to be true in the present state of the world, "the tendency of things in this day towards democracy, and the instance which has been presented to us of democracy within the last fifty years, in those occurrences in France to which I have already alluded".[421]

In these Advent sermons of 1835, there were also echoes of Newman's thoughts in his letters from Rome in 1833 about the pagan city bearing the marks of Antichrist. Indeed, Rome was nothing else but "the woman which thou sawest" in Revelation, xvii. 18, described as cruel, profligate and impious arrayed in all worldly splendour and costliness, shedding and drinking the blood of the saints, till she was drunken with it. Her name was "Babylon the Great", signifying her sensuality and persecuting spirit.[422] The representation of Babylon as pagan Rome was distinct from the institution that it sometimes corrupted, the Roman Church and see. As the city of Antichrist, Newman was convinced that Rome would be destroyed by fire at the last, as Our Lord had prophesied that Jerusalem, like Sodom and Gomorrah and the supreme ancient prototype, old Babylon itself, would also be.[423]

The publication of the first two Volumes of Hurrell Froude's *Remains* in 1838 only exacerbated the situation as to whether Newman actually considered the Pope to be Antichrist or not. In replying to Professor Godfrey Faussett, the Lady Margaret Professor of Divinity, who in his *Revival of Popery* of 1838 had referred to the Tractarian tendency to "palliate the errors of Popery" and to approximate towards "the Roman superstitions concerning the Lord's Supper", Newman explicitly denied that the Pope was the Antichrist.[424]

Newman's last attempt to lay the antipapal ghost to rest was his review in October 1840 of the *Prophecies relating to Antichrist in the writings of Daniel and St Paul* by James Henthorn Todd, a Professor at Trinity College, Dublin.[425] This review is significant for three reasons. First, Newman repeated the argument which he had already used in 1838 in his letter to Faussett, that if the Church of Rome was Antichrist, then what was the Church of

England? If Rome had committed fornication with the kings of the earth, wrote Newman in 1838, then "what must be said of the Church of England with her temporal power, her Bishops in the House of Lords, her dignified clergy, her prerogatives, her pluralities, her buying and selling of preferments, her patronage, her corruptions, and her abuses?"[426] Similarly in 1840, Newman claimed that a Sandemanian, a Ranter or a Quaker might call Rome Babylon, but this argument was not open to Anglicans. If Rome was Antichrist as an establishment, then so was Canterbury, which bore all the other marks of the beast, an episcopal hierarchy, an Apostolic succession, priesthood, formal worship and sacraments.[427] If Christ has indeed appointed a body representative of Him on earth during his absence, then the Pope is not Antichrist. If Christ has not, wrote Newman, then every bishop in England, Bishop Newton, Bishop Warburton, Bishop Hurd is Antichrist. Of course, claimed Newman, Christ had left a representative body on earth. All the more reason, then, that Anglicans were not quite the persons to venture to speak of "that woman Jezebel", meaning thereby the Holy Church catholic, sojourning in Rome.[428]

Secondly, Newman made much of a theme which had been his concern since 1835 when he had preached two sermons on "The Kingdom of the Saints" which presented a picture of the Church as an aggressive political force on the world scene. As Misner has shown,[429] Newman's theme in these sermons was that the "Kingdom of the Saints" was the fulfilment of the prophecy in Daniel. The four Kingdoms were gone but the Kingdom of Christ which was made without human hands remained. Many Kingdoms before or after the coming of Christ had been set up or extended by violent means. The wonderful conquest of the Kingdom of Rome by that of Christ was followed by another wonder, the singular history of Christianity, its continued existence beyond the normal life span of other Kingdoms. In spite of the opposition of the kingdoms of this world, a new Kingdom which disclaimed the use of force was in the world but not of it. It had conquered and it remained. In his review of Todd's article, Newman asked, "Which set of prophecies is more exactly fulfilled in the Church of the middle ages, those of Isaiah which speak of the evangelical kingdom, or those of St Paul and St John which speak of the anti-Christian corruption?"[430]

According to Isaiah, wrote Newman, "Out of Zion shall go forth the law, and the word of the law from Jerusalem, and He shall judge among the nations and rebuke many people". The writings of the Fathers formed an historical comment upon the inspired pages of Isaiah, "supplying numberless instances of the execution of that high mission, whereby the spiritual Israel was set forth in the world, as the elect of God, created as an instrument of righteousness to set forth his Maker's glory, to teach truth and righteousness, 'to relieve the oppressed, to judge the fatherless, to plead for the widow', to feed the hungry, to shield the imperilled, to raise the fallen, to repress the tyrannical, to reconcile enemies, and largely to dispense benefits to and fro. Even what is visibly exhibited in the pages of history is an abundant and a most wonderful accomplishment of the prophetic word".[431] Newman was in no doubt that the history of Christian Rome corresponded more closely and literally to the promises of Isaiah than the denouncements of the Apocalypse. The assumption by the medieval Church of power over kings and her right to define the faith corresponded far more literally to the prophecy of Isaiah than St John.

Thirdly, Misner has illustrated the immense power of Newman's imaginative liberation in the conclusion of his article, an extraordinary literal inversion of Protestant prophecy, in finding the medieval Church, not a realization of Antichrist, as prophesied by St John in the Apocalypse, but an "Imperial Church", anticipated in the glorious prophecies concerning Israel of old and realised in the Church of the Fathers. Newman's conclusion is crucial for an understanding of his image of the Church as an imperial power, a theme of so many of his sermons in the following two years. In reality, claimed Newman, the "wealth and splendour, the rich embellishment of the temples of the medieval Church, the jewelled dress of her ministers, the offerings, shrines, pageants and processions", far from being the purple and pearls of the sorceress of Revelation, were actually the camels and gold and incense and cedar from Midian and Ephah, Sheba and Lebanon, Isaiah's vision of the kings and ships and isles bringing gifts, and the "sapphires" and "agates" of the heavenly Jerusalem.[432] As Gilley has shown, Newman never actually doubted the literal fulfilment of these Old Testament prophecies. In that sense, he remained an Evangelical, whatever else he had also become.[433]

No fewer than eleven of his *Sermons on Subjects of the Day* were concerned with the Church as an imperial power.[434] They are significant for an understanding of Newman's concept of the Church in her relationship with the State and society for three reasons. First, they illustrate the literal Evangelical spirit in which the Old Testament prophecies are interpreted. Newman loved to quote the prophet Isaiah: "Strangers shall stand and feed your flocks, and the sons of alien shall be your plowmen and your vinedressers. But ye shall be named the priests of the Lord, men shall call you the ministers of our God; for ye shall eat the riches of the Gentiles, and in their glory shall ye boast yourselves". Such a passage appealed to Newman for it referred to extended dominion over the kings of other kingdoms. It spoke of "aggression and advance; a warfare against enemies; acts of judgement upon the proud; acts of triumph over the defeated; high imperial majesty towards the suppliant; clemency towards the repentant; parental care of the dutiful".[435] In his interpretation of these Old Testament prophecies, Newman knew that it was an exceedingly difficult task. In his review of 1840, he had written: "There is no department of theology in which ordinary men are more at the mercy of an author than that of prophetical interpretation ... who shall warrant, and who shall verify, discussions which embrace on the one hand the wide range of history, and necessarily plunge on the other into the subtleties of allegory and poetry, which profess to connect and adjust a field so fertile in facts with a page so recondite in character, and that upon no principles, perhaps, but such as approve themselves to the judgement of the individual interpreter?"[436] As Misner has shown, for all Newman's insistence that the "mystical" or "ecclesiastical" sense of Scripture was superior to its "literal" sense, yet in elaborating his Kingdom ecclesiology from Old Testament prophecies, he stood firmly by Hooker's rule in favour of an exclusively literal interpretation. "Where a literal construction will stand, the farthest from the letter", wrote Hooker, "is commonly the worst".[437]

Newman felt that in the kingdom ecclesiology, any allegorical, figurative or mystical interpretation was simply too dangerous. Referring to one set of prophecies in Isaiah and the other in

Daniel, St Paul and St John, which of the two, he asked, was the more literally fulfilled in the history of the Church? Which of the two has fewer difficulties? The answer is obvious. From the Apostles' day to our own, there has been a continuous body politic all over the world, bearing the name of Church. It has maintained itself miraculously against the power of the world. It has taken the cause of the poor and friendless against the great and proud. It has succeeded, not by earthly and carnal weapons, but by righteousness and mercy. It has conquered and flourished against the most appalling odds. It has always been at war with the spirit of the world. Such a concept of the Church as an imperial power was nothing less than a literal fulfilment of the prophet Isaiah: "Arise, shine, for thy light is come, and the glory of the Lord is risen upon thee ... And the Gentiles shall come to thy light, and kings to the brightness of thy rising. ... The sons of strangers shall build up thy walls, and their kings shall minister unto thee ... The nation and kingdom that will not serve thee shall perish; yea, those nations shall utterly perish".[438]

Secondly, the contrast in the sermons of 1841 and 1842 with the *Lectures on the Prophetical Office of the Church* of 1837 is profound. Even in 1837, Newman had been willing to contemplate the possibility of the union of Church and State. In England, wrote Newman, the Church co-operated with the State in exacting subscription to the Thirty-nine Articles, as a test, not only of the Clergy, but also of the governing body in our Universities, – a test against Romanism.[439] Such an alliance with the State was sometimes necessary. By 1841, however, all such understanding of the Church in relation to the State has completely disappeared. Instead, Newman has evolved a theory of the Church in her relationship to the kingdoms of this world which was uncompromisingly triumphalist. In his sermon, "The Church and the World", Newman offered a list of symptoms of a nation's submission to Christ which was a natural consequence of his views on the Church's relationship to society generally. The magistrates were there to defend the Christian faith; tithes were paid; family prayers were said, and the Church's seasons observed; sacrifices were made to prove earnestness. All this, claimed Newman, was "the circumcision of the heart from the world".[440] No alliance with the world was possible, since the Church herself knew that the powers of the world have always been against her. In his sermon, "Condition of the Members of the Christian Empire", Newman drew a sharp contrast between those who only wished to use the Gospel as an antidote to rebellion, sedition, conspiracy, riot and fanaticism and true Christians who put off the love of the world. The strength of the Church did not lie in earthly law, or human countenance, or civil station but in those great gifts which Our Lord had pronounced to be beatitudes – blessed are the pure in spirit, the mourners, the meek, the thirsters after righteousness, the merciful, the pure in heart, the peacemakers, the persecuted.[441]

The only difficulty with Newman's concept of the Church as an imperial power was that it bore no resemblance to Anglicanism. Rather, the theme of imperial power was not dissimilar to Hurrell Froude's theocratic images of the Church,[442] as the third Volume of the *Remains* of 1839 had made clear. The process which had begun for Newman in Froude's lifetime, ending with the loss of faith in the Royal Supremacy, reached its climax in a vision of the Church which reflected the triumphalism of the medieval crusading pilgrim. State and society were consumed by the eternal demands and challenges of Christ's Kingdom; "It is by influence only that the Church reigns, or by what is sometimes called *opinion*. Kings and states still have the power of the sword, and they only. They must still be obeyed by the Church, if they prefer to command and rule over her, to honouring her. They must be obeyed, and they will come to nought. She must leave her cause to God, who has promised to avenge it on every proud kingdom and nation. For herself, she has no arms, but peace, quietness, cheerfulness, resignation and love. 'Being reviled, she blesses; being persecuted, she suffers it; being defamed, she intreats'; she does not defend herself; like her Master, she does not 'cry in the streets, or strive'; but she prevails, because God fights for her".[443]

Finally, it was very much the imperial image of the Church, the kingdom ecclesiology, which influenced Newman as he moved towards Rome between 1842 and 1845. According to the *Apologia*, Newman was on his death-bed from the end of 1841, as far as his membership of the Anglican Church was concerned. The *Via Media* was an impossible ideal. Newman called it "standing on one leg".[444] Indeed, Newman was to claim in his *Certain Difficulties felt by Anglicans in Catholic Teaching* of 1850 that the state of the Church of England was a mere abstract idea, that she had no authentic Notes, only tavern toasts, that she was a department of government, responsible for nothing, that she did not know where she stood or what she held, that she was unable to resist heresies and the people were Protestant and progressive.[445] The Church of England, as far as Newman was concerned as he approached the end of his Anglican ministry, had no life. The contrast with the physical world was obvious, since "whatever has life is characterised by growth, so that in no respect to grow is to cease to live".[446] Anglicanism might be good on paper, but what would Athanasius have made of it?[447] The only life which the Church of England possessed consisted in worldly pursuits. It imparted a tone to the court and Houses of Parliament, ministers of State, law and literature, Universities, schools and society. It was a principle of order in the population, an organ of benevolence and almsgiving towards the poor. It made men decent, respectable and sensible. It refined the family circle, deprived vice of its grossness, shed a gloss over avarice and ambition. The Church of England was the jewel in the Queen's Crown, the highest step to the throne.[448] This was not the supernatural life of the true Church of apostles, martyrs, evangelists and doctors.

Unlike the Church of universal dimensions and imperial authority, the Church of England was a mere slave of the State. Dogma was sacrificed to expedience, sacraments were rationalised and perfection ridiculed. The National or State Church comprised only a section of humanity. "In this country especially", wrote Newman, "there is nothing broader than class religions; the established form is but the religion of a class ... the Church catholic includes specimens of every class among her children. She is the solace of the forlorn 'no less than the chastener of the prosperous', and in every sense 'the guide of the wayward' ".[449] The National Church tolerated all opinions except Catholic and lacked stability, let alone permanence in matters of doctrine. It was incapable of being a spiritual force in the land.[450]

Most seriously of all, the Church of England was not Catholic. How different the Church of England was in 1841 from the Church of the fifth and sixth centuries! Whatever the heresies, challenges, loss of land and prestige, she always approximated to the possession of the *orbis terrarum*. This was the Church which was identified by all parties with Christianity, called always catholic by people and by laws.[451] The Church of England's uncatholic ways were not limited to this or that statute or canon at the time of the Reformation, this or that encroachment of the State, this or that Act of King or Queen. Such actions merely touched the hem of the garment. If the Church of England was not Catholic in 1845, then neither was she in 1833, let alone in 1533.[452]

Newman's total commitment to the imperial image of the Church meant the abandonment of any branch theory of the Church of England. As Misner has shown, between 1841 and 1845 the Cyprianic doctrine of Apostolic succession was taken up into a higher unity, the Catholic international Communion. The logic of this development was that the Church "is a kingdom", and not as heretical churches always turned out to be, merely "a family" which continually divided and sent out branches, each of them as independent as its original head.[453] It was Newman's ecclesiological imperialism, to use Misner's phrase,[454] which drove him away from the *Via Media* with its central notion that universality meant "a number of independent communities, at variance (if so be) with each other even to a breach of communion", even if "all these were possessed of a legitimate succession of clergy, or all governed by bishops, priests, and deacons".[455] Augustine's words, *Securus judicat orbis terrarum*, which made such an indelible impression on Newman's mind in 1839, revealed the utter fallacy of the *Via Media*. The Church was a universal kingdom, an actually united and international communion, which simply did not "admit of independent portions".[456] The true Church, the literal fulfilment of the Old Testament prophecies about the universal Kingdom, was no branch Church, a mere heretical and local sect, but rather "a vast organised association, co-extensive with the Roman Empire, or rather overflowing it. Its bishops were not mere local officers, but possessed a power essentially ecumenical, extending wherever a Christian was to be found".[457] This Church alone was spread over the world and called Catholic. It alone remained one and the same. Heretical churches, on the contrary, were local only, were continually subdividing, fell one after another and made way for new sects.[458]

NOTES 3

1. J. H. Newman, *Apo.*, p. 94. Newman's assessment of Samuel Taylor Coleridge could be applied to himself.
2. J. H. Newman, *U.S.*, p. 201.
3. *Life of F. D. Maurice*, by his son (Vol. 1), p. 217.
4. Keith Feiling, *Sketches in Nineteenth Century Biography*, p. 110.
5. D. J. deLaura, "Matthew Arnold and John Henry Newman", *English Literature and Language*, Vol. VI, pp. 668 ff. deLaura was citing Matthew Arnold that Newman was the most acceptable Conservative since Burke.
6. Anthony Quinton, *The Politics of Imperfection*, pp. 62 ff.
7. L. & C., Vol. I, p. 195.
8. C. S. Dessain, *Newman's Spiritual Themes*, pp. 195 ff.
9. L. & C., Vol. II, p. 323.
10. V.M., Vol. I, p. 262.
11. *British Critic*, Vol. XXVI, No. LII, pp. 414 ff.
12. See J. D. Holmes, "Factors in the Development of Newman's Political Attitudes", J. D. Bastable, ed., *Newman and Gladstone, Centennial Essays*, pp. 57–88.
13. Feiling, op. cit., p. 112 cites Newman: "Conservatives are a spent force. We must take things as we find them".
14. Holmes, op. cit., p. 82.
15. Newman wrote of a mystery as "a statement uniting incompatible notions", *G.A.*, p. 36. See also L. Bremond, *The Mystery of Newman*.
16. L. & C., Vol. II, p. 237.
17. *British Critic*, op. cit., p. 422.
18. R. D. Middleton, *Newman and Bloxam*, p. 24.
19. L. & D., Vol. IV, p. 286.
20. Cited by Feiling, op. cit., p. 111.
21. L. & D., Vol. IV, p. 315.
22. J. N. Figgis, *The Fellowship of the Mystery*, p. 247 for the view that Newman's mystery was that he was conservative in essence, revolutionary in form.
23. *Tract No. XC*, p. 5.
24. N. L. A. Lash, *Newman on Development, The Search for an Explanation in History*, p. 155.
25. *Corr.*, p. 245.
26. ibid., p. 192.
27. This was one of St John Chrysostom's abiding virtues. See E. J. Sillem, *The Philosophical Notebook, Vol. 1, General Introduction to the Study of Newman's Philosophy*, p. 96.
28. Dessain, op. cit., p. 136.

29. F. L. Cross, *J. H. Newman*, p. 48.
30. G. D. Dragas, "Conscience and Tradition, Newman and Athanasius in the Orthodox Church", *Athanasiana*, Vol. 1, p. 183.
31. Figgis, op. cit., p. 234.
32. *H.S.*, Vol. II, p. 476.
33. *L. & D.*, Vol. XII, p. 61.
34. *L. & C.*, Vol. I, p. 205.
35. See William Palmer, *A Narrative of Events Concerned with Tracts for the Times*, p. 105.
36. See W. L. Mathieson, *English Church Reform 1815–1840*, pp. 33–34.
37. The shocks of the world were far greater for those who put their faith in the Nineteenth Century gospel of secular progress. See H. Graef, *God and Myself, The Spirituality of J. H. Newman*, pp. 56 ff. for the gravity of sin in Newman's thought.
38. For the view that the nearest England came to producing a disaffected intelligentsia, see W. Thomas, *The Philosophical Radicals*, p. 451.
39. T. Mozley, *Reminiscences chiefly of Oriel College and the Oxford Movement*, Vol. II, p. 207. Mozley believed that the *British Critic* should be precisely what the title implied. So did Newman.
40. On the background to Roman Catholic Emancipation, see Owen Chadwick, *The Victorian Church*, Part 1, pp. 294–304; G. F. A. Best, "The Protestant Constitution and its Supporters", *Transactions of the Royal Historical Society*, (Series 5), 8, pp. 105–127; Donal A. Kerr, *Peel, Priests and Politics, Sir Robert Peel's Administration and the Roman Catholic Church in Ireland, 1841–1846*, pp. 68–70; G. I. T. Machin, *The Catholic Question in English Politics, 1820–1830*; E. R. Norman, *Anti-Catholicism in Victorian England*, pp. 13–22; *The English Catholic Church in the Nineteenth Century*, pp. 29–68. For Newman's part in the agitation against Catholic Emancipation, see *Apo.*, p. 26, *L. & D.*, Vol. II, pp. 117 ff; *L. & C.*, Vol. I, pp. 173–80; Maisie Ward, *Young Mr. Newman*, pp. 154–158, 224–236.
41. On the importance of the conscience for Newman, see two studies by A. J. Boekraad, *The Personal Conquest of Truth according to J. H. Newman* and *The Argument from Conscience to the Existence of God*. See also J. H. Walgrave, *Newman the Theologian*; Sillem, op. cit., pp. 123–126. For Newman's understanding of conscience, see *G. A.*, pp. 93–109; *A Letter Addressed to His Grace the Duke of Norfolk, On Occasion of Mr. Gladstone's Recent Expostulation*, pp. 54 ff.
42. *Norfolk*, op. cit., p. 55.
43. ibid., p. 57.

44. ibid.
45. *G. A.*, pp. 93 ff.
46. *V. M.*, Vol. I, pp. 132–133.
47. ibid., p. 132.
48. *U. S.*, No. 2, p. 31.
49. Newman's classic sermon, "The World Our Enemy", *PPS*, Vol. VII, pp. 27 ff. has the text from 1 John, "We know that we are of God, and the whole world lieth in wickedness". See C. Egner, *Apologia Pro Charles Kingsley*, pp. 66 ff. for a critique of Newman's views on the world as lacking in grace.
50. Newman preached on this theme in "The Second Spring", *OS*, pp. 190–3.
51. *U. S.*, p. 132.
52. *P. P. S.*, Vol. I, p. 21.
53. ibid., p. 39. See also *P. P. S.*, Vol. III, p. 126.
54. ibid., Vol. I, p. 314.
55. ibid., Vol. VI, p. 80.
56. ibid., Vol. III, pp. 244–245.
57. *Ari.*, p. 270.
58. *V. M.*, Vol. I, pp. 109, 133.
59. *Tract No. 3*, p. 3; *T. T.*, p. 96.
60. *Ath.*, Vol. I, p. 129; p. 165.
61. *Norfolk*, pp. 68–70.
62. Machin, op. cit., pp. 117–118. Keble saw it as another example of laxity in politics, see H. P. Liddon, *Life of Edward Bouverie Pusey*, Vol. I, p. 198.
63. Despite the fact that Peel had opposed Catholic Emancipation for twenty years, he changed his mind in 1828 after the election of O'Connell to Clare and the imminent danger of civil war in Ireland. On 4 February, 1829, he sent a letter of resignation to the Vice-Chancellor of Oxford: "I consider myself bound to surrender to the University without delay the trust which they have confided in me". *Memoirs of the Right Honourable Sir Robert Peel*, I, pp. 312–5, cited in *L. & D.*, Vol. II, p. 117, fn. 2.
64. Letter, 7 February, 1829 to Samuel Rickards; *L. & D.*, Vol. II, p. 119.
65. Letter, 15 February, 1829 to Samuel Rickards; ibid., p. 121.
66. Letter, 17 February, 1829 to Harriett Newman; ibid., p. 122.
67. Letter, 18 February, 1829 to Samuel Rickards; ibid., p. 123.
68. See *Norfolk*, p. 71 for Newman's sentiment that Oxford's great medieval motto had been forfeited to "liberalism and progress" and his plea that the University should go to Parliament or the Heralds' College for a new one.
69. Letter, 1 March, 1829 to Mrs Newman, *L. & D.*, Vol. II, p. 125.

70. For a summary of the way Peel acted in liaison with government Ministers, see P. J. Welch, "Blomfield and Peel, A Study in Co-operation between Church and State, 1841–1846", *The Jl. of Ecc. Hist.*, Vol. XII, pp. 71–84.
71. *Apo.*, p. 39.
72. For the turmoil leading up to the 1832 Bill, see Chadwick, op. cit., pp. 24–48; Olive Brose, *Church and Parliament, The Reshaping of the Church of England 1828–1860*, pp. 22–42; W. L. Mathieson, op. cit.; *Apo.*, p. 506 for Svaglic's view that "Newman's early political thought is a blend of the conservatism of Burke, which dominated Oxford, with the Non-juring principle taught in the Anglican Homily on Wilful Disobedience (1569) that 'rebellion of subjects against their prince was in every conceivable instance a grievous sin'".
73. See Newman's letter, 20 August, 1833, cited by Maisie Ward, op. cit., p. 233.
74. See R. C. Selby, *The Principle of Reserve in the Writings of John Henry Newman*, pp. 89–95.
75. *Ari.*, pp. 136, 225, 272 for Newman's disgust with those who had subjected Christ's religion to rude scrutiny and dishonour.
76. *U. S.*, p. 85.
77. Selby, op. cit., p. 92.
78. *The British Magazine*, Vol. V, p. 129.
79. *The Church of the Fathers*, p. 64.
80. *P. P. S.*, Vol. VI, p. 248.
81. *Corr.*, p. 99.
82. *U. S.*, p. 97.
83. *L. & D.*, Vol. V, p. 46.
84. *L. & D.*, Vol. II, p. 283. See also M. Freeman, *Edmund Burke and the Critique of Political Radicalism*, p. 163. See W. Ward, "Functions of Prejudice", *Dublin Review* (Vol. CXXXVIII), pp. 99–118 for a comparison between Newman and Burke.
85. *L. & D.*, Vol. II, pp. 133, 186.
86. *V. V.*, p. 43.
87. *The Rambler*, Vol. I, p. 128.
88. *U. S.*, p. 150.
89. Dollinger felt that historical facts were hard and unimaginative. See F. L. Cross, op. cit., p. 173.
90. See J. L. Altholz, "Newman and History", *Victorian Stds.*, Vol. VII. This view is rather too simple. For studies of Newman as a historian, see also T. S. Bokenkotter, *Cardinal Newman as an Historian*; J. D. Holmes, "Church and World in Newman", *New Blackfriars*, Vol. 49, pp. 468 ff; N. L. A. Lash, "Can a Theologian Keep the Faith?", *Theology on Dover Beach*, pp. 51 ff.

91. *Tract No. 41*, p. 1, *Tracts for the Times*, Vol. 1.
92. *Tract No. 73*, p. 47, *Tracts for the Times*, Vol. IV.
93. *U. S.*, p. 303. Newman stated that Church history was useless, except to the eyes of faith.
94. J. Holloway, *The Victorian Sage*, p. 201 points out that Newman turned everything into a work of art and enabled his readers to see events with new eyes because the whole experience of the person was involved.
95. *P. P. S.*, Vol. III, p. 363.
96. Henry Tristram (intro.), *John Henry Newman, Centenary Essays*, p. 227.
97. Michael Tierney, *A Tribute to Newman, Essays on Aspects of His Life And Thought*, p. 114.
98. See J. D. Holmes, "A Note on Newman's Historical Method", John Coulson and A. M. Allchin, eds., *The Rediscovery of Newman, An Oxford Symposium*, p. 97.
99. Tierney, op. cit., pp. 101 ff.
100. Dragas, op. cit., pp. 126, 175.
101. cf. *Apo.*, p. 217. "To consider the world in its length and breadth ... all this is a vision to dizzy and appal".
102. *Tract No. 83*, p. 21.
103. *Ath.*, Vol. I, p. 170.
104. *V. V.*, p. 161. Cf. *Dev.*, p. 142.
105. *U.S.*, pp. 150–152.
106. See N. L. A. Lash, *Newman on Development, The Search for an Explanation in History*, pp. 23 ff.
107. A recurring theme in *G. A.*, pp. 95 ff. See also *V. M.* I, pp. 345–5; *Dev.*, pp. 444 ff.
108. ibid.
109. *P. P. S.*, Vol. II, pp. 273 ff.
110. *Diffs.*, pp. 175–80, 325–9.
111. Dragas, op. cit., p. 184.
112. Alexander Knox (1757–1831) upheld the view that the Church of England was Catholic, not Protestant. He anticipated many Tractarian ideas. His opinions are contained in his *Remains* (4 Vols. 1834–7). Newman was quoting from Vol. I, pp. 51 ff; cited by Svaglic, op. cit., p. 536.
113. ibid.
114. *P. P. S.*, Vol. III, p. 247.
115. See Owen Chadwick, *From Bossuet to Newman, The Idea of Doctrinal Development*, p. 71.
116. For a discussion of Newman's views on progress, see pp. 217 ff.
117. Cf. Dragas, op. cit., p. 183. In this respect, Newman was much nearer the method of St Augustine. See Alan Richardson, *History*

Sacred and Profane, pp. 57, 60, 63. On the other hand, Eusebius proudly imagined that Constantine's victory was the final consummation. See Frances Young, *From Nicaea to Chalcedon, A Guide to its Literature and Background*, pp. 13–14.
118. Dragas, op. cit., p. 183.
119. For Newman's understanding of Athanasius, see 3.5.
120. Richardson, op. cit., p. 57.
121. ibid., p. 75.
122. Matthew Arnold, *Literature and Dogma*, p. 5. The controlling factor in the affairs of men was God, "whose right hand is full of righteousness", rather than blind and capricious chance.
123. One of Newman's central themes. See *Apo..*, pp. 241–6.
124. *Tract No. 83*, p. 87.
125. Sillem, op. cit., p. 46.
126. *S. S. D.*, p. 10.
127. *P. P. S.*, Vol. III, p. 117.
128. Lash, op. cit., p. 48; Chadwick, op. cit., pp. 99, 118–9, 142.
129. Lash, ibid., pp. 128 ff.
130. Roderick Strange, *Newman and the Gospel of Christ*, pp. 4 ff; *V. V.*, p. 10.
131. *Tract No. 6*, p. 1, *Tracts for the Times*, Vol. 1.
132. *British Critic*, Vol. XXVI, No. LII, p. 412.
133. ibid., p. 411.
134. ibid., pp. 412–3.
135. *Apo.*, p. 97.
136. *L. & D.*, Vol. IV, p. 227.
137. Dragas, op. cit., p. 178.
138. *L. & D.*, Vol. IV, p. 33.
139. *S. S. D.*, pp. 115–6.
140. *U. S.*, p. 35.
141. *P. P. S.*, Vol. VI, p. 121.
142. *U. S.*, p. 82.
143. *S. S. D.*, p. 393.
144. *V. M.*, II, p. 54.
145. Dragas, op. cit., p. 182.
146. *Ath.*, Vol. I, pp. 249–50.
147. *S. S. D.*, p. 391.
148. *Tract No. 6*, p. 3.
149. Thomas Mozley, op. cit., Vol. II, p. 400.
150. For Newman's correspondence with the Abbé Jager and his understanding of the relationship between the episcopal and prophetic traditions, see Louis Allen, *John Henry Newman and the Abbé Jager*. See also G. Biemer, *Newman on Tradition*; John Coulson, "Newman on the Church – his final view, its origins and

influence", *The Rediscovery of Newman*, op. cit., pp. 121 ff. For Newman's own reactions to the Abbé's promptings, see *L. & D.*, Vol. V, pp. 97, 100–2, 107, 116–9, 132–3, 168–70. For a comprehensive treatment of the seventeenth century Anglican background, see P. E. More and F. L. Cross, *Anglicanism, The Thought and Practice of the Church of England, illustrated from the Religious Literature of the Seventeenth Century*; H. R. MacAdoo, *The Spirit of Anglicanism, A Survey of Anglican Theological Method in the Seventeenth Century.*
151. See Allen, op. cit., p. 35.
152. ibid., p. 36.
153. ibid., p. 83.
154. *V. M.*, Vol. I, p. 256.
155. ibid., p. 257.
156. ibid., p. 251.
157. Allen, op. cit., p. 19.
158. *L. & D.*, Vol. V, p. 101.
159. ibid., p. 101.
160. ibid., pp. 102–3.
161. *V. M.*, Vol. I, p. 249.
162. ibid., p. 250.
163. ibid., p. 255.
164. *H. S.*, Vol. II, p. 365.
165. *P. P. S.*, Vol. I, pp. 19–20.
166. *U. S.*, Sermon V, pp. 91–2.
167. *V. M.*, Vol. I, p. 130.
168. ibid., pp. 142–3.
169. ibid., p. 240.
170. ibid., p. 253.
171. ibid., p. 189.
172. ibid., p. 273.
173. ibid., pp. 268–75.
174. *Ess.*, Vol. II, p. 353.
175. *Ari.*, p. 149.
176. *V. M.*, Vol. I, pp. 191, 192, 250.
177. ibid., p. 263.
178. ibid., p. 262.
179. ibid., p. 159.
180. See John Coulson, *Religion and Imagination, "in aid of a grammar of assent"*, pp. 81–2.
181. Henry Tristam, intro., *John Henry Newman, Centenary Essays*, pp. 168, 176.
182. *Tract No. 11*, p. 5.
183. On this theme, see K. D. Bucher, "Newman on the Theologian in

the Church, Some Kindly Light on a Contemporary Problem", *Louvain Stds.*, Vol. VIII, No. 3, pp. 311 ff.; J. Miller, "Newman's Dialogical Vision of the Church", ibid., pp. 320 ff.
184. *Tract No. 85*, p. 19.
185. ibid., p. 25.
186. *The Church of the Fathers*, p. 136.
187. *T. T.*, p. 116.
188. *P. P. S.*, Vol. VII, p. 36. See also *P. P. S.*, Vol. II, pp. 232–54.
189. *P. P. S.*, Vol. VI, p. 220.
190. Newman referred to the *Epistola ad Diognetum* in *T. T.*, p. 201. in reference to the Logos doctrine. It is inconceivable that Newman was unaware of the writer's splendid references to the Church in the world. See *Library of Christian Classics*, Vol. I, p. 216.
191. *Tract No. 83*, p. 37.
192. See D. Nicholls, "Gladstone, Newman and Pluralism" in J. D. Bastable, ed., *Newman and Gladstone*, op. cit., pp. 31 ff.
193. See John Coulson, *Newman and the Common Tradition, A Study in the Language of Church and Society*, p. 235.
194. *U. S.*, pp. 32–3.
195. *P. P. S.*, Vol. VI, pp. 304–5.
196. See E. J. Sillem, op. cit., p. 49.
197. On the Nineteenth Century aspect of the Church and society, see Haddon Willmer, "Holy Worldliness in Nineteenth Century England", Derek Baker, ed., *Studies in Church History*, Vol. X, *Sanctity and Secularity, The Church and the World*, pp. 193–212.
198. See Hilda Graef, *God and Myself, The Spirituality of John Henry Newman*, p. 56.
199. *V. V.*, p. 42.
200. *U. S.*, pp. 41–2, 316.
201. *P. P. S.*, Vol. V, pp. 70–1.
202. ibid., Vol. VI, p. 325.
203. ibid., Vol. VIII, p. 53.
204. *U.S.*, pp. 314, 81.
205. *P. P. S.*, Vol. II, p. 49.
206. *V. M.*, Vol. I, p. 107.
207. *V. M.*, Vol. II, p. 198.
208. *British Critic*, Vol. XXVI, No. LII, p. 426.
209. *The Church of the Fathers*, p. 115.
210. *P. P. S.*, Vol. IV, p. 159. See D. G. Hawkins, "Cardinal Newman's Social Philosophy", *New Blackfriars*, Vol. 53 for a survey of this aspect of Newman.
211. *S. S. D.*, p. 290.
212. *L. & C.*, Vol. I, p. 75.
213. *L. & D.*, Vol. III, p. 72.

214. ibid., Vol. IV, pp. 33943.
215. *H. S.*, Vol. III, pp. 131 ff.
216. See J. D. Holmes, "Factors in the Development of Newman's Political Attitudes", op. cit., p. 58.
217. *British Critic*, op. cit., pp. 418 ff.
218. *P. P. S.*, Vol. VI, p. 369.
219. *Apo.*, p. 198.
220. *P. P. S.*, Vol. I, p. 343.
221. See *Apo.*, p. xxxi and p. 372 for Kingsley's comments.
222. *V. M.*, Vol. I, p. 233.
223. *Tract No. 11*, p. 3.
224. *P. P. S.*, Vol. VIII, p. 129.
225. ibid., Vol. VI, p. 41.
226. See J. D. Holmes, op. cit., p. 78.
227. *P. P. S.*, Vol. V, p. 295.
228. *S. S. D.*, p. 249.
229. *U.S.*, pp. 231 and 364 for the reference to the beggar woman being superior to many learned people.
230. *Ari.*, pp. 147–8.
231. *P. P. S.*, Vol. I, p. 33.
232. ibid., Vol. III, p. 212.
233. ibid., p. 313.
234. *P. P. S.*, Vol. IV, P. 164.
235. *L. & D.*, Vol. IV, p. 28. In *Lamennais and England, The Reception of Lamennais's Religious Ideas in England in the Nineteenth Century*, pp. 105 ff., W. G. Roe wrote that Newman's conception of the Church as a popular power owed much to Lamennais. It is more likely that Lamennais only confirmed what Newman had already read about that topic in the writings of Ambrose and Athanasius. It is interesting that Roe nowhere refers to any of Newman's patristic writings. It was Froude, not Newman, who was in sympathy with many of Lamennais's ideas.
236. Letter, 10 April, 1836; *L. & D.*, Vol. V, p. 275.
237. ibid., Vol. IV, pp. 35, 41, 44, 162, 227.
238. *The Church of the Fathers*, p. 7.
239. ibid., p. 3.
240. On the role of the laity in the Catholic Councils, see Hans Küng, "The Laity in Conciliar History", *Structures of the Church*, pp. 67 ff.; W. J. S. Simpson, *The Role of the Laity in the Church*, pp. 48 ff. The Councils of the fourth and fifth centuries were primarily episcopal, although deacons and lay persons were present. The lay authority as such was severely limited.
241. *V. M.*, Vol. I, p. 257.
242. *Ari.*, p. 154.

243. ibid.
244. *The Church of the Fathers*, p. 21.
245. *Ari.*, p. 455.
246. *U. S.*, p. 73; *P. P. S.*, Vol. V, p. 268.
247. Selby, op. cit., p. 11.
248. *The British Magazine*, Vol. V, p. 127.
249. *S. S. D.*, p. 317.
250. Roe, op. cit., pp. 100 ff.; see also *Ess.*, Vol. I, pp. 121, 122, 124.
251. *V. M.*, Vol. II, pp. 84–5.
252. ibid., p. 87.
253. *V. V.*, p. 190.
254. *Tract No. 83*, pp. 22–4.
255. *Ess.*, Vol. I, p. 122.
256. *D. & A.*, p. 307.
257. See the *British Critic*, Vol. XXX, p. 47, cited by P. J. Welch, "Blomfield and Peel: a Study in Co-operation between Church and State, 1841–6", *The Jl. of Ecc. Hist.*, Vol. XII, p. 71. For general studies of Peel, see especially N. Gash, *Politics in the Age of Peel*. See also his *Mr Secretary Peel: the life of Sir Robert Peel to 1830*; *Reaction and Reconstruction in English Politics 1832–1852*; *Sir Robert Peel: the life of Sir Robert Peel after 1830*. See also Donal Kerr, *Peel, Priests and Politics, Sir Robert Peel's Administration and the Roman Catholic Church in Ireland 1841–6*, pp. 298 ff.
258. See J. R. Griffin, *Tractarian Politics*, citing from mss. Peel Papers, British Museum, 40310 f. 68 (23 March, 1837).
259. *Apo.*, pp. 220–1.
260. See *H. S.*, Vol. II, p. 340. "A Characteristic of the Popes: St Gregory the Great". A Pope could never be this kind of Conservative.
261. See W. Thomas, *The Philosophical Radicals*, p. 21; N. Gash, *Mr Secretary Peel*, p. 333 for Bentham's letter to Peel, rallying him on his conversion to the cause of reform. "What is this I see? One of his Majesty's Principal Secretaries of State become a Reformist? a Law Reform in good earnest? ... Sir, you have passed the Rubicon". March 1830.
262. W. Harrison, intro., to Jeremy Bentham, *A Fragment on Government and an Introduction to the Principles of Morals and Legislation*, p. xi. For a comprehensive study of Newman's attitude to Benthamism, see Thomas Vargish, *Newman, the Contemplation of Mind*, pp. 114–20.
263. See E. Jay, *The Evangelical and Oxford Movements*, p. 169.
264. See Perry Butler, *Gladstone, Church, State and Tractarianism, A Study of his Religious Ideas and Attitudes 1815–1859*, p. 118.
265. William Palmer, op. cit., p. 200.

266. For a different opinion, that Newman's articles were out of touch with the realities of the Nineteenth Century, see C. Egner, *Apologia Pro Charles Kingsley*, pp. 83–4. In contrast, Ian T. Ker, ed., *Idea* p. liii, refers to Newman's brilliantly satirical letters.
267. *U.S.*, pp. 176 ff. The main studies of Newman's epistemology are A. Louth, *Discerning the Mystery, An Essay on the Nature of Theology*, pp. 135 ff; D. A. Pailin, *The Way to Faith: An Examination of Newman's Grammar of Assent as a Response to the Search for Certainty in Faith*; E. J. Sillem, *The Philosophical Notebook*, op. cit.; see also Nicholas Lash, intro., *G. A.*, pp. 1–23. Useful studies also are A. J. Boekraad, *The Personal Conquest of Truth according to J. H. Newman*; J. H. Walgrave, *Newman the Theologian*.
268. *U. S.*, p. 179.
269. Louth, op. cit., p. 138 is of the opinion that the deepest level of the intellect is essentially moral. Newman may well have been indebted to the Greek Fathers, writes Louth, for this insight.
270. *U.S.*, p. 225.
271. ibid., p. 183.
272. For a discussion as to whether Newman was a fideist or not, see Lash, op. cit., pp. 8–9.
273. *U. S.*, pp. 235–6.
274. ibid.
275. Jay, op. cit., p. 169.
276. F. R. Leavis, ed., *J. S. Mill on Bentham and Coleridge*, p. 63.
277. ibid., p. 74.
278. *Apo.*, p. 262.
279. *V. M.*, Vol. I, p. 92.
280. Jay, op. cit., p. 163.
281. *V. M.*, Vol. I, p. lxix.
282. This whole area was a blank for Bentham. See Leavis, op. cit., p. 62.
283. See D. J. deLaura, *Hebrew and Hellene in Victorian England, Newman, Arnold and Pater*, p. 33.
284. Leslie Stephen, *The English Utilitarians*, Vol. I, p. 241.
285. *Ari.*, p. 149.
286. *V. M.*, Vol. I, p. 22.
287. *Ath.*, Vol. I, p. 296.
288. Jay, op. cit., p. 156. See also *P. P. S.*, Vol. V, pp. 247–8.
289. *U. S.*, p. 30.
290. ibid., p. 66.
291. *G. A.*, p. 323.
292. Jay, op. cit., p. 166.
293. ibid., p. 162.

294. ibid., p. 167.
295. *U. S.*, p. 23.
296. *Ari.*, pp. 27–8.
297. *Tract No. 73*, p. 28.
298. See A. Louth, *The Origins of the Christian Mystical Tradition, From Plato to Denys the Areopagite*, p. xi.
299. Jay, op. cit., p. 164.
300. John Coulson, *Newman and the Common Tradition*, op. cit., p. 98.
301. *P. P. S.*, Vol. I, p. 130.
302. See J. Plamenatz, *The English Utilitarians*, pp. 83 ff.
303. *G. A.*, p. 13.
304. L. Stephen, op. cit., pp. 296, 301, 305.
305. *U. S.*, p. 198.
306. ibid., p. 211.
307. Jay, op. cit., p. 179.
308. ibid., p. 179.
309. ibid., p. 185.
310. See H. M. de Archaval, S. J. and J. D. Holmes, *The Theological Papers of J. H. Newman on Faith and Certainty*, pp. 152–3.
311. *U. S.*, p. 27.
312. Jay, op. cit., p. 179.
313. *G. A.*, p. 82.
314. *V. M. II*, p. 67; *British Critic*, Vol. XXVI, No. LII. p. 406.
315. *U. S.*, pp. 234, 236.
316. *P. P. S.*, Vol. I, p. 317.
317. *P. P. S.*, Vol. V, pp. 44–5.
318. On Newman and Liberalism, see Michael Davies, ed., *Newman Against the Liberals*; Owen Chadwick, *Newman*, pp. 71 ff.; Sillem, op. cit., pp. 40 ff.; Vargish, op. cit., pp. 74 ff.
319. *Apo.*, pp. 254 ff.
320. Henry Hart Milman (1791–1868) was Dean of St Paul's from 1849 to 1868. He was Keble's immediate predecessor as Professor of Poetry from 1821 to 1831. His main books were *History of the Jews* (1829), *History of Christianity to the Abolition of Paganism in the Roman Empire* (1840) and *History of Latin Christianity* (1855). The main study of his life and work is Charles Smyth, *Dean Milman*.
321. H. H. Milman, *History of the Jews*, Vol. I, p. 90.
322. *L. & D.*, Vol. II, pp. 160–1.
323. ibid., p. 299.
324. Newman's review appeared in the *British Critic*, Vol. XXIX and was republished as "Milman's View of Christianity", *Ess.* II, pp. 186–248. For a comprehensive survey of Milman's historical method, see Duncan Forbes, *The Liberal Anglican Idea of History*, pp. 78 ff.

325. On this point, see Nicholas Lash, *Newman on Development, The Search for an Explanation in History*, p. 21. Lash disagrees with Owen Chadwick, *From Bossuet to Newman, The Idea of Doctrinal Development*, who wrote that although Newman repudiated the methods of the German and Liberal Anglicans, he could not help learning from them, p. 21. According to Lash, this is misleading, since it was not the method in question which Newman repudiated but the spirit in which that method was too often conducted.
326. *Ess. II*, p. 188.
327. ibid., p. 213.
328. ibid., p. 230.
329. Chadwick, op. cit., p. 99.
330. *Ess. II*, pp. 196–7.
331. ibid., p. 213.
332. ibid.
333. ibid., p. 196.
334. ibid., p. 208.
335. Forbes, op. cit., p. 105.
336. *P. P. S.*, Vol. II, pp. 260–1.
337. *U. S.*, pp. 151–2.
338. *Apo.*, p. 260.
339. *Ess. II*, pp. 189–90. For a discussion of the accommodation principle among Liberal Anglican historians, see Forbes, op. cit., pp. 76–82.
340. *Ess. II*, p. 233.
341. ibid., pp. 220, 230.
342. ibid., p. 233.
343. ibid., p. 242.
344. ibid., p. 232.
345. Chadwick, op. cit., pp. 98 ff.
346. *Ess. II*, p. 71. In this respect, Newman was not dissimilar to a conservative thinker like Archdeacon Denison. See Joyce Coombs, *George Anthony Denison: The Firebrand 1805–96*.
347. Sillem, op. cit., p. 111.
348. Cf. *P. P. S.*, Vol. II, p. 153; Vol. III, p. 81; *U.S.*, pp. 61, 80–1, 225, 250.
349. *Ari.*, p. 141.
350. *Dev.*, p. 348.
351. *Dev.*, Chapter 1, Section 1.
352. ibid., p. 129.
353. Milman, *Quarterly Review*, Vol. 68, p. 411, cited by Forbes, op. cit., p. 83.
354. Chadwick, op. cit., p. 97.
355. *Diffs.*, p. 109; *Dev.* pp. 116 ff.

356. *Dev.*, p. 114.
357. For a discussion of the differences between development, progress and evolution, see Morris Grinsberg, "The Idea of Progress: A Revaluation", *Essays in Sociology and Social Philosophy*, pp. 71–128, cited by Lash, op. cit., p. 63 ff. For a comprehensive study of the idea of progress in religion, see Christopher Dawson, *Progress and Religion, An Historical Enquiry*.
357. *P. P. S.*, Vol. II, p. 153; Vol. III, p. 81.
358. *V. M.*, Vol. I, pp. 132–3, 201–2.
359. Forbes, op. cit., pp. 106–7.
360. *Ess. II*, pp. 247–8.
361. *Dev.*, p. 356.
362. ibid., p. 325.
363. See Chapter Two on Froude, pp. 132 ff. for Newman's increasing dissatisfaction with the Royal Supremacy.
364. See Paul Misner, *Papacy and Development, Newman and the Primacy of the Pope*, pp. 45 ff. I am much indebted to the research of Misner for much of what follows on Newman's image of the imperial Church.
365. *Apo.*, p. 66.
366. ibid., pp. 66–7.
367. ibid., p. 68.
368. Misner, op. cit., pp. 18 ff.
369. ibid.
370. ibid., pp. 24 ff. Froude's quotation is from the *Remains*, III, pp. 220–5.
371. *V. M.*, Vol. I, pp. 258, 259.
372. ibid., p. 262.
373. ibid., p. 265.
374. *Apo.*, p. 108.
375. ibid., p. 110.
376. ibid.
377. ibid., p. 111.
378. ibid., p. 113.
379. *Ess. II*, p. 11.
380. ibid., p. 6.
381. ibid., p. 17.
382. ibid., p. 20.
383. ibid., p. 23.
384. ibid., p. 24.
385. ibid., p. 25.
386. ibid., p. 28.
287. ibid., p. 29.
388. ibid., p. 31.

389. ibid., p. 35.
390. ibid., p. 39.
391. ibid., p. 39.
392. ibid., p. 41.
393. ibid., pp. 51–3.
394. ibid., p. 59.
395. ibid., pp. 71–2.
396. *Apo.*, p. 130.
397. ibid., p. 109.
398. *L. & C.*, Vol. II, p. 263.
399. *Apo.*, p. 130.
400. See G. D. Dragas, "Conscience and Tradition: Newman and Athanasius in the Orthodox Church", *Athanasiana*, Vol. I, p. 180.
401. See Misner, op. cit., p. 39 for Hooper, *Cardinal Newman*, p. 45 citing the way Newman found the key to his interpretation of the Arian controversy in his letter to Mrs William Froude, 5 April, 1844.
402. *Apo.*, pp. 130–1.
403. ibid., p. 133.
404. See Misner, op. cit., pp. 45 ff. See also Misner's article, "Newman and the Tradition concerning the Papal Antichrist", *Church History*, 42, (1973), pp. 377–95.
405. For a systematic treatment of the Antichrist prophecies, see Sheridan Gilley, "Newman and Prophecy, Evangelical and Catholic", *The Jl. of the United Reform Church History Society*, Vol. III, No. 5, pp. 160 ff. The reference to the *Apo.* is on pp. 20 ff. I am greatly indebted to Dr Gilley's article for much of what follows.
406. Gilley, op. cit., pp. 170–1.
407. Cited by Gilley, p. 171 from R. A. Knox, *Enthusiasm: A Chapter in the History of Religion*, p. 557, comparing Newman with the great Evangelical, Edward Irving.
408. Gilley, op. cit., p. 171.
409. *Ess. II*, pp. 134–5. For Newman's fascination with Thomas Scott, see Gilley, pp. 172–3.
410. For Newman's exegesis in 1822 of Revelation 6, see Gilley, pp. 172–4. For Newman's Advent sermons of 1824–5, see Gilley, pp. 174–5; for Newman's review of Edward Cooper's *The Crisis; or, an attempt to shew from prophecy, illustrated by the signs of the times, the prospects and duties of the Church of Christ, at the present period. With an enquiry into the probable destiny of England during the predicted desolations of the Papal Kingdoms*, see Gilley, pp. 166–7, 175–7.
411. *Apo.*, p. 57.

412. ibid., pp. 59 ff.
413. ibid., pp. 57–8.
414. Gilley, op. cit., p. 178.
415. ibid., p. 180.
416. *L. & D.*, Vol. III, pp. 248 ff.
417. ibid., p. 253.
418. ibid., p. 268.
419. ibid.
420. Tract No. 83, *Tracts for the Times*, Vol. V, pp. 13, 21–2.
421. ibid., pp. 23–4.
422. ibid., p. 29.
423. ibid., pp. 35 ff.
424. See *A Letter addressed to the Rev. the Margaret Professor of Divinity, on Mr R. Hurrell Froude's Statements, Concerning the Holy Eucharist, and Other Matters Theological and Ecclesiastical* (1838), published in *V. M.*, Vol. II, pp. 195–257. Newman nowhere referred to this letter in the *Apo.*
425. See Gilley, op. cit., pp. 184–5. The review, "The Protestant Idea of Antichrist" was published in *Ess.* II, pp. 112–85.
426. *V. M.*, Vol. II, pp. 219–20.
427. *Ess.*, II, pp. 160 ff.
428. ibid., pp. 173–4.
429. See Misner, op. cit., pp. 51 ff. Newman's two sermons are in *P. P. S.* Vol. II, pp. 232–54.
430. *Ess. II*, p. 182.
431. ibid., pp. 175–7.
432. ibid., pp. 184–5.
433. See Gilley, op. cit., p. 187.
434. *S. S. D.*, Sermon VIII, Sermons XIV–XXII, XXV.
435. ibid., p. 234.
436. *Ess. II*, pp. 124–5.
437. See Misner, op. cit., p. 87.
438. *S. S. D.*, p. 233.
439. *V. M.*, Vol. I, p. 235.
440. *S. S. D.*, pp. 109–10.
441. ibid., p. 274.
442. *Remains*, Vol. III, p. 224.
443. *S. S. D.*, p. 254.
444. *Apo.*, pp. 137, 139.
445. *Diffs.*, pp. 6–7; *Apo.*, p. 139; *V. M.* Vol. I, p. 260; *Ess.* I, p. 159.
446. *Dev.*, p. 130.
447. *Ess.* Vol. II, pp. 74–5.
448. *Diffs.*, p. 38.
449. *Ess.* I, pp. 384 ff.

450. ibid., p. 382.
451. *Dev.*, p. 296.
452. *Diffs.*, pp. 41–2.
453. See Misner, op. cit., pp. 79–81. Newman referred to heretical Churches being merely "a family" in *Dev.*, p. 275.
454. Misner, p. 179.
455. *Dev.*, p. 286.
456. ibid.
457. ibid., p. 290.
458. ibid., p. 295.

CONCLUSION

In conclusion, my intention is to summarise the main aspects of Keble, Froude and Newman's attitudes towards Church, State and society between 1827 and 1845. The second main section concentrates on the differences and similarities which existed among them. A final section assesses the contribution of Keble, Froude and Newman to political and social thought.

4.1.1. John Keble

The cornerstone of Keble's whole understanding of the Church in its relationship with the State was the Royal Supremacy. As much as his beloved Hooker, Keble was adamant that this idea was not Erastian. The trust invested in the Christian Prince was supported by an appeal to what was second nature to Keble, the Christian Tradition. In the first three centuries, the Kings of the earth had received their commission to be Nursing Fathers of the Church. Constantine refused to take his seat at the Council of Nicaea until he was requested by the Bishops to do so. St Ambrose resisted Valentinian and excommunicated Theodosius, while St Basil refused to change the Church formularies, though it might have brought Valens into Church communion.[1]

Keble knew exactly what was Erastian. In the *Advertisement* to the sermon, "National Apostasy", Keble wrote of a Legislature which had usurped its commission of those whom Our Lord entrusted with at least one voice in making ecclesiastical laws, on matters wholly or partly spiritual. The Church of England had indeed become one sect among many, and now was a mere

Parliamentarian Church. Occasionally, Keble reflected on the idea of disestablishment, which owed much to the influence of Hurrell Froude. Even Parliament must be excommunicated in 1833! In this way, Keble's stance was radically different from "The Friends of the Church" and Gladstone whom he criticised in 1839 for neglecting the idea of a voluntary system, accepting the Royal Supremacy so uncritically and believing that a National Religion could be truly Catholic.[2]

I have concluded, however, that for all his radical utterances between 1833 and 1839, Keble never seriously contemplated disestablishment. He was far too much of a canon lawyer to ignore the legal difficulties involved in such a move. He was only too well aware of the spiritual advantages of the Establishment. Instead, he advocated supreme perseverance in all adversity.

In his understanding of the Church's relationship with society, Keble was aware that mankind had to be adamant in its beliefs and principles. Society must escape the curse "of continuing for ever wavering and unsteady in all the great rules and principles: 'ever wavering, and never able to come to the knowledge of the truth'".[3] As the pattern of holiness, the Church illustrated what could be achieved. Indeed, wrote Keble, there was enough here "to fill out a whole life – of Catholic opinions, usages and sympathies, wherein we may indulge without a shadow of offence".[4] At Hursley, Keble visualised a national community composed of societies of men, women and children, each tending its own area like a sacred trust or stewardship. Keble's panacea was always God-centred, God-orientated, God-inspired. Few Anglican theologians since have been so utterly convinced that only one temperament would suit the Christian soul, "the temper of perfect resignation and singleness of purpose". Such an attitude in life would inevitably lead to "a constant inward appeal, as it were, from a bad and seducing world to a good God".[5] Such an attitude, such a spirit could only flourish in a society which had intense respect for the small community, "the little platoon" which Burke had opposed to what he had seen as the unnatural universals offered by the political philosophy of the French Revolution.[6] As much as his hero, Homer, Keble "reflected the ideas of those who prefer their own happy conditions, however antiquated, however obsolete and old-fashioned, to the united nostrums of reformers".[7] Such a society spoke of organic wholes, not separate parts, emphasising the preordained station in life of rich and poor alike. Its concern was not what was visibly best for its own inhabitants but what was most pleasing to God.[8] Precisely because its orientation and direction was so Godward, it was a foretaste of heavenly, otherworldly realities. It was a place where its inhabitants seemed to be saying "Holy, Holy, Holy, Lord God of Sabaoth" not merely at divine worship but all day long.[9]

4.1.2. Hurrell Froude

Froude was the only really advanced political thinker among the first founders of the Oxford Movement. Having no wish that the Church should be nourished by the dry husks of vague generalities, Froude wanted positive action. No one seemed able to decide to what degree Churchmen should compromise with a society renowned for its laxity in faith and morals. The real difficulty was that spiritual rulers were not free to use their apostolical authority. Consequently their word was not law. Froude was convinced that desperate times needed desperate measures.[10] He felt that the changes in the Constitution between 1828 and 1833 amounted to a downright revolution.

Yet Froude exaggerated the changed position of the Church during those five cataclysmic years. In principle, the Acts of 1828, 1829 and 1832 did change the Church's position dramatically, and yet the Anglican position suffered only gradual erosion during the next fifty years. In reality, the Church was left as an Establishment with a State connexion with many privileges and rights unaffected.[11]

Such a phenomenon, however, was deemed by Newman to be the real author of the Oxford Movement.[12] Not only did he bring Keble and Newman together but also he influenced both.[13] At times, he proved too strong a medicine. His panaceas could prove inebriating, confusing truth with mendacity, sincerity with impatience. Yet he was the most daring spirit of all. Realising that he must always apply what he read about, he became the advocate of Anglican Ultramontanism.[14]

.Dogmatic religion must never give way to Latitudinarianism. Froude thought that the constitutional power of the realm had been disturbed irrevocably against the interests of the Church. It had not been so once when Becket knew that Christ alone could be head not only of the Church but also the Empire. It would be so again, claimed Froude, when a radical Church would be founded on Catholic truth.[15]

The four Volumes of the *Remains* are adequate witness to the spiritual and political insights of Froude's penetrating, if frequently acerbic, mind. The Church was considered not as a glorified Board of Health but in all its Catholic glory, founded purely on the Rock of Christ with the saints and the "pauperes Christi" as its main pillars. Froude's prophetic witness upset the sacred ministers of the Establishment who, claimed J. A. Froude, were never on the most amenable of terms with their prophets except when the latter prophesied lies.[16] So frequently the most conservative of revivalists make the most adept revolutionaries.[17]

Froude's was a frontier existence. Keen at first to preserve the established order in Church, state and society, he came to realise that a fundamental reassessment was required. His personal misfortune dramatised the urgency of an already revolutionary setting. The *Remains* upset a whole generation of Churchmen. Froude would probably have enjoyed that. Writing of great leaders in his novel *Coningsby*, Disraeli summarised their contribution in a way which could well be applied to Froude: "A cause is a great abstraction, and fit only for students; embodied in a party, it stirs men to action; but place at the head of that party a leader who can inspire enthusiasm, he commands the world".[18]

4.1.3. John Henry Newman

Newman's attitude to the Church and State relationship was a develoment from a view of the Church as an institution protected by the Sovereign power of King and Parliament to the image of the imperial Church commanding respect and devotion in 1842. From 1829 till his death in February 1836, Hurrell Froude acted as a catalyst upon Newman's position of high establishmentarianism.[19] Abandoning formally in April 1836 his faith in the Royal Supremacy, Newman became obsessed with the Catholicity of the Church of England. In 1839 there occurred the Donatist scare when Newman realised the sheer inadequacy of the Ignatian-Cyprianic view of the monarchic episcopate in the crises of the fourth century. In the background, his concern about the Antichrist prophecies began to exert an ever greater fascination over his imagination, as his sermons of 1822, 1824 and 1830 reveal.[20] Before the Oxford Movement began officially on 14 July, 1833, Newman, writing from Italy, associated the pagan city of Rome rather than the Roman Church or the Pope with Antichrist. The Roman Church was conceived in ambiguous terms, was she "Light of the wide west or heinous error-seat?" The same ambiguity appeared in "Home Thoughts from Abroad" in 1833 and in his four Lectures on "The Patristical Idea of Antichrist", published as *Tract No. 83*. It was the pagan spirit of the city of Rome which had invaded the papal Church and throne. After the publication of the first part of Froude's *Remains* in 1838, Newman was involved in reviewing the *Prophecies Relating to Antichrist in the Writings of Daniel and St Paul* by J. H. Todd. If Rome was Antichrist as an establishment, then so was Canterbury, which, like the beast, also had an episcopal hierarchy, Apostolic succession, priesthood, formal worship and sacraments. It was in the conclusion of his article, however, that Newman allowed himself full imaginative rein. The Medieval Church, far from being a realisation of Antichrist, was inverted prophetically as "an imperial Church" with all the necessary embellishments of Isaiah's vision of the kings and ships and isles bringing gifts, and "the sapphires and agates of the heavenly Jerusalem".[21]

It was this image of the Church which formed the essential background to Newman's sermons of 1842 on the Church as an imperial power. He became the advocate of universal triumphalism. The secular kingdoms of the world existed to do obeisance to the Church which was an empire in its own right. Out of the chrysalis of a Church protected by the Sovereign power of King and Parliament, there emerged the glorious, living Church commanding universal respect and devotion. The climax came in 1845 with the theme of the Church as an imperial power renewed, "a vast organised association, coextensive with the Roman Empire, or rather overflowing it". Local, independent union with one's Bishop, the Anglican view, was subsumed in the higher, universal communion, centred around the Vicar of Christ, the Roman Catholic view.[22]

Newman's conception of the Church's role in society has been studied under four heads.[23] First, the role of the individual alongside the Church in her episcopal and prophetic traditions was very much Newman's concern between 1833 and 1837. Newman was utterly convinced of the immortal worth of every individual soul. There was only one Homer, Cicero and Caesar, one Constantine or Charlemagne, one Paul and John, one Athanasius, Augustine or Thomas. The only way to exercise influence was to do it personally. In itself, private judgement was good but it could be abused. Newman devoted three whole chapters to an understanding of this faculty in his *Lectures on the Prophetical Office of the Church*. We must always learn to analyse and state formally our reasons for what we do actually believe. Yet Newman was keen to limit the exercise of private judgement to those issues which had not been determined already by Church authority. If private judgement exceeded the limits of its role, it could move in the direction of innovation. The real task of private judgement was to determine what and where was the Church. That is why collective wisdom was on the whole better than that offered by individuals. Newman's ideal was the comfort of the individual in the unity of the Body of Christ. In matters of doctrine, private judgement was not enough. It was the duty of the individual in such matters to accept what he was told by authority. That is why from the beginning Prophets or Doctors were the interpreters of the Revelation. If the Church was to survive, however, she had to be socially orientated. It was only within the Church that the individual could truly become socially integrated.[24]

Secondly, the Church must spiritualise society and save souls. Newman's concern was not with political reformers but saints. The salvation of souls was infinitely more important than making individuals decent. Political reforms alone could never save men's souls.[25]

Thirdly, Newman's social conscience has been studied. Newman cared about society and was vitally interested in the events of the day. Yet his perspective was always eternal. Everything in this life, mental or physical pain, the loss of friends, was subordinate to the real task of the Christian, the salvation of individual souls.[26]

Fourthly, Newman's enthusiasm for the people between 1833 and 1836 has been considered with much circumspection. He was always at pains to show how the illiterate, the poor, had real faith. He genuinely wished to make the Church more popular, as his letters between 1833 and 1836 reveal. Yet the difficulties of such a concept were insuperable. Why were the Christian masses no longer as they were in the time of Ambrose blockading the Churches against the invasion of the heathen? Theologically, Newman's concern was always with the few. His patristic learning assured him that the laity did have a voice in the formation of Christian doctrine in the Early Church. Yet the voice of the laity was passive only and not active. Their reaction was frequently a test of Orthodoxy.[27]

4.2. SIMILARITIES

4.2.1. Holy Otherworldliness

Ronald Knox's comment that Newman's reaction to the Age of Reform was to foresee and brand as apostasy our modern preoccupation with politics, could also be applied to Keble and Froude.[28] Keble was the author of a sermon which bore the title, "National Apostasy" while Newman wrote about apostasy on a global scale. Keble was of the opinion that contemporary England was besotted with thoughts of political reform. Indeed, the nation was very similar to Israel in the time of Solomon. Here was a society which lacked reserve and moral taste. Hampden as Regius Professor of Divinity denied the importance of Tradition; Malthus provided much of the inspiration for political economists and progressive bishops alike. Keble thought they were no better than heretics, the open enemies of society.[29] Froude castigated the vermin Whigs who were simply the heirs of those who had expropriated the lands of the Church at the Reformation.[30] Newman was sickened by the sight of men attempting to build the earthly Jerusalem to their own glory. Good works alone were essentially Pelagian.[31]

In contrast to the prevailing spirit of Rationalism, Liberalism, Erastianism and Utilitarianism, Keble, Froude and Newman provided other panaceas for men's woes. An otherworldly temperament such as Keble, Froude and Newman possessed should not be confused, however, with a lack of interest, apathy or callousness, an important insight which has been stressed recently by John Saward in *Perfect Fools*. So frequently in the Christian tradition the most valuable discernment of the times has been provided by those who in every age have protested against every attempt to conform the Gospel to secular ideology, the mere wisdom of the world.[32] Keble stated emphatically that not to be concerned about politics was in itself immoral.[33] In *Tract No. 2* Newman wrote, "It is sometimes said, that the Clergy should abstain from politics; and that, if a Minister of Christ is political, he is not a follower of him who said, 'My kingdom is not of this world'. Now there is a sense in which this is true, but, as it is commonly taken, it is very false. It is true that mere affairs of this world should not engage a clergyman; but it is absurd to say that the affairs of this world should not at all engage his attention".[34]

Unlike the Evangelicals who wished to embark on social and political crusades and Christianise culture, Keble, Froude and Newman believed human effort on its own to be a waste of time. The sombre Augustinian vision of the mass of mankind as exiled from God's presence without hope in this world or another was too real to be trivialised and degraded by temporary political expedients. The heresies of the day could not be confounded by human resources, however well conceived. Keble, Froude and Newman advocated far sterner measures.

Unlike his learned peers, J. B. Sumner, Copleston and Whately, who wrote tracts on political and social reform,[35] Keble composed *The Christian Year*. No parish priest was more otherworldly than Keble, so much so that Newman thought him "out of sight" for most of the time.[36] Keble gave the impression of seeking obscurity. He hated publicity. In his poetry, and especially in *The Christian Year* which was intended as a supplement to the Prayer Book, Keble advocated a sacramental, hierarchical and orderly administration of society.

Froude, volatile, flamboyant and controversial was still rigorously ascetic, almost to the point of neurosis. His solution for contemporary problems was a theocratic society with the Church giving harmonious direction to all members of society, according to the pre-Reformation pattern.

Newman was convinced that no amount of political or social reform could ease the burden of inherited sin; moral, religious and spiritual improvement came only with "holiness before peace" and "Growth the only evidence of life" rather than appeals for massive institutional change. The religion of the day, however, was utterly different in its emphasis, since "everything is bright and beautiful. Religion is pleasant and easy; benevolence is the chief virtue; intolerance, bigotry, excess of zeal, are the first of sins". The end result was an aesthetically pleasing millennial kingdom, achieved by human labours, which was, in fact, nothing more than "the elegance and refinement of mere human civilization".[37]

Yet men with such an otherworldly temperament did make a profound contribution to the whole Church, State and society question. They were contemptuous of the world and its praise. They were most scholarly, and yet pursued scholarship for purely religious and moral ends. They were reserved and unobtrusive, yet determined to recover the glory of the Church for Protestant England.

4.2.2 The Church's Mission to Society

Keble, Froude and Newman conceived the Church's mission to society in essentially spiritual terms. Keble knew that whatever happened, the Church of England would always be found in his parish. Here in the local community, around a Prayer Book and Clergyman, Keble saw the Church's mission to society in local, rural and pre-industrial terms. It is in such an environment, the world of Poet Laureates from Southey and Wordsworth to Betjeman and Hughes that the Church of England has always felt most at home. This was the timeless world of English groves and streams, a humble Gothic building in a mossy churchyard, the parish of Wordsworth's honest peasant and pastor, which inspired so much the central ideas of *The Christian Year*.

Froude's emphasis was equally spiritual. He saw the Church restored to her medieval splendour at the centre of communities. The Church of England with her smug parsons and pampered aristocrats had forgotten her mission to the poor of the earth. The *Remains* advocated Colleges of unmarried priests to evangelise the new towns of industrial England. Froude himself did very little about the mission of the Church in society. It was his writing rather than his deeds which influenced people. His ideals summarised in the third and fourth volumes of the

Remains stirred two of the most impressive converts to Roman Catholicism, W. G. Ward and Frederick Faber, who visualised the Church without endowed property, tithes or rates.[38] The attractiveness of the Church was apparent enough in the twelfth century when the poor had supported the martyred Becket against the state Bishops. Such heroism might once again become a reality in contemporary society.

Newman was well aware that the great disease of the Church in all ages was that of serving God for the sake of Mammon, loving religion out of love for the world. Newman wondered how many would truly support Christ's Holy Catholic Church if her cause were not of order but of disorder, as in the time of Christ and the apostles. So many in the Church of England loved her for worldly prosperity, that were the peace of the world and the welfare of the Church at variance with each other, they would gladly side with the world against the Church.[39] The Church of God, the fulfilment of Daniel's prophecy about "the kingdom of the saints", was in the world but not of it. Disclaiming the use of force and carnal weapons, the Church conquered the kingdoms of the world. She alone was a kingdom of truth and righteousness.[40] That is why her task at all times and in all places, in fourth century Alexandria or nineteenth century Oxford, is to sanctify individuals, spiritualise society and redeem the times. Let her be associated with movements which have mere political ends, the result is always the same. Her life is imperilled.[41]

It is only in such a perspective that it is possible to make any sense of Newman's famous saying that it would be better for the whole world to perish in agony by fire than for one man to commit a venial sin. All events of the day were subject to this one central concern of his entire Christian ministry in the Church of England, man's eternal destiny and the salvation of his unique immortal soul.

4.2.3. *Rich and Poor One in Christ*

Keble, Froude and Newman were severe critics of the society in which they lived. They portrayed the Benthamite school of philosophers as unfeeling and rational, the Whig aristocracy as insensitive and mercenary. This was the atomised society built on self-interest, *laissez-faire* and Utilitarianism. Symptomatic of this society was the Reverend Mr Malthus who was one of the most influential writers of the age. Greatly favoured by progressive Bishops and clerics, Malthus gave a sanction to the idea that poverty stemmed from a lack of moral fibre, laziness, drunkenness, or simple thriftlessness.[42] Rather than promote a society where the poor were tolerated, the classical economists made poverty a curse with the only relief on offer the terror of a well-disciplined workhouse. Instead of creating an environment where the poor felt they had a right to relief, the idea evolved of the pure, clinical society in which contentment, morality and wealth would reign supreme and poverty, crime and sloth would be banished for ever.

Keble's understanding of society was the antithesis of the political economists, who would have thought Keble's idea of the rich man wanting the poor man's labour, and the poor man wanting the rich man's meat, and both wanting the love and prayers of each other, as delightfully irrelevant in the new industrial age with the poor masses of the factory towns, children exploited in textile mills and illiterate proletariats living in misery, disease and vice. Keble emphasised preserving closely knit communities and utilising parish officials' intimate knowledge of the lives of the poor, all of which symbolised the pre-industrial culture in which the political structure was dominated by upper-class leadership and in which social tensions were resolved by upper-class paternalism.[43]

Nowhere was this more evident than in Keble's understanding of the poor of the earth. Poverty was a blessing, a sign of God's presence in a broken and divided world. God needs his distressed brethren. In his poetry and sermons, Keble raised the poor from their conditions of misery into a sacramental, mystical world where they were considered the blessed of the earth. Illiterate peasants became the paradigms of God's gracious and mysterious Providence because, if they were true to their vocation, they were living patterns of Christ himself. This was a romantic idealisation of the lot of the English peasant classes, a picture which has always featured prominently in the Catholic understanding of poverty. Holy poverty, however, must be countered by holy charity which took the form of almsgiving, arrangements of the allotment system, concern with the just operation of the Poor Law and criticism of the treatment of the poor in the new

Workhouses. The wealthy were there primarily to perform their duties towards God's poor. This was a vision of charity, spiritually motivated, individually offered, voluntarily maintained in contrast to relief, mechanically administered, impersonally given, coldly calculating and spiritually invalid. Keble knew his parishioners as worthy objects of salvation; the new system conceived people as automata to be classified.[44]

The *Remains* helped considerably to propagandise an interpretation of the Reformation which saw that catastrophic event as the harbinger of all contemporary English woes, not only the submission of the Catholic Church to the ever increasingly secular state, but also the substitution of heartless administrators caring for God's poor for the incomparable charity offered by the monasteries. In his adulation and idealisation of the "pauperes Christi", Froude romantically contrasted an infinitely better system in pre-Reformation times when the poor were seen as worthy objects of charity with the contemporary state of affairs where the poor were seen as miserable proletarians. To understand the Reformation in this way was undoubtedly bad history. Froude's ambition to unMiltonise, unCambridgise and unProtestantise the Church of England shocked the conscience of Protestant England.[45] Little wonder that the reactions to the *Remains* were so violent. Yet ideals have their influence. Faber read the *Remains* and was transferred into fiction by Disraeli as the new model parish priest of the revitalised Church of England. This incumbent's charitable care for the poor of his parish was known to all.[46] In stark contrast to the 1834 Poor Law, with its odious principle that outdoor relief should cease forthwith, was the pre-Reformation ideal of the monastery, possessing no private property, saving no money, bequeathing nothing. England then had deathless landlords; now there was only a harsh guardian, a grinding mortgagee, or a dilatory master in chancery.[47] The *Remains* proved to be an inspiration to the rising tide of Young Tories, epitomised by Young England, whose ideas of "noblesse oblige" were in stark contrast to the progressivist Peelite Conservatism which was all too eager to make its peace with the rising tide of mining Inspectors, Boards of Health and Poor Law Guardians. The whole idea of paternalistic doctrines of mutual help and trust between rich and poor appeared redundant to so many of an enlightened temper, but the appeal to what seemed to be a kinder, more charitable age never lost its fascination in the 1830's and 1840's for those like Froude and members of the Young England Party who believed that the Church's mission was primarily to the poor of the earth.

Newman himself never questioned the social order. Indeed, the Gospel tended to make contented and obedient subjects and kept the lowest orders from outbreaks of violence. Rebellion, sedition and riot were anthematised by the Gospel. "Such is the history of society", wrote Newman, "it begins in the poet and ends in the policeman".[48] But although the benefits resulting from an ordered and orderly society were immense, these were as nothing compared with the unseen spiritual blessings, the true and proper gifts of Christ's Kingdom. The strength of the Church did not lie in earthly law or human countenance or civil station but in those gifts which Christ pronounced to be beatitudes. "Blessed are the poor in spirit, the mourners, the meek, the thirsters after righteousness, the merciful, the pure in heart, the peacemakers, the persecuted".[49]

Newman was only truly at home in an older world which praised the theologians, the poets and philosophers in their daily endeavours. Newman distrusted the new world which was coming into existence, full of shrewd, insensitive men of business. In contrast to the new society with its concern for centralisation, its magistrates and police officers, Newman's idea of society was concerned solely with the propagation of spiritual values.[50] What mattered fundamentally was not to change the material condition of mankind, but to minister primarily to their spiritual needs in the local situation.

In their understanding of the complementary role of the rich and poor in society, Keble, Froude and Newman were completely at odds with the prevalent Utilitarian spirit. The greatest mistake of this popular creed was that it did not recognise that from the moral point of view suffering and happiness could not be treated as symmetrical. Keble, Froude and Newman were of the opinion that the promotion of happiness did not compare with the infinitely more urgent task of rendering help to those who suffered. Human suffering, then and now, makes a direct moral appeal for help. There can be no similar call to increase the happiness of those who are doing well anyway.

4.2.4. Detestation of Democracy

The dominant spirit of the age in which Keble, Froude and Newman lived was Liberalism. Its practical achievement was the modern democratic state and what is popularly called the pluralist society. Bourgeois capitalism was superseding landed aristocracy. Keble, Froude and Newman believed passionately in an ideology of hierarchy and a God-given order. There was theological justification for such a view. The Book of Common Prayer, the Book of Homilies and the Catechism spoke of man's duty towards his neighbour as obeying the King and all that are put in authority under him, ordering himself lowly and reverently to all his betters, not coveting or desiring other men's goods but learning and labouring truly to get their own living and doing their duty in that state of life to which it had pleased God to call him. Such views were there to be read and understood in Book VIII of Richard Hooker's *Laws of Ecclesiastical Polity*. The people must never cast down the Lord's anointed. That was precisely Oliver Cromwell's crime, that was the error that brought in Dutch William and dispossessed the Nonjuring Divines. No priest, no layman, then or since, was more familiar with Hooker's ideas about the importance of obedience, that the lowest must be knit to the highest "by that which being interjacent may cause to cleave unto other, and so all continue one" than Keble.

Keble himself was most enthusiastic about subordination and deference. He thought the 1831 Bristol rioters no better than Romanists and Rationalists, enemies of the Established system. Doctrinal, political and social disturbers of the peace had no idea whatsoever of a fixed law of social life.[51] Similarly, Keble always felt that the laity should not have any power to reverse what the clergy had already decided in matters of Christian doctrine. He had no idea of the Church as a popular power. Such a hierarchical system of Church goverment had to correspond to a similar state in the political realm. Keble had theological reasons for detesting democracy. To appreciate poetry, a due sense of reserve must always be shown. Such a state of affairs was impossible in a democratic state where the poet, to be popular, accepted and heard, must betray the secrets of his heart and become the plaything of the masses.[52]

Of the founding Fathers of the Oxford Movement, Froude alone showed any real sympathy with the idea of making the Church popular. Yet Froude, like Faber, Ward and members of the Young England Party, was never enthusiastic about democracy. A strong and powerful sympathy with the people, combined with the idea of paternalism, never extended as far as giving the people their democratic rights. The "pauperes Christi" must be protected, vindicated and saved but universal suffrage was anathema to Froude, who would have shared the general Tory paternalist distrust of Trade Unions, let alone strikes. This mood was reflected by Disraeli when Dandy Mick in *Sybil*, referring to a strike, had in mind nothing less than the sort of upheaval which would dethrone Kings and Queens.[53]

Froude certainly had much in common with Lamennais but Froude disliked immensely the Frenchman's advocacy of universal suffrage. In that respect, much of what Froude wrote, like the sentiments of Young England, did share a complementarity of aims with the revived Ultramontanism in France, for which Lamennais was partly responsible. Prophetic figures like Frederic Ozanam, the founder of the Society of St Vincent de Paul, the Comte de Melun, the Comte de Falloux and Phillippe Gerbet were exponents of conservative Social Catholicism. This was a social, Roman Catholic version of Froude's Anglican Ultramontanism.[54]

Newman's concern to make the Church more popular appeared to be as great as Froude's between 1833 and 1836. His letters during those years are ample testimony to this. He was always at pains to show how the illiterate and the poor had real faith. Yet, theologically speaking, how could the Church become more popular? Newman's concern was always with the few. His patristic learning assured him that the laity only had a passive voice in the formation of Christian doctrine. His detestation of democracy during his Anglican ministry reflected a fear of apocalyptic proportions. He associated liberals and democrats with infidels. He had an unspeakable aversion to the alliance between the political liberals and O'Connell's Irish Catholics.[55] The spirit of revolutionary France was so odious that Newman kept indoors when he stopped at Algiers, so as not to see the Tricolour. This was the basic failure with Lamennais. He had not heeded the simple lesson that rebellion was always a sin.[56]

Newman's abhorrence to democracy, however, did not blind him to the reality that evil in society was not the exclusive work of those whom he branded as "Socialists, Red Republicans, Anarchists and Rebels"[57] but equally the Whigs and millowners for directing economic discontents into political channels. The calculating political selfishness of the new industrial order was as detestable as the violence of the masses.[58]

4.3. DIFFERENCES

There was a vital difference of emphasis in Keble, Froude and Newman concerning the Church's relationship with the State. Keble's constant emphasis was the spiritual independence of the Church from the State. Writing in *The British Magazine* of 1834, Keble was at pains to point out to the Bishop of Leighlin and Ferns that any arrangement of dioceses was an invasion of a fundamental principle of the Church when the opinions of the episcopal body were overborne. This was a direct contravention of Article 34 of the Thirty Nine Articles of Religion and also of the Second Canon of the Council of Constantinople, whereby the ecclesiastical legislation of each Province was committed to the Bishops of that Province.[59] That is precisely why Keble attached such fundamental importance to the Royal Supremacy, since it was the Monarch's essential task, as Nursing Father, in the spirit of the Coronation Oath, to act as the Guardian of the Church. In 1833 the ideal had been considerably tarnished. It was a strange way for a Nursing Father to behave, casting down at will the thrones of those whom the Father had ordained to govern the whole family. An alliance on such terms involved a great sin. The State enforced the alliance but the Church also consented to it.[60]

In contrast, Froude advocated the actual supremacy of the Church over the state in a truly theocratic manner. Unlike Keble, who always wished to emphasise that the Royal Supremacy was essentially not Erastian, Froude saw Erastianism everywhere. Since the days of Pontius Pilate, it had raised its ugly head in the world and held the Church of God in bondage. Froude had no patience with Cranmer, Latimer and Ridley, who like their contemporary successors, had compromised the interests of the Church with those of the State. Froude's hereoes were those who had behaved in a theocratic manner, Becket and Cardinal Pole, Penry and the Puritan Reformers. Froude's views were far more uncompromising than those of Keble.

Between 1829 and 1833, Newman himself upheld the spiritual independence of the Church within the existing structures. His early enthusiasm for the Royal Supremacy is well documented.[61] Yet after 1836, with his loss of faith in the Royal Supremacy, his position veered increasingly in the direction of Froude's more extreme views, to such an extent that by 1842 the Church could no longer rely upon any secular, atheistic, Erastian concept of the State for support. To be a true Church, she had to be spiritually superior in her own right. In that sense, Newman's final position in 1842 was much nearer in spirit to that of Froude's than Keble's.

4.4. THE CONTRIBUTION OF KEBLE, FROUDE AND NEWMAN TO POLITICAL AND SOCIAL THOUGHT

4.4.1. John Keble

Keble enriched the Toryism of his day by imbuing it with a deep moral and spiritual temper. He showed himself to be the exponent of an understanding of the world which was due in no small measure to his reading of the Fathers, especially Saint Irenaeus, Richard Hooker and the divinity of the seventeenth century. This outlook meant the recovery of a perspective on life, which had been kept alive by the witness of Archbishop Sancroft, Bishop Ken and Kettlewell. Bishop Butler had maintained this elevated moral and spiritual temper in his *Analogy* and his understanding of the sacramentalism of Nature, in stark contrast to what was considered the hedonistic, worldly Latitudinarianism of his day. Edmund Burke was the mouthpiece of this moral outlook after the French Revolution. The Tory humanism of Southey and Wordsworth immortalised this spirit in a poetic, literary fashion against an age which was prosaic and materialistic. This outlook was expressed by Pusey in his sermon of the fifth of November, 1837, "Patience and Confidence the Strength of the Church", preached at St Mary's before the University of Oxford and dedicated to Keble who "in years past unconsciously implanted a truth which was afterwards to take root, himself the dutiful disciple of its ancient guardian and faithful witness in word and action". In a superficial age, eternal truth had been discarded not because it had been disproved but because it was "out of date, as if any changes introduced by men could annul the ordinance of God". This was always Keble's emphatic witness, that the Christian society is based upon eternal realities with the Sovereign placed over the affairs of men, not as the instrument of God's will, but as "ordained of God".

4.4.2. Hurrell Froude

The least theologically educated of the Tractarians, his *imprimatur* was always zealously sought by Keble and Newman. A Jacobite who loved the Roman Breviary, he reflected the deep Medieval and feudal roots of Toryism. If Young England was the Oxford Movement translated by Cambridge from religion into politics, as J. E. Baker first claimed in 1933, then Froude was largely responsible. Althouh Keble and Newman referred to the Middle Ages in their writings, Froude alone was totally fascinated by the pre-Reformation period. Detesting the vermin Whigs and Latitudinarian Tories, hating the Reformation with a perfect hatred, his vision was of a truly theocratic society with the Church at the centre giving direction to the destinies of its citizens. The Hildebrandine outlook signified a radical rejection of the contemporary Conservatism and a quest for an alternative in the feudal past.

4.4.3. John Henry Newman

Convinced of the depravity of the world, a theological belief confirmed by the democratic infidelity which stemmed from the French Revolution, "that arrogant, falsely liberal, and worldly spirit, which great cities make dominant in a country",[63] Newman felt certain that the spirit of Antichrist was a reality in contemporary England. There was nothing new in that. Nations and individuals were mortal. Kingdoms of the world always had their strength of life in bold deeds and bad principles.[64] The tradition of fifteen hundred years threatened, Newman knew that only Orthodoxy, right belief, could stem the tide. As much as royal-hearted Athanasius, Newman knew that his task was to help the human race to distinguish the true God and father of our Lord Jesus Christ from the idols, from the projections of the human mind and condition whose power enslaved the world. The Church had burst into life all over the world, thus becoming a unique phenomenon in human affairs. According to Newman, the Church's mission was not to accommodate itself to the relevant needs of society but rather to be loyal to the Scriptures and the Fathers and oppose the existing course of things. All earthly power rose and fell. The Church alone was eternal.[65]

But Orthodoxy must be lived, since it is bound up with integrity, Orthopraxis. Newman never abandoned during his Anglican days his conservative otherworldliness. In 1829, he had looked in vain to Peel to preserve the traditional Christian polity. Not only did Peel betray the true spirit of Toryism, he also betrayed the everlasting Catholic Church.[66] Newman felt in 1833 that he could hope for nothing good from Tory, let alone Whig, administrations. Peel was largely responsible for the progressivist spirit of the Conservative Party, genuflecting to the reign of Knowledge, the cause of true happiness. This Toryism was not much better than the worship of the goddess Liberty which had led to the pillage and destruction of the French Churches and the spoliation of the Gallican clergy. Such a worldly, materialistic, insensitive political creed was anathema to Newman. Instead, he embraced a moral, religious and spiritual outlook which was transcendental in its dimensions. This accorded well with his idea that the Church would always prevail over the heathen kingdoms of the world. Such an attitude to Church, State and society had existed before when the Gospel had been realised in its fullest perfection, with both Caesar and St Peter knowing and fulfilling their office, Charles the King, Laud as Prelate and Oxford the sacred city of that principle.[67] This kind of Toryism, unlike the cold, unimaginative and prosaic Conservative Party of the day, is based on loyalty to persons and springs immortal in the human breast, with Religion as a spiritual loyalty and Catholicity the only divine form of Religion.[68]

CONCLUSION

NOTES

1. See Chapter 1, pp. 59 ff.
2. See Chapter 2, pp. 109 ff.
3. John Keble, *Tract No. 60*, Tracts for The Times, Vol. II, Pt. I, p. 12.
4. John Keble, *Sermons Acad. and Occ.*, p. lxxi.
5. ibid., p. 103.
6. Edmund Burke, *Reflections on the Revolution in France*, p. 53.
7. John Keble, *Lectures on Poetry*, Vol. I, p. 243.
8. *Sermons Acad. and Occ.*, p. xv.
9. J. T. Coleridge, *A Memoir of the Rev. John Keble*, p. 604.
10. See Froude's article in *The British Magazine*, July 1834, pp. 52 ff.
11. See Chapter 2, pp. 105 ff.
12. *Diffs.*, p. 32.
13. *Remains*, Vol. I, p. 438.
14. Piers Brendon, *Hurrell Froude and the Oxford Movement*, p. 158.
15. Piers Brendon, "Newman, Keble and Froude's Remains", op. cit., p. 190.
16. J. A. Froude, "The Oxford Counter-Reformation", op. cit., p. 250.
17. Brendon, *Hurrell Froude*, op. cit., p. xviii.
18. Benjamin Disraeli, *Coningsby*, p. 133.
19. See Chapter 2, pp. 114 ff.
20. See pp. 233 ff.
21. See pp. 236 ff.
22. See pp. 238 ff.
23. See pp. 186 ff.
24. See pp. 190 ff.
25. See pp. 198 ff.
26. See pp. 201 ff.
27. See pp. 203 ff.
28. Ronald Knox, *Enthusiasm: A Chapter in the History of Religion*, p. 557.
29. See Chapter 1, pp. 36 ff.
30. See Chapter 2, pp. 100 ff.
31. See Chapter 3, pp. 173 ff.
32. John Saward, *Perfect Fools, Folly for Christ's Sake in Orthodox and Catholic Spirituality*.
33. Chapter 1, pp. 36 ff.
34. *Tract No. 2, Tracts for the Times*, Vol. I.
35. See Introduction, p. 4.
36. *Apo.*, p. 28.
37. *P. P. S.*, Vol. I, pp. 309 ff.
38. See Chapter 2, pp. 46 ff.

39. *S. S. D.*, pp. 272 ff.
40. *P. P. S.*, Vol. II, pp. 91 ff.; 232–54; *S. S. D.*, pp. 237–8; *P. P. S.*, Vol. VII, pp. 36 ff.
41. *S. S. D.*, pp. 242–53.
42. Chapter 1, pp. 36 ff.
43. See W. C. Lubenow, *The Politics of Government Growth, English Victorian Attitudes towards State Intervention*, 1833–48, pp. 52 ff.
44. See Chapter 1, pp. 38 ff.
45. See Chapter 2, pp. 140 ff.
46. Benjamin Disraeli, *Sybil*, pp. 156–60.
47. ibid., p. 92.
48. *H. S.*, Vol. III, p. 77.
49. *S. S. D.*, pp. 272–4.
50. See Chapter 3, p. 202.
51. See Chapter 1, pp. 74 ff.
52. *Lectures on Poetry*, Vol. I, p. 243.
53. *Sybil*, Chapter 2, x.
54. See A. R. Vidler, *A Century of Social Catholicism, 1820–1920*, pp. 24 ff., 36–40, 51–4, 64–7.
55. *Apo.*, pp. 142 ff.
56. See Chapter 3, p. 207.
57. *H. S.*, Vol. III, pp. 131 ff.
58. See Chapter 3, p. 202.
59. See Chapter 1, pp. 61 ff.
60. ibid.
61. See Chapter 2, pp. 132 ff.
62. E. B. Pusey, *Patience and Confidence the Strength of the Church*, preface, p. iv.
63. *D. & A.*, p. 91.
64. *S. S. D.*, pp. 242–3.
65. ibid., pp. 70 ff.
66. See Chapter 3, pp. 209 ff.
67. *D. & A.*, p. 22.
68. *A Letter to His Grace the Duke of Norfolk*, p. 72.

BIBLIOGRAPHY

A. PRIMARY SOURCES

(i) Works

Faber, F. W., *The Cherwell Water-Lily and Other Poems* (London, 1840).
——, *The Styrian Lake and Other Poems* (London, 1842).
——, *Sights and Thoughts in Foreign Churches and Among Foreign Peoples* (London, 1842).
——, *The Rosary and Other Poems* (London, 1845).
Froude, R. H., *The Remains of the Late Reverend Richard Hurrell Froude*, Part I, 2 Vols., (London, 1838), Part II, 2 Vols., (London, 1839).
Keble, John, ed., *Library of the Fathers, Five Books of S. Irenaeus, Bishop of Lyons against Heresies* (London, 1872).
——, *The Works of the Learned and Judicious Divine, Mr Richard Hooker: With an Account of His Life and Death by Isaac Walton*, 3 Vols., (Oxford, 1845, 3rd edn.).
——, *The Life of the Right Reverend Father in God, Thomas Wilson, DD, Lord Bishop of Sodor and Man, Compiled Chiefly from Original Documents*, 7 Vols., (Oxford, 1853).
——, *The Christian Year, Thoughts in Verse for Sundays and Holydays Throughout the Year*, (1827; Oxford, 1880 edn.).
——, *Occasional Papers and Reviews* (Oxford, 1877).
——, *Outlines of Instructions and Meditations for the Church's Seasons* (Oxford, 1880).
——, *On Eucharistic Adoration* (Oxford, 1857).
——, *Lectures on Poetry*, 2 Vols., translated by E. K. Francis (Oxford, 1912).

——, *The Christian Year, Lyra Innocentium and Other Poems* (Oxford, 1914).
Newman, J. H., *Apologia Pro Vita Sua* (Introduction by M. J. Svaglic), (Oxford, 1967). *Apo.*
——, *The Arians of the Fourth Century* (1833; London, 1871 edn.). *Ari.*
——, *Certain Difficulties felt by Anglicans in Submitting to the Catholic Church* (1850; Dublin, 1857 edn.). *Diffs.*
——, *Discussions and Arguments on Various Subjects* (London, 1873). *D. & A.*
——, *An Essay in Aid of a Grammar of Assent* (Introduced by Nicholas Lash) (1870; London, 1979 edn.). *G. A.*
——, *Essays Critical and Historical*, 2 Vols., (London, 1871). *Ess. I & II.*
——, *Historical Sketches*, 3 Vols., (London, 1872). *H. S.* I, II, III.
——, *The Idea of a University, Defined and Illustrated* (Edited by Ian T. Ker) (Oxford, 1976). *Idea.*
——, *Select Treatises of St Athanasius in Controversy with the Arians* 2 Vols., (1881; London, 1895 edn.). *Ath.* I, II.
——, *The Church of the Fathers* (London, 1900 edn.).
——, *The Development of Christian Doctrine* (Introduced by J. M. Cameron) (1845; London, 1974 edn.). *Dev.*
——, *The Via Media of the Anglican Church Illustrated in Lectures, Letters and Tracts Written between 1830 and 1841*, 2 Vols., (London, 1911 edn.). *V. M.* I, II.
——, *Tracts Theological and Ecclesiastical* (London, 1874. *T. T.*
——, *Verses on Various Occasions* (1867; London, 1880 edn.). *V. V.*
Pusey, E. B., *The Royal Supremacy, Not an Arbitrary Authority but Limited by the Laws of the Church of England, of which Kings are Members* (Oxford, 1850).
——, *The Councils of the Churches from the Council of Jerusalem AD 51 to the Council of Constantinople AD 381 chiefly as to their Constitutions but also as to their Objects and History* (Oxford, 1857).
Wilberforce, R. I., *A Sketch of the History of Erastianism together with Two Sermons on the Reality of the Church's Ordinances and on the Principle of Church Authority* (London, 1851).

(ii) Sermons

Keble, John, *Plain Sermons by Contributors to the Tracts for the Times*, Vol. I, Sermons I–VIII, XXIII–XXX (London, 1841).
——, *Plain Sermons by Contributors to the Tracts for the Times*, Vol. II, Sermons XLIII–LIV, LXVII–LXII (London, 1845).
——, *Plain Sermons by Contributors to the Tracts for the Times*, Vol. VI, (London, 1845).

——, *Plain Sermons by Contributors to the Tracts for the Times*, Vol. VII, (Sermons CCXV–CCXVI). (London, 1845).
——, *Rich and Poor One in Christ*, A Sermon preached at St Peter's Church, Sudbury, August 1858 (London, 1858).
——, *Sermons Academical and Occasional* (Oxford, 1848).
——, *Sermons Occasional and Parochial* (Oxford, 1868).
——, *Sermons for the Christian Year, from Advent to Christmas Eve* (London, 1875).
——, *Sermons for the Christian Year, from Septuagesima to Ash Wednesday* (London, 1878).
——, *Sermons for the Christian Year, from Lent to Passiontide* (London, 1878).
——, *Sermons for the Christian Year, from Ascension Day to Trinity Sunday* (London, 1878).
——, *Sermons for the Christian Year, Sermons after Trinity I–XII* (London, 1878).
——, *Sermons for the Christian Year, Trinity XIII to the End* (London, 1878).
Newman, J. H., *Fifteen Sermons Preached before the University of Oxford* (Introduction by D. M. Mackinnon and J. D. Holmes) (London, 1970). *U. S.*
——, *Parochial and Plain Sermons*, 8 Vols., (London, 1868 edn.). *P. P. S.*
——, *Sermons preached on Subjects of the Day*, (London, 1873 edn.). *S. S. D.*
——, *Sermons preached on Various Occasions* (London, 1898). *O. S.*
Pusey, E. B., *Patience and Confidence the Strength of the Church*, A Sermon preached on the Fifth of November before the University of Oxford at St Mary's (Oxford, 1837).

(iii) Tracts

Keble, John, *Tract No. 4*, "Adherence to the Apostolical Succession the Safest Course".
——, *Tract No. 40*, "Baptism".
Tracts for the Times, Vol. I for 1833–4 (London, 1840 edn.).
——, *Tract No. 52*, "Sermons for Saints' Days and Holidays, (No. 1 St Matthias)".
——, *Tract No. 54*, "Sermons for Saints' Days and Holidays (No. 2, The Annunciation of the Blessed Virgin Mary)".
——, *Tract No. 57*, "Sermons on Saints' Days (No. 3 St Mark's Day)".
——, *Tract No. 60*, "Sermons for Saints' Days and Holidays, (No. 4, St Philip and St James)".
Tracts for the Times, Vol. II, Pt. I for 1834–5 (London, 1840 edn.).

—, *Tract No. 78*, "Testimony of Writers in the Later English Church to the Duty of Maintaining Quod Semper, quod ubique, quod ab omnibus traditum est".
Tracts for the Times, Vol. II, Pt. II for 1834–5 (London, 1840 edn.).
—, *Tract No. 89*, "On the Mysticism Attributed to the Early Fathers of the Church" in E. Jay, ed., *The Evangelical and Oxford Movements* (Cambridge, 1983).
Newman, J. H., *Tract No. 1*, "Thoughts on the Ministerial Commission respectfully addressed to the Clergy".
Tract No. 2, "The Catholic Church".
Tract No. 3, "Thoughts respectfully addressed to the Clergy on Alterations in the Liturgy".
Tract No. 6, "The Present Obligations of Primitive Practice".
Tract No. 8, "The Gospel a Law of Liberty".
Tract No. 10, "Heads of a Week-day Lecture, delivered to a Country Congregation in – shire".
Tract No. 11, "The Visible Church, Letters I and II".
—, *Tract No. 20*, "The same continued, Letter III".
—, *Tract No. 31*, "The Reformed Church".
—, *Tract No. 38*, "Via Media, Vol. I".
—, *Tract No. 41*, "Via Media, Vol. II".
—, *Tracts for the Times*, Vol. I for 1833–4 (London, 1840).
—, *Tract No. 47*, "The Visible Church".
Tracts for the Times, Vol. II, Pt. I for 1834–5 (London, 1840).
—, *Tract No. 71*, "On the Controversy with the Romanists".
—, *Tract No. 73*, "On the Introduction of Rationalistic Principles".
Tracts for the Times, Vol. III for 1835–6 (London, 1840).
—, *Tract No. 83*, "Advent Sermons on Antichrist".
—, *Tract No. 85*, "Lectures on the Scripture Proofs of the Doctrines of the Church".
Tracts for the Times, Vol. V (London, 1840 edn.).
—, *Tract No. 90*, "Remarks on Certain Passages in the Thirty Nine Articles", (With a Commentary by A. W. Evans) (London, 1933 edn.).
Williams, Isaac, *Tract No. 87*, "On Reserve in Communicating Religious Knowledge", Elizabeth Jay, ed., *The Evangelical and Oxford Movements* (Cambridge, 1983).

(iv) *Letters and Diaries*

Addington, Raleigh, ed., *Faber, Poet and Priest. Selected Letters of F. W. Faber from 1833–63* (Bridgend, 1979).
Bowden, J. E., ed., *The Life and Letters of Frederick William Faber, DD* (London, 1869).

Correspondence of John Henry Newman with John Keble and Others, 1839–45, edited at the Birmingham Oratory (London, 1917). *Corr.*
Dessain, C. S., ed., *The Letters and Diaries of John Henry Newman*, Vols. XI–XX (London, 1961–9) *L. & D.*
Froude, R. H., "Private Excommunication", A Letter to the Editor of *The British Magazine* (Vol. VI, July 1834).
Keble, John, *A Pastoral Letter to the Parishioners of Hursley* (London, 1851).
——, *Letters of Spiritual Counsel and Guidance* (London, 1870).
Ker, I. and Gornall, T., S. J., *The Letters and Diaries of John Henry Newman*, Vols. I–IV (Oxford, 1978–80) *L. & D.*
Gornall, T., S. J., *The Letters and Diaries of John Henry Newman*, Vols. V and VI (Oxford, 1981–4). *L. & D.*
The Bishop of Leighlin and Ferns, Letter to the Editor of *The British Magazine*, (Vol. IV, December 1833).
Mill, W. H., *A Letter to a Clergyman in London on the Theological Character of Dr Hampden's Bampton's Lectures and the Extent and Value of Subsequent Qualifications of their Meaning* (London, 1848).
Mozley, Anne, ed., *Letters and Correspondence of John Henry Newman*, 2 Vols. (London, 1903 edn.). *L. & C.*
Newman, J. H., *A Letter Addressed to His Grace the Duke of Norfolk On Occasion of Mr Gladstone's Recent Expostulation* (London, 1875).

(v) Pamphlets

Alexander, W. L., *Anglo-Catholicism not Apostolical* (Edinburgh, 1843).
Bennett, W. J. E., ed., *State Interference in Matters Spiritual, A Re-Print from a Work entitled* "Remains of Richard Hurrell Froude" (London, 1869).
Bateman, J., *Tractarianism as described in Prophecy* (London, 1845).
Fausett, G., *The Revival of Popery* (London, 1836).
Golightly, C. I., *New and Strange Duties Extracted from the Writings of Mr Newman and his Friends* (Oxford, 1841).
Hampden, R. D., *The Scholastic Philosophy considered in its Relation to Christian Theology* (London, 1832).
——, *The Thirty Nine Articles of the Church of England*, the Eleventh of the Public Course of Lectures in Trinity Term, read before the University in the Divinity School, Oxford, 1 June, 1842 (London, 1842).
Jelf, R. W., *Via Media* (Oxford, 1842).
Liddon, H. P., (Preface), John Keble, "The State in its Relations with the Church", *A Paper re-printed from the British Critic, October 1839 and including an Appendix, a Letter to the Editor of the British Magazine, January 1834* (London, 1869).

Macmullam, R. G., *Two Exercises for the Degree of BD* (Oxford, 1844).
Powell, Baden, *Tractarianism Unveiled* (Oxford, 1838).

(vi) Charges

Bagot, Richard, *A Charge addressed to the Clergy of the Diocese of Oxford* (Oxford, 1838).
——, *A Charge addressed to the Clergy of the Diocese of Oxford* (Oxford, 1843)
Copleston, Edward, *A Charge delivered to the Clergy of the Diocese of Llandaff* (London, 1839).
——, *A Charge delivered to the Clergy of the Diocese of Llandaff* (London, 1848).
Manning, H. E., *A Charge to the Clergy of the Archdeaconry of Chichester* (London, 1841).
——, *A Charge to the Clergy of the Archdeaconry of Chichester* (London, 1842).
——, *A Charge to the Clergy of the Archdeaconry of Chichester* (London, 1843).
——, *A Charge to the Clergy of the Archdeaconry of Chichester* (London, 1848).
——, *A Charge to the Clergy of the Archdeaconry of Chichester* (London, 1849).
Phillpotts, Henry, *A Charge delivered to the Clergy of the Diocese of Exeter* (London, 1839).
Thirlwall, Connop, *A Charge delivered to the Clergy of the Diocese of Saint David's* (London, 1842).
Wilberforce, R. I., *A Charge to the Clergy of the Archdeaconry of the East Riding* (London, 1844).
——, *A Charge to the Clergy of the Archdeaconry of the East Riding* (London, 1845).
——, *A Charge to the Clergy of the Archdeaconry of the East Riding* (London, 1846).
——, *A Charge to the Clergy of the Archdeaconry of the East Riding* (London, 1847).
——, *A Charge to the Clergy of the Archdeaconry of the East Riding* (London, 1848).

(vii) Articles

Froude, R. H., "Thomas à Becket", *The British Magazine*, (Vol. II, September, December, 1832; Vol. III, January to May, 1833; Vol. IV, September to December, 1833; Vol. V, January to June, 1834).

BIBLIOGRAPHY

Keble, John, "Church Reform", *The British Magazine*, (Vol. III, March and June, 1833).
——, "Unpublished Papers of Bishop Warburton", *The British Critic*, Vol. XXIX, (April, 1841).
Newman, J. H., "The Convocation of the Province of Canterbury", *The British Magazine* (Vol. VI, November and December, 1834; Vol. VII, January to March, 1835).
——, "Art. V. 1. Letters from Lord John Russell to the Lords Lieutenant and to the Magistrates in Sessions, and to Mayors in Boroughs in Certain Counties. 2. Return to an address of the Hon. the House of Commons, dated 20th August, 1839; for a Return of all Associations formed and armed for the Protection of Life and Propety under the Authority of Letters from Lord John Russell to Lords Lieutenant of Counties and to Magistrates, dated the 7th day of May, 1839". Editor, *The British Critic*, Vol. XXVI, No. LII (1839).
——, "The Tamworth Reading Room", E. Jay, ed., *The Evangelical and Oxford Movements* (Cambridge, 1983).
——, "Contemporary Events", *The Rambler*, Vol. I (May, 1859).

B. SECONDARY SOURCES

(i) Works

Abbey, C. J. and Overton, J. H., *The English Church in the Eighteenth Century*, 2 Vols. (London, 1878).
Abbott, E. A., *The Anglican Career of Cardinal Newman*, 2 Vols. (London, 1892).
Abrams, M. H., *The Mirror and the Lamp, Romantic Theory and the Critical Tradition* (Oxford, 1976).
Allen, Louis, *John Henry Newman and the Abbé Jager, A Controversy on Scripture and Tradition* (Oxford, 1976).
Altholz, J., *The Liberal Catholic Movement in England* (London, 1962).
Anderson, M. S., *Historians and Eighteenth Century Europe, 1715–89* (Oxford, 1979).
Annan, Noel, *Leslie Stephen, The Godless Victorian* (1951; London, 1984).
Arnold, Matthew, *Literature and Dogma, An Essay towards a better Appreciation of the Bible* (London, 1876).
Ashwell, A. R. and Wilberforce, R. G., *Life of The Right Reverend Samuel Wilberforce, DD, Lord Bishop of Oxford and afterwards of Winchester*,(3 Vols.) (London, 1880).
Avis, Paul D. L., *The Church in the Theology of the Reformers* (London, 1979).

Awdry, Frances, *A Country Gentleman of the Nineteenth Century* (Winchester, 1906).
Bailey, John, *Dr Johnson and his Circle* (1913; London, 1940 edn.).
Baker, Derek, ed., *Studies in Church History*, Vol. 10, *Sanctity and Secularity, the Church and the World* (Oxford, 1973).
——, *Studies in Church History*, Vol. 12, *Church, Society and Politics* (Oxford, 1975).
Baker, J. E., *The Novel and the Oxford Movement* (Princeton, 1933).
——, ed., *The Reassessment of Victorian Literature* (Princeton, 1962).
Bastable, J. D., ed., *Newman and Gladstone: Centennial Essays* (Dublin, 1978).
Batho, E. C., *The Later Wordsworth* (Cambridge, 1933).
Battiscombe, Georgina, *John Keble, A Study in Limitations* (London, 1963).
Beek, W. J. A. M., *John Keble's Literary and Religious Contribution to the Oxford Movement* (Diss Nimjegen, 1959).
Bennett, G. V. and Walsh, J. D., eds., *Essays in Modern English Church History in memory of Norman Sykes* (London, 1966).
Berkeley, George, *A New Theory of Vision and Other Philosophical Writings* (Introduction by A. D. Lindsay). (London, 1956 edn.).
Best, G. F. A., *Temporal Pillars, Queen Anne's Bounty, The Ecclesiastical Commissioners and the Church of England* (Cambridge, 1964).
Blake, Robert, *Disraeli* (London, 1966).
——, *The Conservative Party from Peel to Churchill* (London, 1970).
Blount, Charles, *Miscellaneous Works* (London, 1695).
Boekraad, A. J., *The Personal Conquest of Truth according to J. H. Newman* (Louvain, 1955).
——, *The Argument from Conscience to the Existence of God according to J. H. Newman* (Louvain, 1961).
Bokenkotter, T. S., *Cardinal Newman as an Historian* (Louvain, 1959).
Bonar, J., *Malthus and His Work* (London, 1885).
Boswell, James, *The Life of Samuel Johnson, LLD.*, 2 Vols. (London, 1946 edn.).
Bowen, Desmond, *The Idea of the Victorian Church, A Study of the Church of England 1833-1889* (Montreal, 1968).
Bowle, John, *Politics and Opinion in the Nineteenth Century* (London, 1954).
Bowra, C. M., *The Romantic Imagination* (London, 1964).
Braun, T., *Disraeli the Novelist* (London, 1981).
Bredvold, L. I. and Ross, R. G., eds., *The Philosophy of Edmund Burke, A Selection from His Speeches and Writings* (Michigan, 1970).
Bremond, Henri, *The Mystery of Newman* (London, 1907).

BIBLIOGRAPHY 243

Brendon, Piers, *Hurrell Froude and the Oxford Movement* (London, 1974).
Brett, R. L. and Jones, A. R., eds., *Wordsworth and Coleridge, Lyrical Ballads* (London, 1963).
Brett, R. L., ed., *S. T. Coleridge* (London, 1971).
Bricknell, W., *The Judgement of the Bishops upon Tractarian Theology* (Oxford, 1845).
Brilioth, Yngve, *The Anglican Revival, Studies in the Oxford Movement* (London, 1925).
Brinton, Crane, *English Political Thought in the Nineteenth Century* (New York, 1962).
——, *The Political Thought of the English Romanticists* (New York, 1962).
Brose, O. J., *Church and Parliament, The Reshaping of the Church of England, 1828–60* (Oxford, 1959).
Brown, David, *The Divine Trinity* (London, 1985).
Brown, F. K., *Fathers of the Victorians* (Cambridge, 1981).
Broxap, H., *The Later Non-Jurors* (London, 1924).
Brundage, A., *The Making of the New Poor Law* (London, 1978).
Buckley, J., *The Victorian Temper* (London, 1952).
Burgon, J. W., *Lives of Twelve Good Men* (1888; London, 1891 edn.).
Burke, Edmund, *Works and Correspondence*, 6 Vols. (London, 1852).
——, *Correspondence*, 8 Vols. (Cambridge, 1958–69).
——, *Reflections on the Revolution in France* (Introduction by Conor Cruise O' Brien) (Harmondsworth, 1968).
Burn, W. L., *The Age of Equipoise* (London, 1964).
Burns, J. H. and Hart, H. L. A., eds., *Jeremy Bentham: An Introduction to The Principles of Morals and Legislation* (London, 1982).
Butler, Joseph, *Analogy of Religion* (London, 1736).
——, *Fifteen Sermons preached at the Rolls Chapel and a Dissertation on the Nature of Virtue* (ed. with an introduction by T. A. Roberts) (London, 1970).
Butler, Marilyn, *Romantics, Rebels and Reactionaries, English Literature and its Background 1760–1830* (Oxford, 1981).
Butler, Perry, *Gladstone, Church, State and Tractarianism, A Study of His Religious Ideas and Attitudes 1815–59* (Oxford, 1982).
——, ed., *Pusey Rediscovered* (London, 1983).
Butler, R. A., ed., *The Conservatives: A History from their Origin to 1965* (London, 1977).
Cairns, W. T., *The Religion of Dr. Johnson and Other Essays* (London, 1946).
Calleo, D. P., *Coleridge and the Idea of the Modern State* (London, 1966).

Carlyle, Thomas, *Past and Present* (ed. A. M. D. Hughes) (Oxford, 1921 edn.).
Carnall, G., *Robert Southey and His Age, The Development of a Conservative Mind* (Oxford, 1960).
Carpenter, Edward, *Cantuar, The Archbishops in Their Office* (London, 1971).
Carter, T. T., *The Life and Times of John Kettlewell* (London, 1895).
Cazamian, L., *The Social Novel in England 1830–50, Dickens, Disraeli, Mrs Gaskell, Kingsley* (London, 1973).
Cecil, Hugh, *Conservatism* (London, 1912).
Chadwick, Edwin, *An Article on the Principles and Progress of the Poor Law Amendment Act* (London, 1847).
Chadwick, Owen, *From Bossuet to Newman, The Idea of Doctrinal Development* (Cambridge, 1957).
——, ed., *The Mind of the Oxford Movement* (London, 1960).
——, *The Victorian Church*, 2 Pts. (Cambridge, 1970 edn.).
——, *The Secularisation of the European Mind* (Cambridge, 1975).
——, *Newman* (Oxford, 1983).
Chandler, Alice, *A Dream of Order: the Medieval Ideal in Nineteenth Century English Literature* (London, 1970).
Chapman, Raymond, *Faith and Revolt, Studies in the Literary Influence of the Oxford Movement* (London, 1970).
Chapman, Ronald, *Father Faber* (London, 1961).
Checkland, S. G. and E. D. A., *The Poor Law Report of 1834* (London, 1974 edn.).
Chubb, Thomas, *The Comparative Excellence and Obligation of Moral and Positive Duties* (London, 1730).
Church, Mary, ed., *The Life and Letters of Dean Church* (London, 1894).
Church, R. W., *Essays and Reviews* (London, 1854).
——, *The Oxford Movement, Twelve Years, 1833–1845* (Oxford, 1890).
——, *Occasional Papers*, 2 Vols. (London, 1897).
Clark, J. C. D., *English Society 1688–1832, Ideology, Social Structure and Political Practice During the Ancien Regime* (Cambridge, 1986).
Clarke, M. L., *Paley, Evidences for the Man* (London, 1974).
Clifford, James L., ed., *Man Versus Society in Eighteenth Century Britain: Six Points of View* (Cambridge, 1968).
Cobban, Alfred, *Edmund Burke and the Revolt against the Eighteenth Century, A Study of the Political and Social Thinking of Burke, Wordsworth, Coleridge and Southey* (London, 1960).
Cobbet, William, *A History of the Protestant Reformation in England and Ireland*, 2 Vols. (London, 1829).
Cole, G. H. D., *The Life of William Cobbett* (London, 1947).

Coleridge, J. T., *A Memoir of the Rev. John Keble, MA, Vicar of Hursley* (London, 1870, 3rd edn.).
Coleridge, S. T., *The Friend*, 2 Vols. (ed. B. E. Rooke, Collected Works 4) (Princeton, 1969).
———, *Lay Sermons* (ed. R. J. White, Collected Works 6) (Princeton, 1972).
———, *On the Constitution of Church and State* (ed. J. Colmer, Collected Works 10) (Princeton 1976).
Collingwood, R. G., *The Idea of History* (Oxford, 1946).
Collins, Anthony, *A Discourse of the Grounds and Reasons of the Christian Religion* (London, 1724).
Collins, W. E., ed., *Typical English Churchmen from Parker to Maurice* (London, 1902).
Colmer, John, *Coleridge, Critic of Society* (Oxford, 1959).
Cooke, K., *Coleridge* (London, 1979).
Coots, A. W., ed., *Poverty in the Victorian Age*, 4 Vols. (Farnborough 1972).
Copleston, Edward, *A Second Letter to the Rt Hon. Sir Robert Peel, MP.* (London, 1819).
Cornish, F. W., *The English Church in the Nineteenth Century*, 2 Pts. (London, 1910).
Cornwell, Peter, *Church and Nation* (Oxford, 1983).
Cosslett, Tess, ed., *Science and Religion in the Nineteenth Century* (Cambridge, 1984).
Coombs, Joyce, *George Anthony Denison, The Firebrand* (London, 1984).
Coulson, John, *On Consulting the Faithful in Matters of Doctrine* (London, 1961).
———, *Newman and the Common Tradition, A Study in the Language of Church and Society* (Oxford, 1970).
———, *Religion and Imagination "in aid of a grammar of assent"* (Oxford, 1981).
Coulson, John and Allchin, A. M., eds., *The Rediscovery of Newman, An Oxford Symposium* (London, 1967).
Cragg, G. R., *Reason and Authority in the Eighteenth Century* (Cambridge, 1964).
Crocker, L. G., *The Age of Enlightenment* (London, 1969).
Cross, Claire, *The Royal Supremacy in the Elizabethan Church* (London, 1969).
Cross, F. L., *The Oxford Movement and the Seventeenth Century* (London, 1933).
———, *J. H. Newman* (Oxford, 1933).
———, and E. A. Livingstone, eds., *The Oxford Dictionary of the Christian Church* (Oxford, 1974 edn.).

Culler, A. D., *The Imperial Intellect, A Study of Newman's Educational Ideal* (London, 1965).
Cunningham, V., *Everywhere Spoken Against; Dissent in the Victorian Novel* (Oxford, 1975).
Danielou, J., Couratin, A. H., Kent, J., *Historical Theology, The Pelican Guide to Modern Theology*, Vol. 2 (London, 1969).
Davies, E. T., *Episcopacy and the Royal Supremacy in the Church of England in the Sixteenth Century* (Oxford, 1950).
Davies, G. C. B., *Henry Phillpotts, Bishop of Exeter 1778–1869* (London, 1954).
Davies, Horton, *Worship and Theology in England, from Watts and Wesley to Maurice* (London, 1961).
Davies, H. W. C., *The Age of Grey and Peel* (Oxford, 1929).
Davies, M., ed., *Newman against the Liberals* (Cambridge, 1978).
Dawson, Carl, *Victorian Noon, English Literature in 1850* (Baltimore, 1979).
Dawson, Christopher, *Progress and Religion, An Historical Enquiry* (London 1929).
———, *The Spirit of the Oxford Movement* (London, 1945).
Dearing, T., *Tractarian and Wesleyan Worship* (London, 1966).
de Laura, D. J., *Hebrew and Hellene in Victorian England, Newman, Arnold and Pater* (London, 1969).
———, *Victorian Prose, A Guide to Research* (London, 1973).
Dellheim, Charles, *The Face of the Past: The Preservation of the Medieval Inheritance in Medieval England* (Cambridge, 1982).
Dessain, C. S., *John Henry Newman* (Oxford, 1980 edn.).
———, *Newman's Spiritual Themes* (Dublin, 1977).
Disraeli, Benjamin, *Coningsby, or The New Generation* (1844; London, 1983 edn.).
———, *Sybil, or The Two Nations* (1845; London 1983 edn.).
———, *Tancred, or The New Crusade* (London, 1847).
———, *Endymion* (London, 1879).
Donaldson, A. B., *Five Great Oxford Leaders* (London, 1902).
Dragas, G. D., *Athanasiana, Vol. I, Essays in the Theology of Saint Athanasius* (London, 1980).
———, *The Study of Theology* (Darlington, 1981).
Dugmore, C. W., *Eucharistic Doctrine in England from Hooker to Waterland* (London, 1942).
———, *The Mass and the English Reformers* (London, 1958).
Eccleshall, R., *Order and Reason in Politics, Theories of Absolute and Limited Monarchy in Early Modern England* (Oxford, 1978).
Eden, F. M., *The State of the Poor* (ed. A. L. Rogers) (London, 1928 edn.).
Edsall, N. C., *The Anti-Poor Law Movement* (Manchester, 1971).

BIBLIOGRAPHY 247

Edwards, D. L., *Leaders of the Church of England 1828–1944* (Oxford, 1971).
Egner, C., *Apologia Pro Charles Kingsley* (London, 1969).
Elliott-Binns, L. E., *Religion in the Victorian Era* (London, 1953).
Elton, O., *A Survey of English Literature 1830–80*, Vol. I (London, 1920).
Engels, F., *The Condition of the Working Class in England in 1844* (Introduction by W. O. Henderson and W. H. Chalmer) (Oxford, 1958).
Everett, C. W., *Jeremy Bentham* (London, 1966).
Ewold, A. C., *The Rt Hon. Benjamin Disraeli, Earl of Beconsfield and His Times* (London, 1882).
Faber, Geoffrey, *Oxford Apostles: A Character Study of the Oxford Movement* (London, 1933).
Fairweather, E. R., ed., *The Oxford Movement* (New York, 1964).
Faulkner, R. K., *Richard Hooker and the Politics of a Christian England* (London, 1981).
Feiling, Keith, *Sketches in Nineteenth Century Biography* (London, 1934).
Figgis, J. N., *The Fellowship of the Mystery* (London, 1914).
——, *The Divine Right of Kings* (London, 1914).
Forbes, Duncan, *The Liberal Anglican Idea of History* (Cambridge, 1952).
Freeman, M., *Edmund Burke and the Critique of Political Radicalism* (Oxford, 1980).
Friedman, M. H., *The Making of a Tory Humanist* (New York, 1979).
Froude, J. A., *Nemesis of Faith* (London, 1849).
——, *Short Studies on Great Subjects*, 4 Vols. (London, 1894 edn.).
——, *Lord Beaconsfield* (London, 1915 edn.).
Gash, Norman, *Politics in the Age of Peel* (London, 1953).
——, *Mr Secretary Peel, The Life of Sir Robert Peel to 1830* (London, 1961).
——, *Reaction and Reconstruction in English Politics 1832–1852* (Oxford, 1965).
——, *Sir Robert Peel: the Life of Sir Robert Peel after 1830* (London, 1972).
Gay, Peter, *The Enlightenment: an Interpretation*. Vol. 1, *The Rise of Modern Paganism*. Vol. 2, *The Science of Freedom* (London, 1970).
——, *Deism, An Anthology* (Princeton, 1968).
Gilbert, A. D., *Religion and Society in Industrial England* (London, 1976).
Gilmour, Ian, *Inside Right, A Study of Conservatism* (London, 1977).
Gladstone, W. E., *The State in its Relations with the Church* (London, 1938 edn.).

——, *The Works of Joseph Butler*, 2 Vols. (Oxford, 1896).
——, *Later Gleanings, A new series of Gleanings of past years* (London, 1898).
Glas, D. V., ed., *Introduction to Malthus* (London, 1853).
Gloyn, C. K., *The Church in the Social Order, A Study of Anglican Social Theory from Coleridge to Maurice* (Oregon, 1945).
Graham, James, *Inquiry into the Principles of Population: including a Defence of the Poor Law* (Edinburgh, 1816).
Gray, Robert, *Cardinal Manning, A Biography* (London, 1985).
Griffin, J. R., *The Oxford Movement 1833–1983* (Edinburgh, 1984).
Griggs, E. L., *Unpublished Letters of S. T. Coleridge*, 2 Vols. (London, 1932).
Grisbrooke, W. J., *Anglican Liturgies of the Seventeenth and Eighteenth Centuries* (London, 1958).
Guiney, L. I., *Hurrell Froude, Memoranda and Comments*, 2 Vols. (London, 1904).
Halevy, E., *The Growth of Philosophical Radicalism* (London, 1928).
——, *A History of the English People in the Nineteenth Century*, 6 Vols. (London, 1961 edn.).
Halsted, J. B., ed., *Romanticism, Problems of Definition, Explanation and Evaluation* (Boston, 1965).
Hammond, J. L. and B., *The Village Labourer 1760–1832, A Study in the Government of England before the Reform Bill* (London, 1912).
Hardelin, Alf, *The Tractarian Understanding of the Eucharist* (Uppsala, 1965).
Harrison, W., (Intro.) *Jeremy Bentham, A Fragment on Government and an Introduction to the Principles of Morals and Legislation* (Oxford, 1967).
Harrold, C. F., *John Henry Newman* (London, 1945).
Hart, H. L. A., *Essays on Bentham* (Oxford, 1982).
Hartman, G. H., *Wordsworth's Poetry 1787–1814* (Yale, 1964).
Hawkins, L. M., *Allegiance in Church and State, The Problems of the Non-Jurors* (London, 1928).
Hazard, Paul, *The European Mind 1680–1715*, Eng. Transl. J. L. May (Harmondsworth, 1964).
Hearnshaw, F. J. C., ed., *The Social and Political Ideas of Some Representative Thinkers of the Victorian Age* (London, 1933).
Hennell, Michael, *sons of the Prophets, Evangelical Leaders of the Victorian Church* (London, 1979).
Hibben, J. G., *The Philosophy of the Enlightenment* (London, 1912).
Hill, W. Speed, *Studies in Richard Hooker* (London, 1972).
Hodgson, P. and King, R., eds., *Christian Theology, An Introduction to its Traditions and Tasks* (London, 1983).
Holloway, J., *The Victorian Sage* (New York, 1965).

Holloway, Richard, ed., *The Anglican Tradition* (London, 1984).
Holmes, J. Derek, ed., *Theological Papers of J. H. Newman on Faith and Certainty* (Oxford, 1976).
———, *More Roman than Rome, English Catholicism in the Nineteenth Century* (London, 1978).
———, *The Triumph of the Holy See, A Short History of the Papacy in the Nineteenth Century* (London, 1978).
Honour, Hugh, *Romanticism* (London, 1981).
Hough, G., *The Romantic Poets* (London, 1968).
Houghton, W., *The Victorian Frame of Mind* (Yale, 1957).
Hudson, C. E. and Reckitt, M. B., *The Church and the World*, 3 Vols. (London, 1938).
Hunt, J., *Religious Thought in England in the Nineteenth Century* (London, 1896).
Hutton, R. H., *Cardinal Newman* (London, 1890).
Hutton, W. H., *The English Church from the Accession of Charles I to the Death of Anne* (London, 1903).
Inglis, B., *Poverty and the Industrial Revolution* (London, 1971).
Inglis, K. S., *Churches and the Working Classes in Victorian England* (London, 1963).
Ingram, K. A., *John Keble* (London, 1933).
Jasper, David, ed., *Image and Belief in Literature* (London, 1985).
———, *Coleridge as Poet and Religious Thinker, Inspiration and Revelation* (London, 1985).
Jay, E., ed., *The Evangelical and Oxford Movements* (Cambridge, 1983).
Jones, Peter d'A., *The Christian Socialist Revival* (Princeton, 1968).
Jones, O. W., *Isaac Williams and His Circle* (London, 1972).
Kantorowicz, E. H., *The King's Two Bodies, A Study in Medieval Political Theology* (Princeton, 1957).
Kebbel, T. E., ed., *Selected Speeches of the Late Rt Hon. the Earl of Beaconsfield*, 2 Vols. (London, 1880).
Kenny, T., *The Political Thought of J. H. Newman* (London, 1957).
Kenwick, I., *Bolingbrooke and His Circle, The Politics of Nostalgia in the Age of Walpole* (Cambridge, Mass., 1968).
Kerr, Donal A., *Peel, Priests and Politics, Sir Robert Peel's Administration and the Roman Catholic Church in Ireland, 1841–1846* (1982; 1984 edn.).
Keynes, J. M., *Essays in Biography* (London, 1933).
Kirk, R., *The Conservative Mind* (London, 1954).
Kitson Clark, G., *The Making of Victorian England* (London, 1962).
———, *Churchmen and the Condition of England 1832–1885* (London, 1968).
Knox, E. A., *The Tractarian Movement 1833–45* (London, 1933).

Knox, Ronald, *Enthusiasm, A Chapter in the History of Religion* (Oxford, 1950).
Küng, Hans, *Structures of the Church* (London, 1974).
Kurry, K., *Southey* (London, 1975).
Lash, N. L. A., *Change in Focus* (London, 1973).
——, *Newman on Development, The Search for an Explanation in History* (London, 1976).
——, *Theology on Dover Beach* (London, 1979).
——, *A Matter of Hope, A Theologian's Reflections on the Thought of Karl Marx* (London, 1981).
Laski, H., *Political Thought in England from Locke to Bentham* (London, 1919).
——, *Studies in the Problem of Sovereignty* (London, 1937 edn.).
Lathbury, D. C., ed., *Letters on Church and Religion of W. E. Gladstone* (London, 1910).
Lathbury, T., *A History of the Non-Jurors* (London, 1845).
Leavis, F. R., (Introduction), *Mill on Bentham and Coleridge* (London, 1967).
Leech, K. and Williams, R., *Essays Catholic and Radical* (London, 1983).
Liddon, H. P., *The Life of E. B. Pusey*, D. D., 4 Vols. (London, 1893).
Lindsay, A. D., *The Modern Democratic State* (Oxford, 1943).
Locke, W., *John Keble* (London, 1895).
Lonergan, B., S. J., *A Second Collection* (London, 1974).
Louth, A., *The Origins of the Christian Mystical Tradition, From Plato to Denys* (Oxford, 1981).
——, *Discerning the Mystery, An Essay on the Nature of Theology* (Oxford, 1983).
Lowther Clark, W. K., *Eighteenth Century Piety* (London, 1944).
Lubenow, W. C., *The Politics of Government Growth, Early Victorian Attitudes towards State Intervention* (Newton Abbot, 1971).
Lucas, J., *Romantic to Modern Literature, Essays and Ideas of Modern Culture* (Brighton, 1982).
MacAdoo, H. R., *The Spirit of Anglicanism, A Survey of Anglican Theological Method in the Seventeenth Century* (London, 1965).
Machin, G. I. T., *The Catholic Question in English Politics 1820–1830* (Oxford, 1964).
——, *Politics and the Church in Great Britain 1832–68* (Oxford, 1977).
Mackinnon, D. M., *The Church of God* (London, 1943).
Macpherson, C. B., *Burke* (Oxford, 1980).
Madden, E., ed., *Robert Southey, The Critical Heritage* (London, 1972).
Magnus, Philip, *Gladstone* (London, 1963).
Malthus, T. R., *A Letter to Samuel Whitbread, Esq., MP, on his Proposed Bill for the Amendment of the Poor Laws* (London, 1807).

——, *An Essay on the Principle of Population: or, a View of its Past and Present Happiness; with an enquiry into our Prospects respecting the Future Removal or Mitigation of the Evil which it occasions* (Introduction by T. H. Hollingworth) (London, 1973 edn.).
——, *Principles of Political Economy, with a View to their Practical Application* (London, 1836 edn.).
Manners, Lord John, *England's Trust and other Poems* (London, 1841).
——, *A Plea for National Holy-Days* (London, 1842).
——, *A Political and Literary Sketch* (London, 1862).
Marshall, Dorothy, *The English Poor in the Eighteenth Century* (London, 1926).
Martin, B. W., *John Keble, Priest, Professor and Poet* (London, 1976).
Martin, E. W., ed., *Comparative Development in Social Welfare* (London, 1972).
——, *From Parish to Union; Poor Law Administration 1601–1865* (London, 1972).
Mather, F. C., ed., *Chartism and Society* (London, 1980).
Mathieson, W. L., *English Church Reform 1815–1840* (London, 1923).
Maurice, F. D., *The Kingdom of Christ*, 2 Vols. (London, 1948 edn.).
Maurice, J. F., *The Life of Frederick Denison Maurice*, 2 Vols. (London, 1885).
McDowell, R. B., *British Conservatism 1832–1914* (London, 1959).
Meacham, S., *Lord Bishop, The Life of Samuel Wilberforce* (Harvard, 1970).
Mencher, S., *Poor Law to Poverty Programme* (Pittsburgh, 1978).
Mews, S., ed., *Studies in Church History*, Vol. 18, *Religion and National Identity* (Oxford, 1982).
Micklem, P. A., *The Secular and the Sacred, An Enquiry into the Principles of a Christian Civilization* (London, 1948).
Middleton, conyers, *A Free Inquiry into the Miracles and Powers which are supposed to have subsisted in the Christian Church* (London, 1749).
Middleton, R. D., *Keble, Froude and Newman* (Canterbury, 1933).
——, *Newman and Bloxam* (Oxford, 1947).
——, *Newman at Oxford* (London, 1950).
Milburn, R. L. P., *Early Christian Interpretations of History* (London, 1945).
Milman, H. H., *History of the Jews* (London, 1829).
——, *The History of Christianity from the Birth of Christ to the Abolition of Paganism in the Roman Empire*, 3 Vols. (1840; London, 1892 edn.).
Misner, Paul, *Papacy and Development, Newman and the Primacy of the Pope* (Leiden, 1976).
Moneypenny, W. F. and Buckle, G. E., *The Earl of Beaconsfield*, 6 Vols. (London, 1910–20).

Moorman, Mary, *William Wordsworth, A Biography: The Early Years 1770–1803* (Oxford, 1957).
——, *William Wordsworth, A Biography: The Later Years 1803–50* (Oxford, 1965).
More, P. E. and Cross, F. L., *Anglicanism, The Thought and Practice of the Church of England, illustrated from the Religious Literature of the Seventeenth Century* (London, 1935).
Morley, John, *Life of W. E. Gladstone*, 2 Vols. (London, 1905).
Morse-Boycott, D., *The Secret History of the Oxford Movement* (London, 1933).
——, *They Shine Like Stars* (London, 1947).
Mossner, E. C., *The Life of David Hume* (Oxford, 1970).
Mozley, J. B., *Essays Historical and Theological* (London, 1878).
——, *Letters* (ed. by Anne Mozley) (London, 1885).
——, *Theological Essays* (London, 1901).
Mozley, Thomas, *Reminiscences Chiefly of Oriel College and the Oxford Movement*, 2 Vols. (London, 1882).
Munz, P., *The Place of Richard Hooker in the History of Thought* (London 1952).
Murphy, Dwight D., *Modern Social and Political Philosophies, Burkean Conservatism and Classical Liberalism* (Washington, 1982).
Newsome, David, *Two Classes of Men, Platonism and English Romantic Thought* (London, 1974).
——, *The Parting of Friends, A Study of the Wilberforces and Henry Manning* (London, 1966).
Norman, E. R., *Anti-Catholicism in Victorian England* (London, 1968).
——, *Church and Society in England 1770–1970, A Historical Survey* (Oxford, 1976).
——, *The English Catholic Church in the Nineteenth Century* (Oxford, 1984).
Norton, P. and Aughey, A., *Conservatives and Conservatism* (London, 1981).
Ollard, S. L., *The Anglo-Catholic Revival* (London, 1925).
——, *A Short History of the Oxford Movement* (1915; London, 1963).
Overton, J. H., *The English Church in the Nineteenth Century, 1800–33* (London, 1894).
——, *The Non-Jurors* (London, 1902).
Overton, J. H. and Relton, F., *The English Church from the Accession of George I to the end of the Eighteenth Century, 1714–1800* (London, 1906).
Owen, D., *English Philanthropy 1660–1940* (Harvard, 1964).
Oxley, G. W., *Poor Relief in England and Wales* (Newton Abbot, 1974).
Pailin, David, *The Way to Faith: An Examination of Newman's*

Grammar of Assent as a Response to the Search for Identity in Faith (London, 1969).
Paley, William, *The Principles of Moral and Political Philosophy* (1785; London, 1811 edn.).
——, *View of the Evidences of Christianity* (London, 1794).
——, *Natural Theology* (London, 1802).
Palmer, William, *A Treatise on the Church of Christ*, designed chiefly for the Use of Students in Theology, 2 Vols. (London, 1838).
——, *A Narrative of Events connected with the Tracts for the Times* (London, 1883 edn.).
Parkin, C., *The Moral Basis of Burke's Political Thought* (Cambridge, 1956).
Peck, W. G., *The Social Implications of the Oxford Movement* (London, 1933).
Plamenatz, J., *The English Utilitarians* (Oxford, 1966).
Plummer, Alfred, *The Church of England in the Eighteenth Century* (London, 1910).
Porter, Roy and Teich, M., *The Enlightenment in National Context* (Edinburgh, 1983).
Poynter, J. R., *Society and Pauperism: English Ideas on Poor Relief 1795–1834* (London, 1967).
Prevost, George, *The Autobiography of Isaac Williams* (London, 1892).
Prickett, Stephen, *Romanticism and Religion; The Tradition of Coleridge and Wordsworth in the Victorian Church* (Cambridge, 1976).
——, ed., *The Romantics* (London, 1981).
Pugin, A. W. N., *The True Principles of Pointed or Christian Architecture* (London, 1841).
Quinton, Anthony, *Utilitarian Ethics* (London, 1973).
——, *The Politics of Imperfection* (London, 1978).
Ravitch, Norman, *Sword and Mitre, Government and Episcopate in France and England in the Age of Aristocracy* (The Hague, 1966).
Reardon, B. M. G., *Religious Thought in the Nineteenth Century* (Cambridge 1966).
——, *From Coleridge to Gore, A Study of Religious Thought in Britain* (London, 1971).
Reckitt, M. B., *From Maurice to Temple, A Century of Social Movement in the Church of England* (London, 1947).
——, *Prospect for Christendom* (London, 1945).
——, *The World and the Faith* (London, 1954).
Redwood, J., *Reason, Ridicule and Religion: The Age of Enlightenment in England 1660–1715* (London, 1976).
Rice, H. A. L., *The Life of Bishop Ken* (London, 1958).
Richardson, Alan, *History Sacred and Profane* (London, 1964).

Richardson, Cyril C., ed., *Early Christian Fathers*, Vol. I, Library of Christian Classics (London, 1953).
Rigg, J. H., *Oxford High Anglicanism and its Chief Leaders* (London, 1899).
Roe, W. G., *Lamennais and England: The Reception of Lamennais's Religious Ideas in England in the Nineteenth Century* (Oxford, 1966).
Rose, M. E., *The English Poor Law 1780–1930* (Newton Abbot, 1971).
Round, J. T., ed., *The Prose Works of the Right Rev. Father in God, Thomas Ken, DD, Sometime Lord Bishop of Bath and Wells* (London, 1838).
Rowell, Geoffrey, *The Vision Glorious, Themes and Personalities in the Catholic Revival of Anglicanism* (Oxford, 1983).
——, *Tradition Renewed, The Oxford Movement Conference Papers* (London, 1986).
Russell, G. W. E., *Dr Pusey* (London, 1907).
——, *The Household of Faith* (London, 1902).
Sarolea, C., *Cardinal Newman and His Influence on Religious Life and Thought* (Edinburgh, 1908).
Saward, John, *Perfect Fools, Folly for Christ's Sake in Catholic and Orthodox Spirituality* (Oxford, 1980).
Schwarz, D. R., *Disraeli's Fiction* (London, 1979).
Scruton, Roger, *A Dictionary of Political Thought* (London, 1985).
——, *The Meaning of Conservatism* (London, 1985).
Selby, Robin, *The Principle of Reserve in the Writings of John Henry Newman* (Oxford, 1975).
Sencourt, R., *The Life of Newman* (London, 1948).
Sherlock, Thomas, *The Trial of the Witnesses of the Resurrection of Jesus* (1729; London, 1743 edn.).
Shipley, O., ed., *The Church and the World* (London, 1867).
Shirley, F. J., *Richard Hooker and Contemporary Political Ideals* (London 1949).
Sillem, E. J., *George Berkeley and the Proofs for the Existence of God* (Louvain, 1957).
——, ed., *The Philosophical Notebook, John H. Newman, Vol. I, General Introduction to the Study of Newman's Philosophy* (Louvain, 1969).
Simpson, W. J. S., *The Role of the Laity in the Church* (London, 1918).
Smart, Ninian, Clayton, John, Sherry, Patrick and Katz, T., *Nineteenth Century Religious Thought in the West*, Vol. II (Cambridge, 1985).
Smith, P., *Disraelian Conservatism and Social Reform* (London, 1967).
Smith, B. A., *Dean Church, the Anglican Response to Newman* (London, 1966).
Smith, S. M., *The Other Nation, the Poor in English Novels of the 1840's and 1850's* (Oxford, 1980).

Smyth, Charles, *Dean Milman* (London, 1949).
——, *The Church and the Nation, Six Studies in the Anglican Tradition* (London, 1962).
Soloway, R. A., *Prelates and People, Ecclesiastical Social Thought in England 1783–1852* (London, 1969).
Southey, Robert, *The Book of the Church*, 2 Vols. (London, 1825).
——, *Colloquies on the Progress and Prospects of Society* (London, 1829).
——, *The Poetical Works*, 8 Vols. (London, 1830).
——, *Essays Moral and Political*, 2 Vols. (London, 1832).
Stanley, A. P., *The Life and Correspondence of Thomas Arnold, DD*, 2 Vols. (London, 1844).
Stanlis, P. J., *Edmund Burke and the Natural Law* (Michigan, 1965).
Stephen, Leslie, *Hours in a Library*, 3 Vols. (London, 1900 edn.).
——, *History of English Thought in the Eighteenth Century*, 2 Vols. (London, 1881 edn.).
——, *The English Utilitarians*, 2 Vols. (London, 1900 edn.).
Stonyk, M., *Nineteenth Century English Literature* (London, 1983).
Storr, V. F., *Development of English Theology in the Nineteenth Century* (London, 1913).
Strange, Roderick, *Newman and the Gospel of Christ* (Oxford, 1981).
Stranks, C. J., *Anglican Devotion, Studies in the Spiritual Life of the Church of England between the Reformation and the Oxford Movement* (London, 1961).
Sumner, J. B., *A Treatise on the Records of Creation, Consisting of the Principle of Population with the Wisdom and Goodness of the Deity* (London, 1816).
Sutcliffe, Tom, ed., *Tracts for Our Times 1833–1983* (London, 1983).
Sykes, Norman, *Church and State in England in the Eighteenth Century* (Cambridge, 1934).
——, *From Sheldon to Secker: Aspects of English Church History 1660–1768* (Cambridge, 1959).
Sykes, Stephen W., *The Integrity of Anglicanism* (London, 1979).
——, *The Identity of Christianity, Theologians and the Essence of Christianity from Schleiermacher to Barth* (London, 1984).
Symondson, A., ed., *The Victorian Crisis of Faith* (London, 1970).
Tagliacozzo, G., *Vico and Contemporary Thought* (London, 1980).
Tellenbach, G., *Church, State and Christian Society at the Time of the Investiture Contest* (Oxford, 1940).
Tennyson, G. B., *Victorian Devotional Poetry, The Tractarian Mode* (Harvard, 1981).
Thomas, W., *The Philosophic Radicals, Nine Studies in Theory and Practice 1817–1841* (Oxford, 1979).

Thompson, E. P., *The Making of the English Working Class* (1963; London, 1980 edn.).
Tierney, M., ed., *A Tribute to Newman, Essays on Aspects of His Life and Thought* (Dublin, 1945).
Tillotson, G. and K., *Mid-Victorian Studies* (London, 1965).
Tindal, Matthew, *Christianity as Old as the Creation or the Gospel, a Republication of the Religion of Nature* (London, 1730).
Todd, F. M., *Politics and the Poet* (London, 1957).
Toland, John, *Christianity not Mysterious* (London, 1696).
Toynbee, A. J., *Civilization on Trial* (New York, 1948).
Trevor, Meriol, *Newman, The Pillar of the Cloud* (London, 1962).
Tristram, H., (introduction), *John Henry Newman: Centenary Essays* (London, 1945).
Tulloch, John, (Introduction by A. C. Cheyne), *Movements of Religious Thought in Britain during the Nineteenth Century* (Leicester, 1971 edn.).
Vargish, T., *Newman: The Contemplation of Mind* (Oxford, 1970).
Vidler, A. R., *The Orb and the Cross, A Normative Study in the Relation of Church and State with Reference to Gladstone's Early Writings* (London 1945).
——, *Prophecy and Papacy, A Study of Lamennais, the Church and the Revolution* (London, 1954).
——, *A Century of Social Catholicism 1820–1920* (London, 1969).
Voll, D., *Evangelical Catholicism* (London, 1963).
Wakefield, Gordon, ed., *A Dictionary of Christian Spirituality* (London, 1983).
——, *Kindly Light, A Meditation on Newman's Poem* (London, 1984).
Walgrave, J. H., *Newman the Theologian* (London, 1960).
Warburton, William, *The Alliance between Church and State* (London, 1736).
Ward, Maisie, *Young Mr Newman* (New York, 1964).
Ward, W., *The Life of John Henry Cardinal Newman*, 2 Vols. (London, 1912).
——, *William George Ward and the Oxford Movement* (London, 1889).
——, (Introduction) *Newman Apologia Pro Vita Sua, The Two Versions of 1864 and 1865 preceded by Newman's and Kingsley's Pamphlets* (Oxford, 1931 edn.).
Warren, A. H., *English Poetic Theory 1825–65* (Princeton, 1950).
Watson, J.R., ed., *An Infinite Complexity, Essays on Romanticism* (Edinburgh, 1983).
——, *Wordswoth's Vital Soul* (London, 1984).
Watson, Richard, *An Apology for Christianity in a Series of Letters addressed to Edward Gibbon* (London, 1776).

BIBLIOGRAPHY

Weatherby, H. L., *Cardinal Newman in His Age, His Place in English Theology and Literature* (Vanderbilt, 1973).
Webb, C. C. J., *Religious Thought in the Oxford Movement* (London, 1928).
——, *The Philosophy of the Oxford Movement* (London, 1928).
Webb, Sydney and Beatrice, eds., *The Break-up of the Poor Law: being Part I of the Minority Report of the Poor Law Commission* (London, 1909).
——, *English Poor Law History, Part II, the Last Hundred Years* (London, 1929).
Webster, Alan, *Joshua Watson, The Story of a Layman* (London, 1954).
Whately, Richard, *Letters on the Church by an Episcopalian* (Oxford, 1826).
——, *Introductory Lectures in Political Economy* (Oxford, 1831).
Whibley, C., *Lord John Manners and his Friends*, 2 Vols (London, 1925).
White, J. F., *The Cambridge Movement* (Cambridge, 1962).
White, R.J., *The Political Thought of Samuel Taylor Coleridge* (Cambridge, 1938).
——, *Political Tracts of Wordsworth, Coleridge and Shelley* (Cambridge, 1938).
Willey, Basil, *The Eighteenth Century Background, Studies on the Idea of Nature in the Thought of the Period* (London, 1957).
——, *Nineteenth Century Studies* (London, 1969).
Williams, N. P. and Harris, C., *Northern Catholicism, Centenary Studies in the Oxford and Parallel Movements* (London, 1933).
Williams, Raymond, *Culture and Society 1780–1950* (New York, 1958).
——, *The Country and the City* (Oxford, 1973).
——, *Cobbett* (Oxford, 1983).
Wilson, Mona, ed., *The Place of a Dictionary of the English Language in Samuel Johnson's Prose and Poetry* (London, 1959).
Wolf, William J., ed., *The Spirit of Anglicanism* (Edinburgh, 1982).
Woodring, Carl, *Politics in English Romantic Poetry* (Harvard, 1970).
——, *Wordsworth* (Harvard, 1968).
Woodward, E. L., *The Age of Reform 1815–70* (Oxford, 1938).
Woolaston, William, *The Religion of Nature Delineated* (London, 1722).
Woolston, Thomas, *Discourses on the Miracles of Our Saviour* (London, 1727–30).
Wordsworth, William, *The Poetical Works*, 5 Vols., ed. by Ernest de Selincourt and Helen Darbishire (Oxford, 1940–9).
——, *The Prelude*, ed. by Ernest de Selincourt (Oxford, 1959).
——, *The Prose Works*, 3 Vols., ed. by W. J. B. Owen and J. W. Smyser (Oxford, 1974).

Wright, J. R., *Life High the Cross, The Oxford Movement 1833–1983* (New York, 1983).
Young, Frances, *From Nicaea to Chalcedon, A Guide to the Literature and its Background* (London, 1983).

(ii) Articles

Allen, Peter, "Samuel Taylor Coleridge's 'Church and State' and the idea of an Intellectual Establishment", *Journal of the History of Ideas*, Vol. XLVI, No. 1, (1985).
Altholz, J. L., "Newman and History", *Victorian Studies*, Vol. VII, No. 3, (1964).
Aydelotte, W. O., "The England of Marx and Mill as reflected in Fiction", *Journal of Economic History*, Vol. VIII (1948).
Backstrom, P. N., "The Practical Side of Christian Socialism in Victorian England", *Victorian Studies*, Vol. VI (1962/3).
Baillie-Cochrane, Alexander, "In the Days of the Dandies III: The Young England Party", *Blackwood's Magazine*, Vol. XLVI (1890).
Baker, W. J., "Hurrell Froude and the Reformers", *The Journal of Ecclesiastical History*, Vol. XXI, No. 3 (1970).
Bebbington, D. W., "Gladstone and the Nonconformists: A Religious Affinity in Politics", Derek Baker, ed., *Studies in Church History* Vol. 12, *Church, Society and Politics* (Oxford, 1975).
Best, G. F. A., "The Protestant Constitution and its Supporters", *Transactions of the Royal Historical Society* (Series 5), 8 (1980).
Blaug, M., "The Myth of the Old Poor Law and the Making of the New", *The Journal of Economic History*, Vol. XXIII (1963).
Booty, J. E., "Richard Hooker", W. J. Wolf, ed., *The Spirit of Anglicanism* (Edinburgh, 1982).
Branthinger, Patrick, "The Case against Trade Unions in Early Victorian Literature", *Victorian Studies*, Vol. XIII (1969).
Brendon, Piers, "Newman, Keble and Froude's Remains", *English Historical Review*, Vol. CCCXLV (1972).
Briggs, Asa, "Middle-class Consciousness in English Politics, 1780–1846", *Past and Present*, Vol. XXII (1956).
Bright, Michael, "English Literary Romanticism and the Oxford Movement", *Journal of the History of Ideas*, Vol. XL (1979).
Bucher, K. D., "Newman on the Theologian in the Church – Some Kindly Light on a Contemporary Problem", *Louvain Studies*, Vol. VIII (1981).
Butler, J. A., "Wordsworth's 'Tuft of Primroses': an Unrelenting Doom", *Studies in Romanticism*, Vol. XIV (1975).
Cameron, J. M., "John Henry Newman and the Tractarian Movement", Ninian Smart, John Clayton, Steven Katz and Patrick Sherry,

Nineteenth Century Religious Thought in the West, Vol. II (Cambridge, 1985).
Chadwick, Owen, "The Limitations of Keble", *Theology*, Vol. LXVII (1964).
Chandler, Alice, "Sir Walter Scott and the Medieval Revival", *Nineteenth Century Fiction*, Vol. XIX (1964).
de Laura, D. J., "Matthew Arnold and John Henry Newman", *English Literature and Language*, Vol. VI, University of Texas Studies (1965).
Dowling, W. C., "Burke and the Age of Chivalry", *The Yearbook of English Studies*, Vol. XII (1982).
Dragas, G. D., "Conscience and Tradition: Newman and Athanasius in the Orthodox Church", *Athanasiana*, Vol. I (London, 1980).
Eliot, George, "The Natural History of German Life", *Westminister Review* (1856).
Figgis, J. N., "William Warburton", W. E. Collins, ed., *Typical English Churchmen from Parker to Maurice*, (London, 1902).
Force, J. E., "Secularization, The Language of God and the Royal Society at the turn of the Seventeenth Century", *History of European Ideas*, Vol. 2 (1981).
——, "Hume and the relation of Science to Religion among certain members of the Royal Society", *Journal of the History of Ideas*, Vol. XLV (1984).
Fulweiler, H. W., "Tractarians and Philistines", *Historical Magazine of the Protestant Episcopal Church*, Vol. XXXI (1962).
Gilley, Sheridan W., "Vulgar Piety and the Brompton Oratory, 1850–1860", *Durham University Journal* (1981).
——, "Nationality and Liberty, Protestant and Catholic: Robert Southey's 'Book of the Church'", S. Mews, ed., *Studies in Church History*, Vol. 18, *Religion and National Identity* (Oxford, 1982).
——, "Christianity and Enlightenment, An Historical Survey", *History of European Ideas*, Vol. I (1981).
——, "John Keble and the Victorian Churching of Romanticism" J. R. Watson, ed., *An Infinite Complexity, Essays in Romanticism* (Edinburgh, 1983).
——, "Newman and Prophecy, Evangelical and Catholic", *The Journal of the United Reformed Church History Society*, Vol. 3, No. 5 (1985).
Graham, W., "Politics of the great Romantics", *Publications of the Modern Language Association*, Vol. XXXVI (1921).
Greaves, R. W., "The Working of an Alliance: a Comment on Warburton", G. V. Bennett and J. D. Walsh, eds., *Essays in Modern English Church History in Memory of Norman Sykes* (London, 1966).
Griffin, J. R., "John Keble, Radical", *Anglican Theological Review*, Vol. LIX (1971).

——, "Dr Pusey and the Oxford Movement", *Historical Magazine of the Protestant Episcopal Church*, Vol. XIL (1972).
——, "The Radical Phase of the Oxford Movement", *The Journal of Ecclesiastical History*, Vol. XXVII (1976).
Hamill, Paul, "Other People's Faces: The English Romantics and the Paradox of Fraternity", *Studies in Romanticism*, Vol. XVII (1978).
Harrison, B., "Religion and Recreation in Nineteenth Century England", *Past and Present*, No. XXXVIII (1967).
Harrold, C. F., "Newman and the Alexandrian Platonists", *Modern Philology*, Vol. XXXVII (1939–40).
——, "The Oxford Movement, A Re-interpretation", J. E. Baker, ed., *The Re-interpretation of Victorian Literature* (Princeton, 1950).
Hart, J., "Sir Charles Trevelyan at the Treasury", *English Historical Review*, Vol. LXXV (1960).
——, "The Tory Interpretation of History", *Past and Present*, Vol. 31 (1965).
Hawkins, D. G., "Cardinal Newman's Social Philosophy", *New Blackfriars*, Vol. 54 (1973).
Helsinger, E. K., "Ruskin on Wordsworth: The Victorian Critic in Romantic Country", *Studies in Romanticism*, Vol. XVII (1978).
Holmes, J. Derek, "Church and World in Newman", *New Blackfriars*, Vol. 49 (1968).
——, "A Note on Newman's Historical Method", John Coulson and A. M. Allchin, ed., *The Rediscovery of Newman* (London, 1967).
——, "Factors in the Development of Newman's Political Attitudes", J. D. Bastable, ed., *Newman and Gladstone; Centennial Essays* (Dublin, 1978).
Hughes, P., "Newman and his Age", *Dublin Review* (1945).
Huzel, J. P., "Malthus, the Poor Law and Population in Nineteenth Century England", *Economic History Review*, Vol. XXII (1969).
——, "The Demographic Impact of the Old Poor Law; more reflexions on Malthus", *Economic History Review*, Vol. XXXII (1980).
Kemp, B., "The General Election of 1841", *History*, Vol. XXXVII (1952).
Kennedy, W. F., "Humanist v's. Economist. The Economic Thought of Samuel Taylor Coleridge", *University of California Publications in Economics*, Vol. XVII (1958).
Kenyon, Ruth, "The Social Aspects of the Catholic Revival", N. P. Williams and C. Harris, eds., *Northern Catholicism, Centenary Studies in the Oxford and Parallel Movements* (London, 1933).
Ker, Ian, "Development or Continuing Revelation", J. D. Bastable, ed., *Newman and Gladstone: Centennial Essays* (Dublin, 1978).
Kirk, R., "The Conservative Mind of Newman", *Sewanee Review*, Vol. LX (1952).

Lewis, C. J., "Theory and Expediency in Disraeli's Policy", *Victorian Studies*, Vol. V (1961).
Lively, Jack, "The Europe of the Enlightenment", *History of European Ideas*, Vol. I (1981).
Louth, Andrew, "Manhood into God: the Oxford Movement, the Fathers and the Deification of Man", K. Leech and R. Williams, ed., *Essays Catholic and Radical* (London, 1983).
Machin, G. I. T., "Gladstone and Nonconformity in the 1860's, the Formation of an Alliance", *History Journal*, Vol. XVII (1974).
Manning, P. J., "Wordsworth, Margaret and the Pedlar", *Studies in Romanticism*, Vol. XV (1976).
Martin, B. W., "Wordsworth, Faber and Keble: Commentary on a Triangular Relationship", *Review of English Studies* (Vol. XXVI, (1975).
Matthew, H. C. G., "Edward Bouverie Pusey, From Scholar to Tractarian", *The Journal of Theological Studies*, Vol. XXII (1981).
McGreevy, M. A., "John Keble and the Anglican Church and the Church Catholic", *Heythrop Journal*, Vol. V (1964).
Misner, Paul, "Newman and the Tradition concerning the Papal Antichrist", *Church History*, 42 (1973).
Nef, J. U., "The Industrial Revolution reconsidered", *Journal of Economic History*, Vol. III (1943).
Newsome, David, "J. H. Newman and the Oxford Movement", A. Symondson, ed. *The Victorian Crisis of Faith* (London 1970).
Nicholls, Aidan, "Newman and the Illative Sense, a Reconsideration", *The Scottish Journal of Theology*, Vol. 38 (1985).
Nicholls, D., "Gladstone, Newman and Pluralism", J. D. Bastable, ed., *Newman and Gladstone: Centennial Essays* (Dublin, 1978).
Nockles, Peter, "Pusey and the Question of Church and State", Perry Butler, ed., *Pusey Rediscovered* (London, 1983).
——, "The Oxford Movement: Historical Background 1780–1833" in Geoffrey Rowell, *Tradition Renewed, The Oxford Movement Conference Papers* (London, 1986).
O'Kell, R., "Disraeli's 'Coningsby': Political Manifesto or Psychological Romance", *Victorian Studies*, Vol. XXIII (1979).
O'Leary, J. J., "Malthus's general Theory of Employment and the Post-Napoleonic Depression", *Journal of Economic History*, Vol. III (1943).
Parker, T. M., "The Rediscovery of the Fathers in the Seventeenth Century Anglican Tradition", John Coulson and A. M. Allchin, ed., *The Rediscovery of Newman* (London, 1967).
Pattison, Mark, "Tendencies of Religious Thought in England, 1688–1750", *Essays and Reviews* (London, 1859).
Pitt, Valerie, "'The Oxford Movement: a case of Cultural Distortion?",

K. Leech and R. Williams, ed., *Essays Catholic and Radical* (London, 1983).
Porter, Roy, "The Enlightenment in England", Roy Porter and M. Teich, *The Enlightenment in National Context* (Edinburgh, 1983).
Raleigh, J. H., "What Scott meant to the Victorians", *Victorian Studies* Vol. VII (1963/4).
Roberts, D., "Tory Paternalism and Social Reform in Early Victorian England", *American Historical Review*, Vol. LXIII (1958).
——, "How cruel was the Victorian Poor Law?", *History Journal*, Vol. VI (1963).
Rock, H. D., "Christ's Kingdom not of this World, Benjamin Hoadly versus William Law", D. Baker, ed., *Studies in Church History*, Vol. 12, *Church, Society and Politics* (Oxford, 1975).
Ryan, A. S., "The Development of Newman's Political Thought", *Review of Politics*, Vol. VII (1945).
Sharp, Richard, "New Perspectives on the High Church Tradition: Historical Background", Geoffrey Rowell, ed., *Tradition Renewed, The Oxford Movement Conference Papers* (London, 1986).
Straten, H., "Newman on Self and Society", *Studies in Romanticism*, Vol. XVIII (1979).
Townsend, R. D., "The Caroline Divines", Gordon Wakefield, ed., *A Dictionary of Christian Sirituality* (London, 1983).
Walgrave, J. H., "The Rediscovery of Newman", *New Blackfriars*, Vol. XIL, (1968).
Ward, W., "Functions of Prejudice", *Dublin Review* (1900).
Waterman, A. M. C., "The Ideological Alliance of Political Economy and Christian Theology, 1798–1833", *The Journal of Ecclesiastical History*, Vol. XXXIV (1983).
Welch, P. J., "Blomfield and Peel, A Study in Co-operation between Church and State, 1841–1846," *The Journal of Ecclesiastical History* Vol. XII (1961).
Wilmer, Haddon, "Holy Worldliness in Nineteenth Century England", D. Baker, ed., *Studies in Church History*, Vol. 10, *Sanctity and Secularity, The Church and the World* (Oxford, 1973).

(iii) Unpublished Thesis

Griffin, J. R., "Tractarian Politics: A Study of the Political Thought of the Major Tractarians", (Trinity College, Dublin, PhD thesis, 1972).

POETRY

of considerable distinction from

CHURCHMAN

POETRY OF THE WORD: At Christmas
by Bishop Kenneth Cragg

"It is good to have these poetic Christmas meditations in print. They are the fruits of a long life in the Middle East and in the service of the Church as a pastor. The poems have been well printed and set out, and the book includes several line drawings."
—*The Bishop of Oxford*

"A deeply spiritual compilation of Christmas poetry which will be welcomed by the searcher after the mystery of the Incarnation."
—*The Methodist Recorder*

"Having served as an assistant bishop in Jerusalem he has some unusual insights and his verse is never bland."—*The Baptist Times*

"He has the gift of fine-honed phrases and striking coherent symbolism. Several of these poems will find their way into worship at Christmas, and they will enrich it."—*The Expository Times*

"An attractive book, cheaply priced, excellent for bedside or coffee table reading."—*The Church of England Newspaper*

ISBN 1 85093 077 5   **Illustrated**   **£1.95**

The Editorial Director of CHURCHMAN PUBLISHING

will always be ready to consider manuscripts on most non-fiction subjects especially Theology and Religion. A preliminary letter is usually advisable and return postage in case of unsuitability would be appreciated.

Please write to:
>   Peter Smith
>   Churchman Publishing Limited
>   117 Broomfield Avenue, Worthing
>   West Sussex, BN14 7SF